A Newcomer's Guide to the Bible

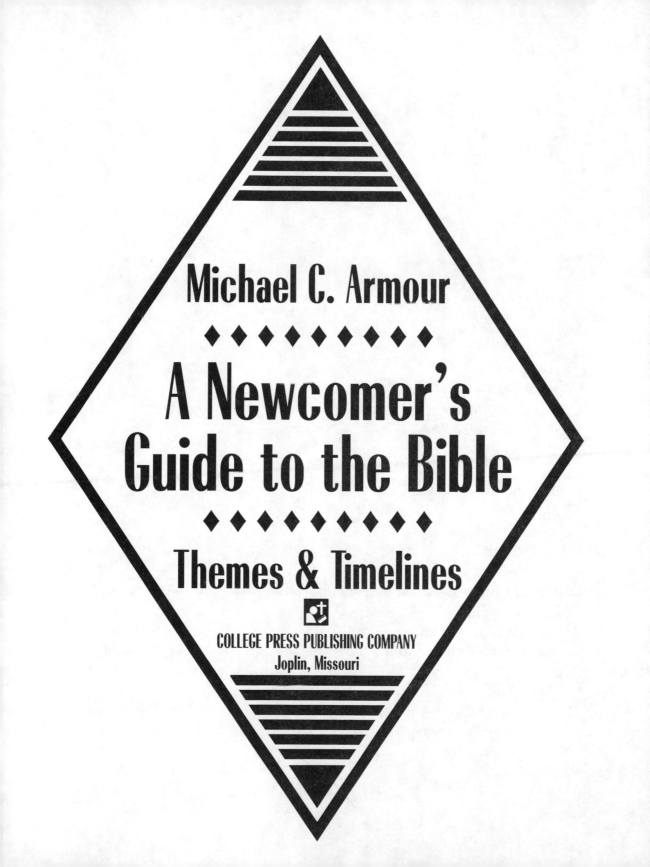

Michael C. Armour

◆ ◆ ◆ ◆ ◆ ◆ ◆ ◆ ◆

A Newcomer's Guide to the Bible

◆ ◆ ◆ ◆ ◆ ◆ ◆ ◆ ◆

Themes & Timelines

COLLEGE PRESS PUBLISHING COMPANY
Joplin, Missouri

Library of Congress Cataloging-in-Publication Data

Armour, Michael C. (Michael Carl), 1944–
    A newcomer's guide to the Bible: themes and time lines / Michael C.
Armour.
        p.   cm.
    ISBN 0-89900-859-3 (pbk.)
    1. Bible Introductions.   I. Title.
BS475.2.A76 1999
220.6'1—dc21   99-30558
                                                                    CIP

TABLE OF CONTENTS

PREFACE

A Newcomer's Guide to the Bible serves thousands of readers that other introductions overlook. The typical guide to the Bible aims at readers who already know most Biblical terms and events. But half of our population comes to adulthood today without even cursory knowledge of the Bible. In many cases, even the most common Biblical terms are foreign to them.

When these adults develop an interest in Christianity, as millions of them do, they find that the average Bible class is "over their heads." They also discover that basic reference materials about the Bible may exceed their level of understanding.

A Newcomer's Guide was written for just these people. In fact, several who reviewed the manuscript initially were exploring the Bible for the first time. Who were these people? Successful, well-rounded adults who, for whatever reason, were unfamiliar with the Bible. One was an internationally renowned scholar who shuttles between faculty appointments in Europe and North America.

Another was a brilliant young physician who was reared in a totally secular Jewish home. Others were ordinary, workaday people with a genuine thirst for truth.

All these readers had one thing in common. They wanted to gain a broad grasp of the Bible and its most important concepts. To a person, they achieved their goal with *A Newcomer's Guide*. They discovered that it presents the themes and structure of the Bible in a style that is easy to read and simple to grasp.

This same simplicity benefits others who hardly qualify as "newcomers" to the Bible. Perhaps they grew up hearing Bible stories in childhood. Or they may know the basics of Christianity from sermons and classes. Yet much of the Bible seems like alien territory. Key events in the Bible are little more than isolated episodes in their minds, not interconnected developments in a seamless whole. For these people *A Newcomer's Guide* provides a full, comprehensive picture of the Bible's unfolding themes.

To be honest, I did not initially write *A Newcomer's Guide* with American readers in mind. This project began as a labor of love for the people of Russia. This book came about in response to a request from Dr. Vladimir Skovorodnikov, at the time minister of education for the sprawling Altai region of Russia. Following the fall of Marxism, he pioneered the reintroduction of Christian thought and themes to Russian classrooms.

Yet most of his teachers had never seen a Bible before, much less read one. When dealing with Christian motifs in art, literature, and philosophy (not to mention religion), they had no background from which to explain Biblical concepts and allusions to their students. "What we need for our schools," Dr. Skovorodnikov said one morning over breakfast, "is an introduction to the Bible written for someone who knows absolutely nothing about it."

I agreed to help him find such a guide, assuming that something appropriate already existed. It would be reasonably simple, I thought, to find a book that met Dr. Skovorodnikov's requirements and persuade the publisher to let us translate it into Russian. But I soon learned how much I had miscalculated. Although we were able to identify some excellent nontechnical introductions to the Bible, none of them was basic enough for our purposes in Russia.

Thus, three years ago I turned my attention to writing *A Newcomer's Guide* in order to fill that need. As word spread of what I was doing, church leaders and Christian educators from across the U.S. started asking for copies to use in their own settings. Finding this guide highly useful with those they were teaching, they constantly urged me to make this work available in English. As their encouragement continued, and as I reflected on the growing challenge of Biblical illiteracy in our own land, I started looking for an American publisher who would join hands with me in this project.

I am grateful to College Press for seeing the value of placing *A Newcomer's Guide* in the hands of English-speaking readers. Quite by coincidence the English and Russian versions will come from the press within days of each other. Work is already under way to put *A Newcomer's Guide* in other foreign languages, especially Spanish, Ukrainian, and Romanian, with other translations to follow. It was purposefully written in a non-idiomatic style to facilitate the process of translation. This same style, however, gives it the clarity of expression that makes it so easily grasped in English.

Some who read this book, I know, will already possess an advanced knowledge of the Bible. For their benefit I should offer a word or two about the assumptions that shaped *A Newcomer's Guide.* Because I was writing for readers who are absolutely new to the Bible, I thought it best to deal with the story of the Bible straightforwardly, without delving into technical difficulties that surround certain portions of it. Otherwise I risked losing the newcomer in a maze of views and counterviews on topics that are not easily resolved, even among experts.

Nor was it wise, I thought, to raise issues that I could not thoroughly address in the finite length of this volume. *A Newcomer's Guide* was originally targeted for regions of the globe where no religious bookstores or libraries exist. In those areas I would do readers a disservice if I opened debated issues that they have no local resources to examine.

In a similar vein I have also avoided controversies about Old Testament dating. This accounts for the very conservative dates that appear throughout this book. Trying to establish precise dates for Biblical events prior to the 10th century BC — and even as late as the 8th century BC — is a difficult, often impossible task. For one thing, our archaeological evidence is still quite limited and subject to conflicting interpretations. Second, the Bible is prone to state intervals of time in round numbers, with a particular tendency to round off lengthy periods to 40 years.

Rather than delve into all the intricacies of creating an accurate chronology, I have simply set an arbitrary date of 925 BC for the death of Solomon (most scholars place it between 930 BC and 920 BC). Then I have "worked back" from that point to determine the date of earlier events. To do so I have used a chronology that most naturally emerges when we take Old Testament statements about time spans at face value, treating none of them as generalizations or approximations. For those who realize that this is a terribly simplistic solution to a thorny problem, I can only beg your indulgence. Such complex questions, I believe, are best addressed at a later, more advanced level of study.

Decisions about what to include and what to omit from *A Newcomer's Guide* were the most difficult part of this effort. On every page I fought the temptation to say more. But I did not want this book to become so long that it discouraged someone just starting to explore the Christian faith.

Still, with all the tough decisions, writing *A Newcomer's Guide* was a constant joy. I deeply appreciate the release time my congregation gave me to devote several months of intensive writing to this project. And a special "thank you" goes to my wife Fran and my children Deborah, David, and Rebekah who never once complained when I disrupted family plans and commitments (as I often did) to bring this work to completion.

They remained supportive throughout the writing because they believed, as I believe, that *A Newcomer's Guide* will be an immense blessing to thousands of people. I pray that you will be one of those thousands and that the chapters that follow will enrich your life.

Chapter One

THE BIBLE'S LASTING IMPACT

Most people know that the Bible teaches about religion, morals, and God. But its influence spreads far beyond religion. In fact, the Bible has shaped human values and culture more than any other book.

This seems like a bold claim, to be sure, but history confirms it. For 2000 years the Bible has steadily transformed legal and social institutions everywhere, beginning with the Roman Empire. Before Christianity came along, Roman justice and social policy were harsh, often cruel. But Christianity, armed with the Bible, tempered that brutality and elevated respect for human life and dignity.

Medieval states continued this process. They took over Roman law, bound it more tightly to Biblical principles, and adopted it as their own. During the Middle Ages criminal trials moved into church courts and lawyers were schooled in Biblical precedents. In addition, the universities taught law and theology side by side.

As modern European nations emerged in the fifteenth and sixteenth centuries, they adopted law codes that enforced Biblical standards of justice. Later, as these same governments raced to plant colonies around the globe, they took the Bible with them. And wherever they flew a colonial flag, they imposed European law, now thoroughly infused with values from the Bible.

This law proved so effective that former colonies tended to retain its basics even after throwing off colonial rule. As a result, today's legal systems in Europe, the Americas, and Australia, as well as many parts of Africa and Asia, trace their roots to Biblical concepts. And today's international law first took shape in the writings of men like Hugo Grotius, a serious student of the Bible, as well as a great legal mind.

Likewise, the quest for democracy owes much to the Bible. Democratic movements in the West first arose among people who turned to the Bible for moral guidance. They based their call for universal rights and personal freedom on Biblical ideals of individual worth

<< **The Bible and law**

< **The Bible and democracy**

and dignity. It was also people dedicated to the Bible who led worldwide efforts to eradicate slavery, improve the status of women, and secure the equal treatment of all races.

Thus, the Bible has molded human history for hundreds of years. We could fill volumes talking about its lasting imprint on art, literature, and social policy. But its most telling influence has been in the realm of faith and personal religion. Both Judaism and Christianity grew out of the Bible. The Bible also left a mark on Islamic culture, for Mohammed, the founder of Islam, held the Bible in high regard. He even considered Jesus a prophet from God.

The Bible and faith ➤

It is only natural, then, to ask why the impact of the Bible has been so monumental. What accounts for its attractiveness over the centuries? How has it had such enduring influence? And why is it still the best selling book in the world?

The character of mankind ➤➤

The answer lies in the great ideas conveyed by the Bible, the great truths it unfolds. No other book has ever surpassed its exalted view of God and His love for mankind. In a word, the Bible stretches our sense of who God is and what we have the potential to become because of His love.

God and the Human Race

At the very outset the Bible declares that God created human beings in His own image. This does not mean that God resembles us physically, for the Bible is equally clear that God is a spirit-being. He does not have a body. But as a spirit-being Himself, God imparted a spirit to each of us. Thus, we are like him — created in His image — because we have a spirit-essence, like He does.

This inner spirit sets the human race apart from every other species. It gives us unique abilities, unknown to other creatures. We can reason abstractly. We can comprehend truth. We can create splendid works of art. We can make moral judgments. We can invent powerful technologies. In short, we can be distinctly human because we possess a spirit that makes creativity possible.

Unfortunately, we tend to behave in ways that pollute this spirit-nature. God as a spirit-being is loving, just, and truthful. But as spirit-beings ourselves, we are often unloving, unjust, and untruthful. When we act this way, we corrupt the spirit within us. If corruption goes unchecked, we become wicked, hateful people, and evil overruns society.

The Bible tells us that God foresaw this problem from the beginning. Fortunately, He did not give up on us and abandon us, even when evil gripped mankind. Rather, God chose to stay in a relationship with us. Out of His love, He longed to see us escape from the effects of corrupt lives, corrupt governments, and corrupt societies. The Bible is the story of what God has done over countless generations to make that escape possible.

As this story unfolds, the Bible shows us a God who cares deeply for every individual. He also is a God who actively involves Himself with the events of our lives. The Bible details how He guided human destiny, including the rise and fall of civilizations, beginning with man's first steps on our planet.

< **God works in people's lives**

The Old and New Testaments

The Bible uses a variety of literary forms. Within its pages we find books of history and engrossing narrative. There are also great poems and songs, along with dozens of moving speeches and letters. These elements of the Bible were pulled together between 1500 BC and 100 AD in two great collections. We commonly refer to the first collection as the Old Testament. The other is called the New Testament.

The Old Testament is respected by Christians, Jews, and Moslems alike. It describes how God dealt with individuals and nations prior to the birth of Jesus. For Christians the most important part of the Bible is the New Testament. This is where we learn about Jesus and what He taught. The New Testament also tells us how Christianity started and what the earliest churches were like.

The Old and New Testaments are somewhat like small libraries, for they both contain dozens of books. There are 66 books in all, 39 in the Old Testament and 27 in the New Testament. Some of them are relatively short, no longer than a tract or a pamphlet. Others are rather lengthy and require several hours to read.

The Lands and People of the Old Testament

The pages of the Bible take us into renowned empires of the ancient world, places like Egypt, Assyria, Babylon, Persia, Greece, and Rome. But most events in the Bible occur in the narrow strip of land between the Jordan River and the Mediterranean Sea. The people of antiquity called this area Canaan.

Strategically Canaan was far more important than its small size would indicate. Within its borders the major trade routes connecting Asia, Europe, and Africa came together. Thus, every rising empire wanted to control Canaan. The Bible tells of frequent wars as first one power, then another tried to seize this valued territory.

<< **Ancient nations**

Early in the Bible we meet a man named Abraham who moved to Canaan at God's command. Abraham came from the Tigris-Euphrates Valley, home of a highly advanced civilization. God promised the entire sweep of Canaan to Abraham's family. But God made it clear that actual ownership of the land would take place in the distant future, long after Abraham's death. In fact, almost 600 years passed before God carried out this promise.

< **Abraham**

<< **Canaan**

During those years God created a special working relationship with

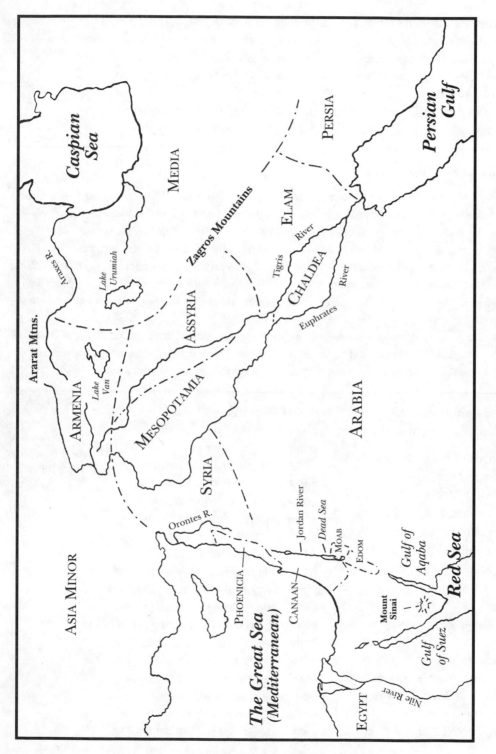

THE OLD TESTAMENT WORLD

one branch of Abraham's family. This branch descended from Jacob, Abraham's grandson. Jacob was a wanderer, living first in Canaan, then in Mesopotamia, and later in Egypt. In the course of those wanderings he also became known as "Israel."

Jacob had twelve sons, each the head of a large household. In time these households grew into twelve huge clans, or tribes. From Jacob they took the name Israel and referred to themselves as Israelites or "the children of Israel." By the end of the Old Testament they were also called Jews.

The Bible is largely the account of how God used Abraham's family, especially the Israelites, to reveal His promises, hopes, and expectations for humanity. Eventually God brought Jesus into the world through the Israelites. Most writers of the Bible were also from Israel.

Near the close of Jacob's life the Israelites started an extensive sojourn in Egypt. They migrated there after Joseph, Jacob's favorite son, gained prominence in the Egyptian government. Things went well for the Israelites at first. But following Joseph's death, Egyptian rulers turned against the Israelites and reduced them to slavery.

This enslavement continued for four centuries under harsh conditions. During those years the Israelites grew into a vast nation. Then God raised up a man named Moses, who led them to freedom.

With Moses at their head, the Israelites made their way from Egypt into the wilderness of the Sinai peninsula, where they lived as nomads for 40 years.

Shortly after Moses died, the Israelites marched into Canaan as a mighty military force. They subdued several Canaanite kingdoms and took possession of the land, just as God had promised Abraham. Israel's second king, a man named David, conquered Jerusalem and made it his national capital. Then Solomon, David's son, established a small empire that took up most of the area between the Euphrates River and the northeastern border of Egypt. He also built a magnificent temple in Jerusalem.

All this success, according to the Bible, was a direct gift from God. But despite His kindness, Israel drifted away from Him. She turned to other gods and openly set aside His commands. As this disobedience grew unchecked, God warned His people that they were risking the loss of their land, for He would drive them from Canaan if they continued to disobey.

After centuries of warnings, God finally carried out His threat. First the Assyrians and then the Babylonians overran Canaan. Not only did the Israelites lose their independence, their enemies literally hauled them away and gave their land to other people. Several books of the Old Testament describe Israel's suffering at the

◄◄ Chosen family

◄ Wilderness wanderings

◄ God's kindness; man's unfaithfulness

◄◄ Slavery and freedom

hands of their conquerors. But suffering had the benefit of turning the Israelites back to God.

God responded by granting them a return to Jerusalem, which Babylon had demolished in 586 BC. During the next century the Israelites rebuilt the city and reconstructed the temple.

Resurrection »

With the rebuilding of Jerusalem, the Old Testament comes to a close. About 400 years then pass before the events of the New Testament begin. During that interval Alexander the Great marched through Canaan en route to his conquest of Egypt and the Middle East. Israel came under Greek control, but later regained her independence, at least for a few decades. Then the Romans came in and subjugated Israel, as well as her neighbors.

Growth of the church »

Jesus and the Earliest Christians

The Romans ›

When the New Testament opens, the Romans are still in control. But they have granted the Israelites considerable freedom to maintain their temple worship and to have their own courts and laws. This is the setting in which Jesus lived.

Apostles ›

He began His teaching career by surrounding Himself with twelve special students. The New Testament calls them "apostles," from a Greek word that means "one sent out." Jesus planned to train these men and send them out with His message.

Makeup of the New Testament »

He worked with them for only three years before the Romans crucified Him. At first His death sent the apostles into despair. But then, in a series of striking events, He appeared among them, alive. He announced that God had raised Him from the dead. (The Biblical term for this is "resurrection.") He also said that God was preparing a resurrection for every person who accepts the teachings of Jesus and follows them.

Armed with this message, the apostles went out and immediately began telling the story of Jesus. Within 30 years they had established communities of Christians from Jerusalem to Rome and beyond. As these communities matured, they occasionally needed fuller guidance on how a Christian should live. To provide that guidance, the apostles and others around them wrote a group of books called Gospels. These are detailed accounts of what Jesus did and taught.

In addition, the apostles often sent personal letters to various Christian communities. These letters usually addressed moral and spiritual questions that followers of Jesus commonly face. As you might imagine, the early Christians treasured these letters. As a result, the letters were carefully copied and circulated. Eventually 21 of them — along with four Gospels, a history of early Christianity, and a book called Revelation — were pulled together in a single collection to form the New Testament.

Revelation, the last book in the New Testament, was written about 95 AD. It anticipates a great persecution of Christians that broke out a short time later. The highest levels of the Roman government sponsored this persecution. The book of Revelation urges Christians to remain faithful to God, even in the face of official repression. By staying faithful, Revelation assures them, they will secure their own resurrection — a life beyond death in the presence of God.

With this assurance the Bible comes to an end. But the principles and ideals in its pages are as relevant today as ever. Throughout the Bible, God upholds an exalted standard of moral excellence for every man and woman. He calls on us to live extraordinary, upright lives. While the people of the Bible lived in a world vastly different from ours, we still struggle with the same moral and spiritual issues that they faced. The Bible thus speaks to us as meaningfully as it did to them.

Names for God

In the chapters ahead you will become familiar with the Biblical themes that have sustained God's people for ages. Beginning with the first books of the Old Testament, we will examine the Bible section by section, highlighting vital insights and central truths. You will learn what the Bible says about the nature of God, the nature of mankind, the nature of the universe. You will discover what God tells us about building strong families, loving homes, and healthy communities. You will become familiar with Jesus, who He was, and what He taught. And through it all, you will ask fresh questions about yourself and the meaning of your life.

◄ Discovering who God is

In short, you are about to embark on a rewarding journey. But one note before we begin. On this journey we will encounter different names for God. Since no one name can fully describe Him, the Bible relies on a variety of terms to refer to Him. Often it speaks of Him simply as the Lord, or as the Lord God. In the Old Testament (which was originally written in Hebrew) the name "Lord" is usually a translation of the Hebrew word "Yahweh." The Jews considered this the most sacred name for God, so sacred that they hesitated even to pronounce it. Consequently, they eventually forgot how to pronounce it at all.

However, Yahweh is the name God uses for Himself in the Bible when He wants to emphasize His personal involvement in human existence; when He is revealing His laws for us to follow; or when He is making promises to us. The name Yahweh frequently appears in combination with some other word to highlight a particular quality of God's existence. For instance, He is referred to by the name "Yahweh Shalom," Hebrew for "Yahweh Is

◄ God's personal name

Descriptive names of God ➤

Peace." Or in another place as "Yahweh Jireh," which means "Yahweh Who Sees," affirming that God sees the plight of people who are afflicted.

The Hebrew word that we normally translate as "God" is "Elohim," or in its shortened form, "El." This points to God's great power and majesty. In general this is the name God uses when He speaks of His ultimate control over the universe, nature, and mankind. Many people in the Old Testament have names that include a shortened form of Yahweh or Elohim, or sometimes both. We will point out several names like this as we work through the Bible.

A third name for God in the Old Testament is "Adonai." The term calls attention to His sovereign rule over mankind. It closely parallels the concept of a lord over a group of subjects.

In this study we will restrict ourselves to the terms "God" and "Lord," with occasional references to "Yahweh." Moreover, we will use "God" and "Lord" interchangeably, since modern languages do not distinguish between these names the way the Israelites did. Simply remember that God reveals Himself under different names, but He is the same God wherever we encounter Him.

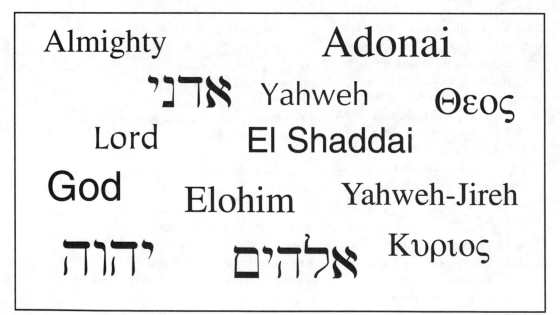

Chapter Two

FINDING YOUR WAY
AROUND IN THE BIBLE

As you know from chapter one, the Bible has two major sections. One is the Old Testament, the other the New Testament. The Old Testament was originally written in Hebrew, the New Testament in Greek. Modern Bibles are therefore translations of ancient Hebrew and Greek manuscripts.

In terms of length, the Old Testament is three times the size of the New Testament. Several factors account for this.

➤ First, there are 39 books in the Old Testament, only 27 in the New Testament.

➤ Second, Old Testament books are typically much longer than those in the New Testament.

➤ And third, the Old Testament covers a far broader span of time. More than 1500 years separate Abraham from the final events of the Old Testament. By contrast, the events in the New Testament all unfold in the first century AD, most of them within less than 50 years.

How the Bible Is Organized

Whatever its length, each book of the Bible is divided into chapters and verses. These divisions did not appear in the original writings. They have been added to make it easier to study the Bible. Before book-binding was invented, the Bible was copied on long scrolls of parchment or papyrus. Since a single copy of the Old Testament required several scrolls, reading the Bible was a tedious process of constantly rolling and unrolling scrolls. This was cumbersome, to say the least.

‹ Scrolls

‹‹ Size of the Bible divisions

Once the Bible began to appear in book form (about the fourth century), moving from one section to another became as simple as turning a few pages. But it still might take several minutes of searching to locate a specific passage. To solve this problem scholars in the Middle Ages added chapter divisions to each book. The number of chapters in a book varied widely. A few short books were assigned only one chapter. Longer books were given as many as 40 or 50 chapters, even more.

‹ Chapter divisions

Verse divisions ➤

Books with the
same name ➤➤

Chapter divisions now made it easier to find a precise location. This innovation proved so helpful that chapters were later divided into verses. A verse contains the general equivalent of a sentence, although complex sentences may spread across several verses. The number of verses in a chapter follows no set pattern. Chapters range in length from as few as two verses to as many as 176.

In modern editions of the Bible, a chapter usually covers no more than one or two printed pages. The numbering of chapters starts anew in each book, so that every book begins with chapter one. Verse numbers also start over with each new chapter.

As a result of this arrangement, we can identify the exact location of any statement in the Bible by referring to a specific book, chapter, and verse. We call this "citing" a passage. Printed citations follow a generally accepted convention of placing the name of the book first, followed by the chapter number, a colon, and the verse number.

Thus, Genesis 3:15 refers to the fifteenth verse of the third chapter of the book named Genesis. To cite several consecutive verses, we use a hyphen to separate the beginning and ending verse numbers. For example, Genesis 3:15-18 refers to verses fifteen through eighteen of the third chapter of Genesis.

In some citations a number *precedes* the name of the book. This allows us to distinguish between books that otherwise have identical names. There are three reasons why two or more books may have the same name.

➤ First, there are three books in the Old Testament that are so long that they have been split into two volumes apiece. The resulting six books are 1 Samuel and 2 Samuel, 1 Kings and 2 Kings, and 1 Chronicles and 2 Chronicles.

➤ Second, some books of the New Testament are named for their author. If the same writer gave us two or three books, they may all bear his name, as with 1 Peter and 2 Peter.

➤ And third, New Testament books that were originally written as letters commonly take the name of the people to whom they were addressed. Where the same individual or Christian community received two different letters, we can end up with duplicate names. For instance, 1 Corinthians and 2 Corinthians are both letters to Christians in the city of Corinth.

When a number precedes the name of book, the numeral represents the words "first," "second," or "third," as in "First Samuel" or "Second Corinthians."

Abbreviations and Cross-References

To conserve space when citing a passage, publishers often abbreviate the names of books. The most common way to do this is to drop all but the first two or three letters in the book's name. Instead of Genesis 3:15, we would have Gen. 3:15. A reference to 1 Samuel 2:2 would become 1 Sam. 2:2. Until you are familiar with all the books of the Bible, these abbreviations can prove confusing. For that reason, we have avoided them in this introductory study.

You will see these abbreviations quite often in a Bible that includes cross-references. A cross-reference is a type of footnote. It points the reader to other places in the Bible where we find phrases or ideas similar to the ones in the current verse. Cross-references are not part of the Bible itself. They are simply a helpful aid for study.

Because it is costly to print cross-references, not all Bibles contain them. You can quickly determine if you are using a Bible that includes these special notes. They usually appear in a narrow vertical column, set in a small typeface and running the length of the page. This column may be in the middle of the page or along the outer margin. Some publishers prefer another approach and put cross-references at the bottom of the text, much like a conventional footnote. If you are fortunate enough to have a Bible with cross-references, you will benefit from using them often.

The Arrangement of Books

Now that you understand books, chapters, verses, and cross-references, you can move effortlessly from one part of the Bible to another. You will soon discover, however, that its books are not in strict historical sequence. Instead, they are grouped according to literary style. The Old Testament begins with

- ➤ five books by Moses, followed by
- ➤ twelve books of history, then
- ➤ five books of songs, poetry, and writings about wisdom, and finally
- ➤ seventeen books by prophets.

The prophets were men (and occasionally women) through whom God communicated specific mes-

▽ 🗐 Old Testament
　　▷　🗐　Law/Moses
　　▷　🗐　History
　　▷　🗐　Poetry/Wisdom
　　▷　🗐　Prophets
▽ 🗐 New Testament
　　▷　🗐　Gospels
　　▷　🗐　History
　　▷　🗐　Letters
　　▷　🗐　Prophecy

◀◀ Divisions of the Old Testament

sages to mankind. The message from a prophet was called "prophecy." Often these messages included a prediction of future events, so the word "prophecy" can also mean "a foretelling of the future."

In the New Testament the grouping of books follows this pattern:

Divisions of the
New Testament ➤

➤ four books on the life of Jesus (the Gospels),

➤ one book about early Christian history,

➤ twenty-one letters written mostly by apostles, and

➤ one book of prophecy about widespread persecution that would befall Christian communities.

By keeping these groupings in mind, you will quickly learn to find a book of the Bible by simply remembering the general section it is in.

But what if you wanted to locate a specific story? How would you know where to look for it? One way is to learn a basic timeline of Biblical events. Nor is it difficult to do so. The Bible falls naturally into 14 periods of history. By the time you complete this study, you will know these periods by heart. Not only that, you will be able to identify the books and major developments that go with each period. With those skills in place, you will be able to find key sections of the Bible with little difficulty.

Periods of Bible History

14 historical
periods ➤

As a preview of what you soon will learn, we want to briefly identify each of the 14 historical periods in the Bible. Do not be concerned with remembering all the details in this outline right now. You will master them naturally as our study continues.

The Period of Beginnings — This covers all the events leading up to the story of Abraham. The Period of Beginnings tells about God creating the earth, its creatures, and the first human family. This period also relates how a great flood once destroyed the earth, how life reemerged after the flood, and how various nations got their start.

The Period of Abraham's Family — In this period the Bible introduces us to Abraham, tells his life story, and then follows his family for three more generations as the Lord works with them. By the end of this period Abraham's grandson Jacob and his twelve sons have moved their households to Egypt.

The Period of Egyptian Bondage — During these 400 years the descendants of Jacob undergo harsh treatment. The Egyptians force them into slavery, then intensify that slavery as time goes by. This enslavement comes to an end when Moses leads his people to freedom after God uses a series of powerful disasters to cripple Egypt.

The Period of Wilderness Wanderings — Once they gain their freedom, the Israelites leave Egypt for the wilderness region of the Sinai peninsula, east of the Red Sea. Moses leads them through this desolate area for 40 years. It is here that God gives Israel His law. At the heart of this law are ten principles — the Ten Commandments — that serve as Israel's basic moral code from this time forward. It is also here that Moses begins writing the first books of the Bible. During this time the Israelites live as nomads, growing in size and preparing to conquer Canaan. By the end of his life Moses has brought them to the border of Canaan and positioned them to invade it.

The Period of Conquest — Under Joshua, Moses' successor, the Israelites enter Canaan, fight a series of pivotal battles with God's help, and take over the region. They divide the land among themselves according to tribes, so that specific sections of Canaan will hereafter bear the name of an Israelite tribe.

The Period of Judges — After Joshua dies, no national leader appears immediately. All government is at a local level. The only exception occurs when military emergencies arise. Then the Israelites turn to some exceptional individual to lead them. These individuals are known as judges, because they often settle legal disputes, in addition to providing military leadership.

The Period of the United Kingdom — Israel ultimately wants a permanent leader and Samuel, the last of the judges, appoints the nation's first king. For more than a century, over the lifespan of three rulers, all of Israel answers to one crown. Jerusalem becomes the capital of this kingdom, and Solomon, the third king, builds a great temple

there. But following his death, internal rivalries break the nation apart and two separate kingdoms emerge.

The Period of the Divided Kingdom — In this period ten tribes band together to form a kingdom in the northern portion of Canaan. Two others pull together in the south. Sometimes these two kingdoms stand side by side against invaders. At other times they turn on one another in pitched battle. Of the two, the northern kingdom is shorter lived, for it was an early victim of the rising Assyrian Empire.

The Period of Judah Alone — The southern kingdom took the name of its larger tribe, Judah. (This is the name that eventually gives us the word "Jew.") Assyria never succeeds at toppling Judah. Yet Judah does eventually fall to the Babylonians, who supplant the Assyrians and become rulers of the Middle East.

The Period of Babylonian Exile — Like the Assyrians before them, the Babylonians transplant conquered people from their homes to distant lands. The Babylonians take thousands of families in Judah to Babylon, where they live in exile for decades. During this period the Medes and Persians overthrow the Babylonians and seize their empire.

The Period of Restoration — Under the rule of the Medes and Persians, conditions improve for the displaced Israelites. They are permitted to return to Jerusalem and rebuild it. They also reconstruct the temple, which the Babylonians had leveled. As the rebuilding of Jerusalem nears completion, the Old Testament comes to an end.

The Period Between the Testaments — This era, some 400 years long, is addressed only indirectly in the Bible. The book of Daniel foretells some of the events that play out in this period, including the rise of both Greece and Rome. Toward the end of this period Israel falls under Roman rule, as does most of the Middle East.

The Period of the Life of Jesus — The New Testament opens by giving us four parallel accounts of Jesus' life. In these accounts we have the most exhaustive statement of what Jesus taught. We also learn how He trained His followers and prepared them to spread His teachings far and wide.

The Period of the Early Church — The remainder of the New Testament is about the first Christian com-

munities in the Middle East, Asia Minor, Greece, and Rome. We learn about how they began, the challenges they faced, and the rapid growth they experienced. In general, the New Testament focuses on the Christian communities that came into existence within 30 years after Jesus died.

With this series of periods in mind, you will grasp Biblical developments more fully. There is no correlation between the length of a period and the number of books devoted to it. The earlier periods are sometimes covered in just a few chapters. Other periods are the subject of several lengthy books. As we introduce each book, we will place it in its proper time period so that you see God's story unfold in historical sequence. The charts on the next two pages lay out a time line for the Old Testament, identifying the primary books that cover each period. You will want to refer to this time line often as your study continues.

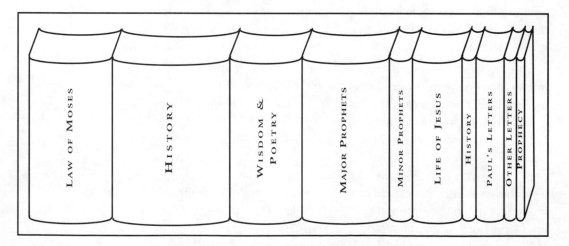

LAW OF MOSES   HISTORY   WISDOM & POETRY   MAJOR PROPHETS   MINOR PROPHETS   LIFE OF JESUS   HISTORY   PAUL'S LETTERS   OTHER LETTERS   PROPHECY

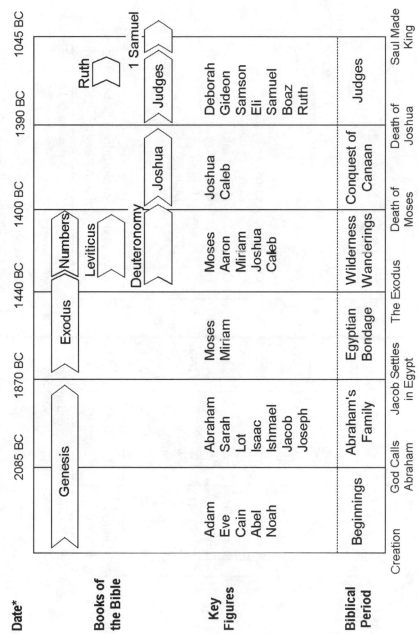

PERIODS OF OLD TESTAMENT HISTORY

Date*	2085 BC	1870 BC	1440 BC	1400 BC	1390 BC	1045 BC
Books of the Bible	Genesis	Genesis	Exodus / Leviticus / Numbers / Deuteronomy	Deuteronomy / Joshua	Ruth / Judges / 1 Samuel	
Key Figures	Adam Eve Cain Abel Noah	Abraham Sarah Lot Isaac Ishmael Jacob Joseph	Moses Miriam	Moses Aaron Miriam Joshua Caleb	Joshua Caleb	Deborah Gideon Samson Eli Samuel Boaz Ruth
Biblical Period	Beginnings	Abraham's Family	Egyptian Bondage	Wilderness Wanderings	Conquest of Canaan	Judges
	Creation	God Calls Abraham	Jacob Settles in Egypt	The Exodus	Death of Moses	Death of Joshua	Saul Made King

*Prior to the 11th century BC we cannot set precise dates for Biblical events. For instance, the Exodus may have occurred as late as 1250 BC. About 1100 BC dates become more accurate, but may still be off as much as ten years. Beginning in the 8th century we can establish exact dates for the first time.

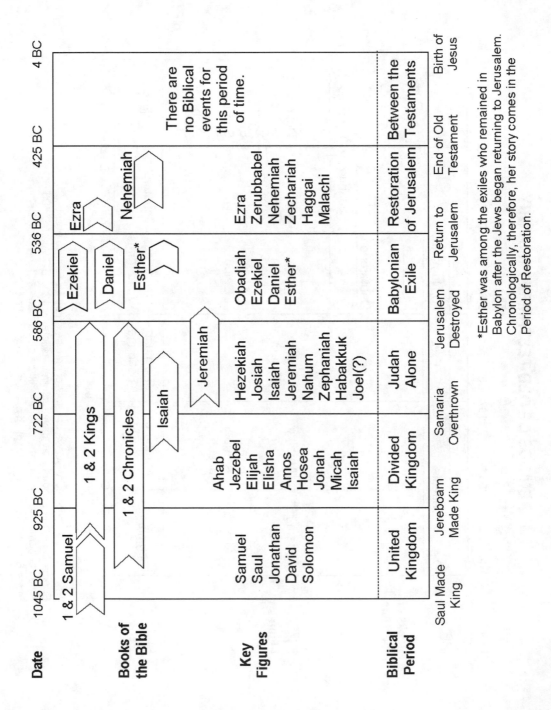

Date	1045 BC	925 BC	722 BC	586 BC	536 BC	425 BC	4 BC
Books of the Bible	1 & 2 Samuel	1 & 2 Kings — 1 & 2 Chronicles	Isaiah	Jeremiah — Ezekiel — Daniel — Esther*	Ezra — Nehemiah	There are no Biblical events for this period of time.	Birth of Jesus
Key Figures	Samuel Saul Jonathan David Solomon	Ahab Jezebel Elijah Elisha Amos Hosea Jonah Micah Isaiah	Hezekiah Josiah Isaiah Jeremiah Nahum Zephaniah Habakkuk Joel(?)	Obadiah Ezekiel Daniel Esther*	Ezra Zerubbabel Nehemiah Zechariah Haggai Malachi		
Biblical Period	United Kingdom	Divided Kingdom	Judah Alone	Babylonian Exile	Restoration of Jerusalem	Between the Testaments	
	Saul Made King	Jereboam Made King	Samaria Overthrown — Jerusalem Destroyed	Return to Jerusalem	End of Old Testament		

*Esther was among the exiles who remained in Babylon after the Jews began returning to Jerusalem. Chronologically, therefore, her story comes in the Period of Restoration.

Chapter Three

THE BIBLE'S RELIABILITY

The Bible was written by dozens of men whose lives spanned more than 1500 years. As you might expect, each one had a unique way of expressing himself. Yet they all wrote as though they were seeing life through a single set of eyes. Their picture of God and His nature is consistent, from the beginning of the Bible to the end.

They also agree completely in the way they portray human nature and in what they say God expects of mankind. In fact, we would need several pages just to list the views they shared in common. The list would include what they said about such vital questions as:

➤ What is morally right and what is morally wrong?

➤ How do we distinguish what is good from what is evil?

➤ How does the spiritual realm differ from the physical realm?

➤ How does God respond when we violate His moral code?

➤ What promises has God made, and how has He carried them out?

➤ Does life continue beyond the grave?

➤ What happens to my personal existence and identity at death?

The Inspiration of the Bible

Since these writers lived centuries apart, it is altogether amazing that they answered such profound questions with total consistency. But they explained it quite simply — what they wrote originated beyond themselves, with God. He was the one who told them what to say. They agreed in what they wrote because their words reflected the underlying mind of God.

Naturally, we would like to know how God communicated with these penmen. But none of them ever gave us the details of the process. We do know that God's Spirit played a role in this communication, for the Bible repeatedly makes that point. We also know that these men yielded themselves to God's control as they wrote (2 Peter 1:21). They made themselves available as instruments or conduits through

<< Consistency of the Bible

< God the source of the Bible

The meaning of
inspiration >>

which God conveyed truth to the world. Or as one of them put it, they were imparting "spiritual words taught by the Spirit of God" (1 Corinthians 2:12-13). As God revealed His thoughts to His spokesmen, they transformed those thoughts into words in print.

Thus, while dozens of writers gave us the Bible, we can also think of God as its sole author. This is why those who follow the Bible often call it the Word of God. It contains His commands, promises, warnings, and instructions, captured in the unique style of men who actually committed His truth to writing. Because it embodies God's words in written form, the Bible is also known as Scripture, which literally means "what is written." God speaks, man writes, and the result is Scripture.

Therefore, whenever we attribute a particular statement in the Bible to a specific author, we should always keep in mind that God was a partner in this process. He was the one who ultimately gave the Bible its form and substance. What sets the Bible apart from all other books is God's direct role in writing it.

The common way to describe His involvement is to say that the Bible is "inspired." This means that God's Spirit brought the Bible into existence and continues to work through its pages. We derive this concept from a statement in 2 Timothy 3:16, which says that all Scripture is inspired by God.

To understand this idea completely, we might notice the Greek term behind it. (Remember that the Bible was first written in Greek and Hebrew.) Where we say that Scripture is "inspired," the Greek wording is artfully vague. It uses a term that could mean either "God-breathed" or "God-spirited."

What we have here is a subtle play on words. In the Greek language the same term meant both "breath" and "spirit." Since we must exhale in order to speak, this passage suggests that God spoke the words of Scripture by "breathing" them. At the same time, by "breathing" these words, He placed His Spirit within them. Thus, Scripture is both God-breathed (it contains His words) and God-spirited (it contains spiritual power).

What adds to this imagery is the fact that the Bible uses God's breath as a symbol for life-giving power. The symbol appears for the first time in Genesis 2, which tells how God created man. Having fashioned a human body, the Lord next "breathed into man's nostrils the breath of life, so that man became a living soul" (Genesis 2:8).

On another occasion God's breath restored life to men long dead. The story is related by a prophet named Ezekiel, who one day saw a vision of a desolate valley. Scattered across that valley were human bones, bleached by the sun. But as the vision continued, God's breath swept over those bones and they came back to life. One by one, bones joined together, then sinews reappeared, and finally vibrant bodies of muscle and flesh arose from the valley floor (Ezekiel 37:1-10).

Just as the breath of God gave physical life at the creation of man and again in the valley of dry bones, so God's breath fills the words of Scripture with life-giving power. This is what Jesus was talking about when He said, "The words I have spoken are spirit and are life" (John 6:63). The life He had in mind, of course, was spiritual life. Thus, we turn to the Bible to feed and nurture the spirit within us.

The Power of the Bible to Change Lives

Life-changing power is one of the most compelling proofs that the Bible is no ordinary book, that it is from God. One leader in the Protestant Reformation called this the "self-validating" nature of Scripture. He offered a simple exercise to anyone who questioned the Bible's divine origin. First, he would tell the doubter to study the Bible thoroughly enough to understand its primary moral and spiritual principles. "Put those principles to work in your life consistently for two years or so," he would say. "By then your own experience will authenticate the Bible's claims for itself." Thousands have since taken his advice and discovered that what he said is true.

The Accuracy of the Bible

Since the Bible is from God, we should expect it to be truthful throughout. For example, the Bible describes thousands of historical events. If these descriptions are filled with inaccuracies and misrepresentations, then we have reason to question the reliability of the rest of the Bible. After all, how can we trust what the Bible says about God and spiritual realities if we cannot trust its details on things we can verify? For that reason, many who reject God and the Bible attack the accuracy of Biblical narratives.

Impressively, the Bible has withstood these attacks time and again. It has repeatedly proven itself a dependable and truthful record of what happened in the ancient world. For instance, in the early nineteenth century there were skeptics who ridiculed the idea that Moses could have written the first five books of the Bible. These critics argued that writing was an unknown art in Moses' day. But now, from the discoveries of archaeology, we know that writing had been around for more than a thousand years when Moses came on the scene.

< Moses and the art of writing

Others tried to discredit the Bible by saying it describes nations that never existed. Nineteenth-century critics of the Bible singled out the Hittites as an example. These

< The Bible and unknown nations

Canaan

Sargon

Syria

Archaeology

Ebla Tablets

Assyria

Hittites

Israelites

Hebrews

Hittites ➤

people are mentioned dozens of times in Scripture, but at one time there was no other record of them. Not so today. Early in the twentieth century archaeologists uncovered impressive remains of an extensive Hittite empire. Their findings have thoroughly verified what the Bible said about Hittites all along.

Sargon the Great ➤

In a similar fashion others accused the Bible of fabricating the exploits of a man named Sargon. The Bible identifies him as an Assyrian king who came against the city of Ashdod and subdued it (Isaiah 20:1). There was no such king, experts in Assyrian history contended. They could not find his name in any ancient record. As with the Hittites, historians reversed themselves when archaeologists uncovered Sargon's palace in modern-day Iraq. Carved on the

Ebla tablets ➤➤

walls of his palace was a description of his campaign against Ashdod. Another archaeological expedition, digging at Ashdod itself, uncovered a stone memorial commemorating Sargon's victory. Once more the Bible was vindicated.

And this process of verification is still under way. New discoveries continue to substantiate the Biblical record. This happened again in the 1960s and 1970s in Syria, where searchers uncovered a city named Ebla. Ebla had flourished about the time of Abraham, some 300 miles from where he lived. It was the capital of a thriving kingdom, with economic and political ties throughout the Middle East.

Archaeologists first identified the ruins of Ebla in 1968. A few years later they dug into the royal archives. There they found a vast array of well-preserved documents (some 17,000 in all) describing the world of Abraham's day. This discovery was vital, since it offered the possibility of clarifying long-disputed details in the story of Abraham in Genesis.

For instance, many scholars maintained that Canaan was more or less unbroken pastures at the time of Abraham, with few towns of significance. In the Bible, however, as Abraham travels the region, he and his family come in contact with one city after another. The documents from Ebla clearly tell us that Canaan was indeed populated with scores of cities, just as the Bible indicates.

The Ebla archives also confirm that the Bible was correct in referring to the region as Canaan in Abraham's day. Before Ebla was found, many historians believed that this name came into use only at a much later date. Genesis was wrong, they claimed, in calling the place where Abraham lived Canaan. But official records at Ebla tell a different story. Long before Abraham, documents at Ebla used the term Canaan with regularity.

While many documents from Ebla are still to be deciphered,

others have already demonstrated that customs and cultures around Abraham were just as the Bible describes them. What happened in the case of Ebla resembles a pattern that often repeats itself when the Bible comes under attack. First, based on some widely-accepted "truth," skeptics voice doubt about the accuracy of specific statements in the Bible. Then, years later — sometimes decades later — a major discovery invalidates the so-called truth that had been used to indict the Bible. With a fuller set of facts in hand, it turns out that the Bible is indeed correct.

This is not to say that we have resolved every discrepancy between the Bible and what specialists tell us about the ancient Middle East. But archaeology remains in its adolescence, relatively speaking. There are thousands of sites in the Middle East yet to be excavated. Much is still to be learned about the people of Bible times and how they lived. What we do know is that new discoveries, far from discrediting the Bible, have served to affirm its credibility. It is thus reasonable to expect that as investigations continue, they too will vouch for its reliability.

◄ Customs and cultures confirmed

◄◄ The name Canaan

Chapter Four

THE BOOKS OF MOSES

Moses, the man who led Israel from Egypt, wrote the first five books of the Bible. Their names are

▷	📖 Genesis
▷	📖 Exodus
▷	📖 Leviticus
▷	📖 Numbers
▷	📖 Deuteronomy

Moses ▷▷

Genesis covers a broad time span, the largest of any book in the Bible. Its opening chapters describe how God created the universe, fashioned the earth, and brought human beings into existence. From the very beginning Genesis shows God in a close, personal relationship with mankind. After tracing how the early human race expanded in the Middle East, Genesis turns specifically to Abraham and his family. Starting about 2050 BC, Genesis follows the life of Abraham and his descendants for four generations.

Genesis ends with Abraham's great-grandchildren (now known as Israelites) living in Egypt. They have been invited to settle there by the pharaoh, the Egyptian king. Exodus picks up their story 400 years later. The intervening centuries have not been friendly to Israel. The Egyptians have grown hostile toward the Israelites and forced them into slavery.

Moses was born to one of these slave families. But through an exceptional set of circumstances, the king's daughter adopted him and raised him in the royal family. At 40, knowing the truth of his origins, Moses made a daring attempt to free his people. When his effort failed, Moses fled as a fugitive to wilderness regions east of Egypt. There he lived another 40 years.

Then God appeared to Moses and told him to return to Egypt, rally his people around him, and free them from enslavement. Moses obeyed immediately, going straight to the pharaoh and demanding liberty for Israel. When the pharaoh refused the demand, God delivered a series of crippling, deadly blows against Egypt.

These devastations finally convinced the reluctant Egyptians that they could not prevail against God's will. In a moment unparalleled in history, they released the Israelites and allowed them to leave the country. Historians refer to this event as "the exodus," from a Greek word for "going out." Of course, this is also where the book of Exodus gets its name.

The last 28 chapters of Exodus describe what happened in the first months after the Israelites left Egypt. During these weeks the Lord gave Moses a set of laws to guide the people of Israel. Among these laws were specific regulations known today as the Ten Commandments. Carved on two stone tablets, the Ten Commandments served as a basic statement of what God expected from His people. Four commandments spelled out how to show proper respect for God and six others detailed how to act toward family and neighbors. We will examine these commands more fully at a later point.

Leviticus, the third book of Moses borrows its name from the Levites, one of the tribes of Israel. The Levites descended from Levi, Jacob's fourth son. Moses was a Levite, and this was the tribe that God chose to serve as Israel's priests. In the book of Leviticus God gives the Levites specific guidance on how to conduct their nation's worship. The book also includes hundreds of other regulations that were to govern the social and family life of Israel.

Of all the books in the Bible, Leviticus is among the most difficult for modern people to understand. The problem lies in the great cultural distance that separates us from the days of Moses. Leviticus refers to many customs, rituals, and social conventions that disappeared centuries ago in most of the world. Nevertheless, there are important principles in Leviticus, and we will touch on these along the way.

The fourth book of Moses is called Numbers, because it opens with the first census ever taken in Israel. This census is only a minor event in Numbers, however. The book is primarily a historical account of the first 40 years after Israel left Egypt. Throughout that time the Israelites lived as nomads in the arid wilderness of the Sinai peninsula.

<< The Ten Commandments

Along the way they began to encounter hostile nations. Numbers recounts Israel's first battles with these nations and shows how God sustained His people in victory. Through all of this, Israel's military prowess grew steadily more refined. And by the end of Numbers, we find the Israelites camped on the border of Canaan, prepared to possess it.

< Israel's enemies

It was also at this point that Moses died. Anticipating his approaching death, he wrote and delivered a lengthy farewell speech to Israel. This speech forms the core of his fifth book, Deuteronomy, a name that basically means "a second statement of the law."

<< Regulations for worship and life

As he said good-bye, Moses reviewed for his people all the good things God had done for them. He reminded them, one by one, of the moral principles God had called on them to respect. And he asked the Israelites to commit themselves afresh to these principles. The entire nation then made a vow to honor God's commands as they moved into Canaan. Finally, Moses entrusted the leadership of Israel to a man named Joshua, who had been at Moses' side ever since the exodus. With his successor in place, Moses retired to a remote mountain, where a short time later he died.

Death of Moses ➤

Moses left behind not only a vast nation ready to secure a new homeland, but five of the most important books in the Bible. These books — especially Genesis and Exodus — lay out the fundamental concepts on which the rest of the Bible builds. Only by understanding these principles can we grasp the full meaning of later Biblical developments. Given that fact, we will devote the next five chapters to the major themes from these books.

In the process we will trace four of the fourteen periods of Biblical history:

➤ The Period of Beginnings

➤ The Period of Abraham's Family

➤ The Period of Egyptian Bondage

➤ The Period Of Wilderness Wanderings

Genesis covers two of these, the Period of Beginnings and the Period of Abraham's Family. The first twelve chapters of Exodus are about the Period of Egyptian Bondage. The rest of Exodus guides us through the first months that Israel spent in the wilderness of Sinai. The remaining years in the wilderness are the subject of Leviticus, Numbers, and Deuteronomy.

The following chart lists the major events and key people we will encounter in these periods. You may find it helpful to return to this chart from time to time for a quick overview of what happened in a particular period.

Period	Major Events	Key Figures
Beginnings	Creation of the world	Adam and Eve
	Creation of the human race	
	Man's first acts of disobedience toward God	
	The first murder	Cain and Abel
	Universal wickedness in the human family	
	A flood that spares only one man and his family	Noah
	Repopulation of the earth	
Abraham's Family	God's promises to Abraham	Abraham, Sarah, and Hagar
		Lot
	The birth of Abraham's sons	Ishmael
	The sacrifice of Isaac	Isaac
	Isaac's marriage and the birth of his sons	Rebekah Esau Jacob
	Jacob's travels and family struggles	Rachel Leah
	Joseph's career in Egypt	Joseph
	Relocation of Jacob's family to Egypt	
Egyptian Bondage	Birth of Moses	Moses Miriam
	An encounter between God and Moses at a burning bush	
	Plagues on Egyptian society	Aaron
	The exodus	
	Egypt's army destroyed	
Wilderness Wanderings	The Ten Commandments	Moses
	Building the tabernacle as Israel's center of worship	Aaron
	Social and religious law codes established	Miriam
	The report of twelve spies	Joshua Caleb
	God's punishment of Israel's distrust	
	Initial conquest of territories near Canaan	Balaam Balak
	Moses' farewell address	
	Moses' death	

Chapter Five

THE PERIOD OF BEGINNINGS

Creation of all
things ➤

The Bible opens with a simple, straightforward statement of how everything we know had its start: "In the beginning God created the heavens and the earth." This is the first of several "beginnings" in Genesis. Others include:

➤ the beginning of humanity

➤ the beginning of evil and wrong-doing in the human family

➤ the beginning of death and suffering

➤ the beginning of cities and civilizations

➤ the beginning of God's special promises (called covenants)

As Genesis describes the creation of the world, it uses a mixture of history and symbolism. Students of the Bible do not always agree on how much of this language is literal and how much of it is figurative. Nor does it serve our purpose to delve into that discussion here. Instead, we will focus on principles that emerge from Genesis, whether the language is taken literally or symbolically.

The first of those principles is already on bold display in the book's opening words.

> In the beginning God created the heavens and the earth. And the earth was formless and void, and darkness was over the surface of the deep. And the Spirit of God was moving over the surface of the waters. Then God said, "Let there be light"; and there was light. — Genesis 1:1-3

The near poetic nature of this wording can obscure the profound truth it affirms. To sense the significance of that truth, we need to look at what was going on when Moses wrote Genesis. He had just led the Israelites from Egypt, where they had felt the influence of Egyptian religion for centuries. Like most people in the ancient world, the Egyptians worshiped objects of nature as though they were gods. Sun-gods, moon-gods, wind-gods, river-gods, ocean-gods — the list goes on and on. In fact, ancient pagan religions tended to share a common worldview, which included the ideas that:

➤ the material universe is eternal

➤ time existed before the gods

➤ the gods evolved from the material universe

➤ whatever we call "spirit" is a by-product of the material universe

Genesis, by contrast, begins by staking out a position completely opposed to these notions. Its simple declaration about the creation holds that

➤ when the material order started, God already existed

➤ when time as we know it began, God was already active

➤ when the physical universe was still formless, God's Spirit was already moving

Centuries later, especially among Greek philosophers, others developed similar ideas. But it was a thousand years after Moses before the Greeks reached these conclusions. At the time of Moses no other people had such a view of reality.

Moses had led his people into the wilderness to enter a special relationship with God. They were going to commit, unequivocally, to be God's people. It was essential, therefore, to purge their thinking of distorted ideas about God and who He was. Otherwise they might confuse Him with the gods their neighbors worshiped.

So Moses opened Genesis by drawing a clear distinction between the God he served and all other deities. With the same stroke of his pen, Moses took the offensive in a debate that is still raging. It is a debate about the underlying nature of reality. To be specific, is the world ultimately spiritual in nature? Or is it material?

The Ultimate Nature of Reality

As we have noted, the pagans said with one voice that reality is ultimately material. Today many schools of philosophy still advance the same idea. We call this type of philosophy "materialism," for it teaches that there is no reality beyond the realm of matter. Materialism explains everything in terms of matter in motion. In materialism even thought itself is nothing more than electrical impulses and chemical firings in the brain.

◄ Pagan concepts of reality

The Bible, on the other hand, affirms that ultimate reality is spiritual — that spirit existed *before* the material universe, that it exists *independent* of the material universe, and that it exercises power *over* the material universe. The mind is not only a set of electrochemical reactions. It is also the product of a spiritual essence within us. Of all the creatures on the planet, the Bible describes humans alone as having a spirit. This spirit separates us from the animal kingdom. While animals share a few basic emotions in common with us, only humans can know such things as wonder, beauty, hope, and awe. In a word, only humans look at life in terms of meaning and values.

◄ The spiritual and the material

This very aspect of human existence unmasks the fatal flaw in materialism. Materialism cannot adequately account for our deep drive to give meaning and value to what we experience. We speak of things as being rational or irrational, true or false, beautiful or ugly, moral or immoral. But where do

Source of value judgments ➤

such values come from if our mind is nothing but electrons flowing along neural pathways? If the mind is only matter in motion, how can it give rise to values?

The best materialism can do is to describe values as a by-product of the brain's evolution. But this begs the question, for if the brain is merely matter in motion, where did these by-products come from? Matter in motion, whether inside our heads or elsewhere, has no value in and of itself. We can combine and recombine matter as many ways as we like, but the end result is only moving matter, not values.

To illustrate, what would you think if I should say, "Polaris is a very rational star, but Sirius is not." Or what if I asked, "Which phase of the moon is the most moral?" You would quickly conclude that I was talking nonsense. There is nothing rational or moral about glowing stars and phases of the moon. They are simply a manifestation of matter in motion.

But what is true of stars and the moon is equally true of molecules in the brain. Just as billions of stars blazing in the night cannot give rise

to a single rational thought, billions of electrons flashing through the brain cannot create a single value. There must be something over and above the material realm that endows us with appreciation for beauty, truth, and goodness. The Bible says there is — the spirit that God placed within us.

The Days of Creation

In Genesis 1 the creation of humanity occurs at the end of a process that moves through six stages of development. Genesis 1 describes these six stages as days.

➤ On day one God creates light and separates it from darkness.

➤ On day two He creates the expanse we know as the sky. With it He separates the water vapor of the clouds from the endless waters of the ocean.

➤ On day three he causes dry land to appear and produces vegetation on the earth.

➤ On day four He sets the sun, moon, and stars in place.

➤ On day five He creates birds and marine creatures.

➤ And on day six He creates the land animals and mankind.

We can view this progression as two groups of three days each. That is, the first three days make up one group, with days four, five, and six comprising a second one. In both groups:

Day	What God Does	Day	What God Does
1	Divides light from darkness	4	Fashions light bearing and light reflecting objects of outer space
2	Stretches the sky as a canopy over the oceans	5	Creates birds of the sky and sea creatures
3	Separates dry land from the sea	6	Populates the land with life forms

> ➤ the first day deals with light and darkness

> ➤ the second day centers on the atmosphere and the seas

> ➤ the third day involves developments on the land

Worded another way, on each of the first three days God creates a specific habitat or environment. On the corresponding day in the second group He creates the things that reside in that habitat, as the above chart indicates.

By picturing the creation this way, Moses declared God's total control over the universe. God has created both creature and habitat, from the tiniest seed in the ground to the most gigantic star in the distant galaxies.

Once God completed His six days of creation, the Bible describes Him as "resting" on the seventh day. His "rest" became the precedent for what the Israelites called the Sabbath, their name for the seventh day of the week. The Sabbath was a day of complete rest for everyone in Israel.

It is important to note that God ends each day in Genesis 1 by looking at His handiwork and saying, "It is good." These words stand in contrast to those religions, both ancient and modern, that celebrate the spirit as good, but perceive anything material as evil. Oriental religions in particular tend to reject the value of the material world. Several schools of Greek philosophy took a similar stance, which had a lasting influence on religion in the West. Over the past 2000 years dozens of religious movements in Europe and the Americas have encouraged their followers to withdraw from any enjoyment of material pleasure and comfort.

What the Bible teaches is altogether different. God, the ultimate

◄◄ God has total control

◄ What God makes is good

Man and the
image of God **>>**

Human
sexuality **>>**

Spirit, fashioned every element of the material universe. At each stage of creation He paused to say of this universe, "It is good." He then continued on this course, confirming the value of the physical realm throughout Scripture. God never hesitated to promise material blessings to those who serve Him. To Israel He said, "I will give you the land of Canaan, a place flowing with milk and honey" (Exodus 13:5) His calendar for Israel included several feast days each year. He provided for soldiers in Israel to be excused from military duty in the first year of their marriage so they could stay home and enjoy time with their wives.

In short, God encourages us to delight in the good things of life. He only asks that we never go beyond what is moral and upright in our pursuit of pleasure. The Bible's instruction is intended to help us know when we have taken pleasure-seeking too far. We are to act responsibly, the Bible says, not irresponsibly.

The Nature of Man

In describing the creation of humanity, Genesis emphasizes four aspects of our nature. Each of these aspects involves some sphere of personal responsibility. Specifically, Genesis says that God created us as:

Man's sovereignty
over nature **>>**

- ➤ spiritual beings
- ➤ sexual beings
- ➤ sovereign beings
- ➤ social beings

We have already seen that God gave us a *spiritual* essence by creating us in His own image and likeness (Genesis 1:27). This implies that we are to live at a level of responsibility that is impossible for animals, who have no spirit. The same passage says that God created us male and female. *Sexuality* is a fundamental drive in human nature because God created us that way. But just as there are proper and improper ways to enjoy material delights, the Bible frequently sets out guidelines for appropriately enjoying sex.

We will note these principles on sexuality as we come to them. For now we can summarize all God says on the subject like this: God's design is for sex to be enjoyed exclusively in the bonds of a husband-wife relationship. God speaks of sex outside of marriage as a violation of His will and calls it sin. On the other hand, within marriage God always encourages full sexual enjoyment. As if to emphasize that point, He placed a very striking book in the Bible. It is called the Song of Solomon, a highly erotic piece of literature that celebrates the sexual bonding between a husband and wife.

Moses points to our *sovereign* nature when he quotes God as saying that man and woman were to "subdue the earth," that is, to tame its natural forces. Humanity was to "rule over the fish of the sea and over the birds of the sky and over every living thing that moves on the earth" (Genesis 1:28).

This does not mean that God turned us loose to exploit the earth in a way that is environmentally destructive. Quite the contrary. In the Bible, God constantly expects those with authority to use their power for the benefit of the ones they govern. Our sovereignty over nature is thus a trust. God has entrusted mankind with caring for His creation. He told the first man and woman that they were to cultivate and keep the habitat in which He had placed them (Genesis 2:15). As He gave them this command, God used a verb that carried the sense of a mother nursing her child. It suggests that we are to nurture the environment as something precious to us.

Genesis underscores our *social* nature when it shows God looking at the first human (a man by the name of Adam) and saying, "It is not good for the man to be alone" (Genesis 2:18). Remember that God completes each phase of creation with the words, "It is good." And once He caps off the creative process by placing man and woman together in their habitat, He says, "It is *very* good" (Genesis 1:31). The first thing He ever says is *not* good is for man to be alone.

This is why God gives so much guidance in the Bible about building a safe, just, and honest society. We have an innate need to be with people. We need to feel free to associate openly with others. But in a world that is unsafe, unjust, and dishonest, we are forced to pull into a protective shell and limit social interaction. The result is a life that quickly becomes emotionally and psychologically impoverished.

◄◄ Man's responsiibility to nature

The Garden of Eden

To have a healthy society there must be standards of behavior that everyone respects. Thus, as we move into Genesis 2, the focus changes from the *physical* realm and how it came into existence to the *moral* realm and how it came into existence. For the first time God sets down behavioral guidelines for man and woman, with warnings of the consequence if they disobey.

◄ Standards of behavior

The backdrop for Genesis 2 is a lush, extensive garden called Eden. In its midst was a plant called "the tree of life." By eating the fruit on this tree, a person could live forever. Once God created Adam and his wife Eve, he placed them in this beautiful setting to live. In keeping with His desire for us to enjoy the pleasures of our existence, He told them they could eat freely from all the trees in the garden, with one exception. They were not to touch what He called the "tree of the knowledge of good and evil."

◄ The tree of life

◄ The tree of knowledge of good and evil

We do not know what kind of tree this was or what type of fruit it bore. Nor do we know how eating its fruit would have deepened their understanding of good and evil.

◄◄ Mankind in society

What we do know is that God told them to leave the tree alone. He said they would bring death on themselves if they violated this instruction (Genesis 2:16-17).

With this injunction the Bible introduces themes that repeat themselves throughout Scripture.

➤ First, God has given us the *freedom to choose*, even to choose what is neither good for us nor in line with what He wants for us.

➤ Second, He sometimes warns us to avoid things that He knows are dangerous for us or society.

➤ Third, He does not always go into detail as to *why* we should avoid the things He prohibits. He merely says to stay away from them.

➤ Fourth, when He makes a prohibition without telling us why, *we are expected to trust Him* and obey anyway. The Bible term for trusting Him is to "have faith" in Him. What He asked of Adam and Eve, then, was to put their faith in Him.

Satan makes an appearance ➤

Sin defined ➤➤

For a while they did. But in Genesis 3 another creature shows up in the garden and begins to undermine their trust. Genesis 3 does not name this being, but elsewhere the Bible identifies him as Satan or the Devil. The Bible offers little information about his origins. He seems to have once been part of the angelic circle around God. At some juncture he rebelled and led a large contingent of other angels in his rebellion. (Angels, like human beings, apparently have the freedom to choose their course of action.)

When Satan slipped into the Garden of Eden, he took on the guise of a cunning, crafty serpent. Through a series of cleverly worded questions he managed to undermine Eve's trust in God. He flatly denied that she would die if she ate fruit from the tree of the knowledge of good and evil. Instead, he asserted that she would become like God Himself in her wisdom (Genesis 3:1-6). Pondering that possibility, Eve began to look at the forbidden fruit in a new light. The Bible says that she noticed three things about it.

➤ It was lovely to look at.

➤ It held the promise of tasting good.

➤ And it seemed like a gateway to great wisdom and power.

She therefore succumbed to Satan's temptation and ate the fruit. She also drew Adam into her disobedience.

By their action Adam and Eve set in motion the process of sin that has polluted human existence ever since. Sin is simply a violation of what God commands. Sin, moreover, follows a consistent pattern that the story of Eve and Satan plainly illustrates. When we allow ourselves to be drawn away from God, the underlying motive is one of three things.

➤ Either we choose to pursue something that looks attractive on the surface, like Eve seeing the fruit to be lovely.

➤ Or we give in to the entice-ments of basic drives and sen-sual appetites (she pictured the fruit as tasting good).

➤ Or we let pride get the upper hand, as Eve did in wanting the fruit because it would make her wise.

The New Testament refers to these three motivating forces as "the desire of the eye, the desire of the body, and the pride of life" (1 John 2:16). One way or another, all wrongdoing in the human family can be traced back to our failure to put proper controls on one of these three forces.

Sin and Death

What Adam and Eve soon learned is that Satan had deceived them. While eating the forbidden fruit did open their eyes to new real-ities, they did not gain Godlike power at all. What they experienced more than anything else was shame. Sin and shame make it impossible to feel comfortable in God's presence. So the next time God came to the garden, Adam and Eve hid from Him (Genesis 3:8-10).

Due to their disobedience, God banished them from the garden. No longer could they eat fruit from the tree of life. Theirs was now a world where death reigned unchecked.

From the Garden of Eden onward, sin has grown in magnitude and scope. Every man and woman has become its victim. And wherever sin spreads, it puts barriers between God and mankind, just as it caused Adam and Eve to hide when He drew near.

To remove those barriers, God made a special promise to Eve. Before He sent her from the garden, He promised that one of her descendants would eventually crush Satan's head, receiving a painful bruise in the process (Genesis 3:15). Without being spe-cific, God seemed to imply that this act would somehow reverse the damage that occurred when Satan deceived Eve.

We will understand this promise more fully when we come to the New Testament. There we will see Jesus dealing Satan a crushing blow. For now we only need to recognize that God had a plan from the begin-ning to rescind what Satan had done. Shame and death would not be the last word. God had a plan to overcome them both.

As for Adam and Eve, heartache and tragedy awaited outside the garden. Genesis 4 opens with Eve giving birth to a son. She calls him Cain. In Hebrew his name speaks of a great hope that she placed in him. Perhaps she thought he was the one who would reverse what sin had set in motion. But her hopes proved sadly mistaken. Cain became a criminal, murdering his

◀◀ The consequences of sin

◀ God's plan

Eden

Sin

Adam & Eve

Cain

Murder

Tree of Knowledge
of Good and Evil

Abel

Noah

World full
of sin

Flood

own brother Abel. Eve had looked to her son for hope, to no avail. Others in the Bible will also anchor their hope to some person or group of persons. But as Eve learned, building our hopes around human beings can be deeply disappointing. That is why God wants us to center our hope on Him, His promises, and His steadfast promise-keeping.

After Cain's crime, sin seems to explode on the human scene. The next section of Genesis talks about rising arrogance, hunger for power, and violence that swept over the earth. Things finally degenerated to the point that every thought and intention of the human spirit was evil, and that continually (Genesis 6:5-12). There was one notable exception. A man named Noah had managed to stay true to God, despite the immoral people around him.

The Flood (Genesis 6–9)

God warned Noah that He was about to destroy the blatant wickedness of the human race by wiping out all human life in a vast flood. But God planned to spare Noah and his family so that they could rebuild the population. God instructed Noah to build a huge boat (the Bible name for it is an ark) to house Noah's family and hundreds of animals. Genesis 7–8 tells of Noah making those preparations and of the flood that came, just as God had said. When the waters finally subsided, Noah and his family emerged from the ark and began life anew.

Following the flood the human race resumed its expansion. Genesis tells about the founding of Babylon and other cities and nations of the ancient world. But soon these nations slipped into arrogance and immorality, just like the people destroyed by the flood.

The flood thus stands as powerful testimony that sin is a serious, relentless problem. We might have expected the fresh start with Noah and his family to return humanity to a path of goodness. But soon after the flood, sin held sway again. Sin is a dangerous spiritual infection. All it needs is a slight opening. From there it has the power to draw us under its power, if we fail to actively resist it.

As we come to the end of Genesis 11, then, God has shown us just how vulnerable we are to the influence of evil. We need that reminder. We are prone to believe that people would turn their back on evil if they lived in a lush, comfortable, well-supplied world like Eden. But the story of Adam and Eve tells us otherwise. It also seems logical that goodness would reign forever if we simply wiped out every evil person and started society all over again. But the story of the flood and its aftermath puts that notion to rest.

We live in a world where evil is entrenched. While we can marshal our own human resources to fight it — which God calls on us to do — we lack the ability to rid the world entirely of evil. If we hope to reverse what evil has done, we must depend on something beyond ourselves.

◄◄ Sin returns again and again

Knowing that, God promised Adam and Eve that He would bring a person into the world who would help us triumph fully and completely over evil. As we move into Genesis 12, God sets that process in motion by building a special relationship with Abraham, one of the most important figures in the Bible. We turn next to him and his extraordinary life.

◄ God starts his plan for salvation

Chapter Six

ABRAHAM, THE MAN OF FAITH

The Bible first introduces us to Abraham when he was 75 years old. At the time he was still known as Abram. Because Hebrew was his native tongue, the Bible refers to Abram and his descendants as Hebrews (Genesis 14:13; 39:14-17). His wife was Sarai, a strikingly beautiful woman even as she approached old age. Although Abram had achieved considerable prominence and wealth, he and Sarai lived with deep heartbreak, for they were without a child.

Abram's father and grandfather had made their home in Mesopotamia, along the Euphrates River, an area already noted for its advanced economy and civilization. In Genesis 12, God appeared to Abram and instructed him to leave the comforts and culture of this homeland. Without specifying where He was taking Abram, God simply said, "Leave for a land I will show you."

Abram called out of his homeland ➤

In turn, God promised to bestow a series of blessings on Abram:

God's promises to Abram ➤

> I will make you a great nation. I will bless you, and make your name great. Thus you shall be a blessing. And I shall bless those who bless you, and the one who curses you I will curse. And in you all the families of the earth will be blessed.
> — Genesis 12:2-3

Trusting God, Abram began an arduous migration with his herds, his servants, his wife, a nephew named Lot, and Lot's family. Although we cannot pinpoint the exact date when they began their journey, Bible chronology would place it sometime before 2050 BC. Over time God brought them to Canaan, where He told Abram, "I have given your descendants this land, from the river of Egypt as far as the great river, the river Euphrates" (Genesis 15:18).

These two promises — that all the families of the earth would be blessed through Abram's family and that his descendants would be a great nation between the Euphrates River and Egypt — must have been quite difficult for the old man to believe. Not only was Sarai childless, she was now at an age when having children seemed no longer

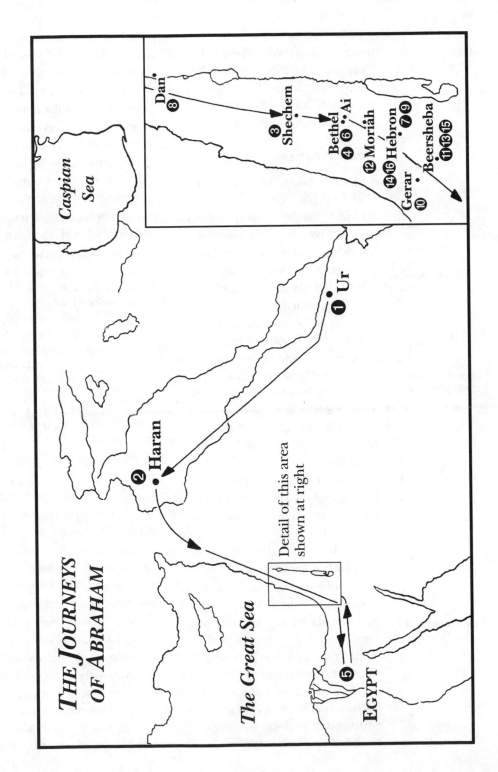

THE JOURNEYS OF ABRAHAM

Caspian Sea

Dan
⑧

Shechem
③

Bethel
④ ⑥ ·Ai

Moriah
⑫

Hebron
⑭⑯   ⑦⑨

Gerar
⑩

Beersheba
⑪⑬⑮

Ur
❶

Haran
❷

The Great Sea

Detail of this area
shown at right

EGYPT
❺

possible. But to confirm His promise, God renamed Abram. "You shall be called Abraham," He said, which means "the father of a multitude." Sarai also became Sarah, meaning "princess."

God's Promise Keeping

One by one God carried out each of these promises. As God had said, Abraham received great personal blessings. His wealth and prestige grew immensely in Canaan (Genesis 13:2). And not just one, but several nations emerged from his family, either as direct descendants or descending from his nephew Lot. These included the Israelites, the Ishmaelites (ancestors of today's Arabs), as well as a number of lesser nations that appear regularly in the Bible, people like the Edomites, the Midianites, the Moabites, and the Ammonites.

Father of many nations ➤

Egyptian slavery predicted ➤➤

Over a much longer period of time God also carried through on His promise to bless all families of the earth through Abraham's descendants. The New Testament says that God fulfilled this promise in the person of Jesus (Galatians 3:16).

All families of the earth blessed ➤

God had assured Adam and Eve that one of their descendants would remove the harm brought to the human race by sin. In choosing Abraham, God selected the family tree from which that descendant, Jesus, would come. Eventually God narrowed this selection to the nation of Israel, then to the tribe of

God's timetables ➤➤

Judah, and finally to the family of David, the second king of Israel (2 Samuel 7:12-13).

While God did fulfill every promise to Abraham, some in only a few years, others went unfulfilled for ages. In the case of Jesus, 2000 years passed before He was born. Even ownership of Canaan, promised to Abraham's family, did not occur until centuries after his death. God told Abraham,

> Your descendants will be strangers in another land, where they will be enslaved and mistreated for 400 years. Then I will punish that nation and bring your descendants back to Canaan and give it to them as a lasting possession.
> — Genesis 15:13-16

This was God's way of foretelling the slavery that Israel would undergo in Egypt, beginning some 200 years later.

Here, in this early promise-making, God is showing us that He does not always look at time the way we do. From our perspective a promise that goes unhonored for decades seems like nothing but empty words. But with God a thousand years is like a single day, as the New Testament confirms (2 Peter 3:8). To Him a promise made a thousand years ago is like a promise made just yesterday. By not rushing to carry out every promise, God tests our confidence both in Him and in His word. Throughout the Bible God offers hope to those who trust Him. But hope, by its very nature, involves patient waiting. Thus, from the earliest scenes of the Bible, God starts showing us the importance of waiting patiently, never losing faith that He will keep His word.

Ishmael and Isaac (Genesis 16–21)

Still, some progress toward the fulfillment of God's promise had to begin in Abraham's lifetime. If great nations were to come from him, he had to have a child. Time was passing and Sarah was getting no younger. Finally Sarah took things in her own hands. She had a handmaid by the name of Hagar, an Egyptian slave. Sarah suggested that Abraham have a child by Hagar. This was a common practice in the ancient world, somewhat akin to our modern concept of surrogate mothering, except that the modern world induces pregnancy through a medical procedure rather than sexual intercourse.

Just as Sarah hoped, Hagar became pregnant and delivered a son, Ishmael. But Ishmael was not the son that God had promised. When Ishmael was 13 years old, God appeared once more to Abraham. "I will bless Ishmael," God said, "and I will create a nation out of his descendants. But the son through whom I plan to bless the world will come from Sarah" (Genesis 17:18-21).

When Abraham heard that Sarah would have a child, he laughed (Genesis 17:17). He probably did not laugh from derision, but from the humorous notion that a couple at their age should be preparing for a firstborn. When God later affirmed His promise to Sarah, she laughed, too (Genesis 18:9-12). But God was true to His word and they indeed soon had a son. Fittingly, they gave him the name Isaac, which means "laughter."

◄ Birth of Isaac

Obviously, Isaac's birth was far from ordinary. It was made possible because God suspended the normal rules of nature. He apparently delayed Isaac's birth to make a vital point to Abraham, Sarah, and all others who would follow Him. Just because what He promises seems impossible, that does not preclude it from happening. As God said to Sarah when she laughed, "Is anything too difficult for Me?" (Genesis 18:14.) To truly trust God, we must be willing to maintain our trust even when what He says exceeds our comprehension. That is the essence of faith.

The Sacrifice of Isaac (Genesis 22)

◄◄ Birth of Ishmael

As for Abraham and Sarah, they were now persuaded that God could indeed do what men think impossible. But had they truly learned to trust Him? God put a special test before Abraham to find out. When Isaac began to mature (tradition says he was about 12 years old), God told Abraham to take the boy to the heights of a

◄ God tests Abraham's faith

What God
asks of us >>

Trust in unusual
circumstances >

Abraham's final
years >>

mountain called Moriah, build an altar, put the boy on the altar, and sacrifice him to God. Moriah later became known as Mount Zion. It is the place where Jerusalem would eventually stand and the place where Jesus Himself was killed.

Amazingly, Abraham's trust in God had become so strong that he set out immediately to obey. Obviously, God's command made no sense. Since God had insisted that He would bless the world through Isaac, why would He now ask Abraham to slay the boy? And given God's commitment to what is right and moral, how could He demand that Abraham sacrifice a child the way pagans did in some of their religions?

Yet, even though the command was illogical and morally troubling, Abraham was ready to submit to it. The New Testament, commenting on this event, suggests that Abraham had reasoned out in his mind what God would do. After Isaac died, Abraham concluded, God would raise the boy back to life (Hebrews 11:17-19). But as Abraham and Isaac approached Mount Moriah, God had a plan of His own. Just as Abraham was about to plunge the knife into Isaac's chest, God froze the muscles of Abraham's arm. He praised Abraham for his faith and pointed him to a ram, snarled in some brambles, which could be sacrificed as a substitute for Isaac.

The story of Isaac is a great lesson about the nature of faith. To follow God, we may sometimes face situations in which He asks us to respond in ways that seem unreasonable. For example, the teachings of Jesus include many principles that violate our sense of reasonableness and fair play. He tells us not to retaliate when someone strikes us (Matthew 5:39). He tells us to forgive those who mistreat us, even if they do it hundreds of times (Matthew 18:21-22). He tells us to do good to those who would do us evil (Luke 6:27-28). These are not the things we would do if we followed what common sense and our natural instincts dictate. But God invites us to trust Him and discover how fruitful it is to live this way.

Covenant Relationships

With the near-sacrifice of Isaac, the last major episode of Abraham's life draws to an end. The Bible gives some concluding details about his final years: the marriage of Isaac to Rebekah, his cousin; the death and burial of Sarah; and Abraham's second marriage to a woman named Keturah, who gave him several additional sons. But these stories are basically postscripts to his life of faith.

One aspect of Abraham's story, however, remains to be explored, namely, the way God couched His promises to Abraham. God put these promises in the form of a covenant (Genesis 15:18; 17:10). Covenant-making is characteristic of God in Scripture. Earlier He had entered a covenant with Noah, promising never again to destroy mankind in a flood (Genesis 9:9). And in the course of the Bible God makes a host of covenants, both with individuals and with entire nations.

It is obviously important, then, to understand the concept of covenant. We can think of covenants as a solemn way of pledging oneself to a promise. In God's own words, His covenant with Abraham was the equivalent of His "swearing with an oath" that He would carry out what He promised (Genesis 26:3).

Covenants were quite common in the ancient world. Archaeologists have uncovered hundreds of documents that record covenant transactions. In some ways they were like contracts in the modern world, but with significant differences. The typical covenant in Abraham's day was initiated by a man of prominence, often a king. He would enter the covenant with someone who was subject to him. The covenant itself would promise specific blessings to be given to the subject.

It is noteworthy that covenant documents often omitted any reference to what the subject would do. There was no need to detail the subject's duties, for everyone knew what was expected of him — he would be ready to do whatever his master asked. The same is true of God's covenant statements in the Bible. They sometimes read as though He is giving a unilateral blessing to the one to whom He

extends a covenant. But in the background is the reality that those who are in covenant with Him are expected to obey. When they do not, He reserves the right to revoke His covenant promises.

The book of Numbers gives an example of this. There God made a covenant with a man named Phinehas, the grandson of Aaron, Moses' brother. Phinehas had been particularly zealous to keep the worship of God pure in Israel. God therefore promised that the office of high priest would remain in the family of Phinehas forever (Numbers 25:10-13). On the surface, this seems like an unconditional promise. But the unspoken assumption, understood by God and Phinehas alike, was that wholesale disregard for obeying God could invalidate the covenant.

And that very thing occurred a few generations later. Eli, a descendant of Phinehas, served as high priest for 40 years. He had two sons, one named Phinehas (no doubt in honor of his famous forefather), the other Hophni. Yet, unlike Phinehas of old, these men were totally corrupt. They stole sacrifices that people brought to God's altar. They committed adultery with women who served in the place of worship. And to make matters worse, Eli did little more than verbally chastise his sons for their misconduct (1 Samuel 2:22-25).

God therefore sent a messenger to Eli, revoking the long-standing

◄ Conditional nature of God's covenants

◄◄ Covenants in the ancient world

◄ Eli the priest

covenant with his family. The messenger's words were to this effect:

> The Lord God of Israel declares, "I did truly say that your house and your father's house should stand before me forever." But now the Lord declares, "Far be it from Me. For I will honor those who honor Me, but those who despise Me I will dishonor."
>
> —1 Samuel 2:30

God also said He would take the priesthood from Eli's family and give it to someone else who would be faithful to Him (1 Samuel 2:31-36). Shortly thereafter Eli and his sons all died on the same day (1 Samuel 4:17-18), and God removed the high priesthood from their household.

Progression of God's love »

Covenants and Grace

It is also important to notice that in making a covenant, God offers blessings first, then calls on those who benefit from His kindness to obey Him out of appreciation. This is exactly opposite to the way many people think of serving God. Our natural tendency is to believe that we must first obey Him perfectly, and only then will He bless us. Or to put it another way, we are inclined to think we must earn God's favor.

Grace ›

The Bible replies that we can do nothing to earn God's favor. His kindness toward us is always unmerited (Ephesians 2:8-9). The Biblical word for this type of kindness is "grace." God shows us grace — unmerited kindness —

because He loves us. He wants the best for us. He therefore provides the blessings and resources we need to have powerful spiritual lives.

When we genuinely appreciate what God has given us, we repay Him with respect for His laws and His commands. Ingratitude is always treated as a grave sin in the Bible (see Romans 1:21, for example). Through the prophets God frequently reminded Israel of all He had done for them and then asked why they were repaying His kindness with indifference and disobedience.

To put this another way, God's love sets in motion a progression that moves

- ➤ from grace
- ➤ to covenants that express His grace
- ➤ to blessings that flow from God's covenant
- ➤ to appreciation for those blessings
- ➤ to obedience based on appreciation

One way God expects us to show appreciation is by being covenant-keepers ourselves as we deal with one another. Just as God gives His word, then keeps it, He calls on us to be people who keep our word. When people consistently honor their covenants and commitments, even when it is costly to do so, human society reaches its highest potential.

Chapter Seven

ABRAHAM'S FAMILY

The Bible is the story of God doing extraordinary things through the most ordinary of people. The men and women we meet in the Bible are real people, like you and me, living in a real world and struggling with real-life issues. The Bible neither idealizes their achievements nor ignores the flaws in their character. Instead, it simply relates what they did, both good and bad.

There is a purpose for this candor. It negates any tendency to believe that God works only with people whose lives are perfect. That misconception, so common in every age, keeps many from trying to serve Him. To dispel this misunderstanding, the Bible lets us see the blemished character of those through whom God performs great deeds.

Nowhere is this more fully the case than in the last half of Genesis. There we meet the later generations of Abraham's family. In general, these were upright people, men and women of faith and principle. But they could slip into pettiness, jealousy, strife, and deceit.

Still, God never gave up on them. To each succeeding generation He renewed the promise made to Abraham. And God continued to seek a relationship with them, even when they behaved poorly.

◀◀ Real people

Strife and envy ran deep in this family as early as the days of Abraham himself. He and his nephew Lot parted company because their servants argued incessantly over water and grazing rights (Genesis 13:5-13). In Abraham's own household there was constant bickering between his wife Sarah and his concubine Hagar. Later their sons were at odds, for Ishmael seemed to delight in treating Isaac with contempt. The problem became so intense that Sarah finally refused to tolerate it any longer. She demanded that Abraham send Hagar and Ishmael away, which he did with regret (Genesis 21:8-21).

◀ Family quarrels

Family feuds continued to follow Isaac long after he left his father's tent. The man whose name meant "laughter" ended up facing frequent sorrow because of a wife and son who perfected the art of deception

◀ Isaac's problems

and betrayal. His wife was Rebekah and his son was Jacob, the man who later became the father of the Israelites.

Jacob and Esau (Genesis 27–28)

From birth Jacob was totally different from his twin brother Esau, both in appearance and personality. Esau was hairy, from head to foot. He loved hunting and the outdoors. Jacob, by contrast, was smooth-skinned and liked to putter around the household. Today we would call him a "Mama's boy."

Favoritism ➤

Esau, the firstborn, happened to be Isaac's favorite. Rebekah countered by practicing favoritism toward Jacob. This set the stage for open rivalry between the boys as they grew into manhood. One day Jacob was tending a stew that simmered on the fire when Esau came in from a lengthy hunting trip. Exhausted and virtually at the point of collapse, Esau asked for something to eat. Never one to forgo an advantage, Jacob responded by saying, "Give me the special rights of inheritance you have as the firstborn, and I will give you food." Esau, famished and on the verge of death, consented.

Jacob's deceit ➤➤

Esau gives up his rights ➤

But Jacob's treachery was far from over. Later, when Isaac was old and blind, Jacob deceived his own father in order to defraud Esau again. And this time Rebekah was Jacob's accomplice. In fact, she instigated the plot. It began when she overheard a conversation between Isaac and Esau. Fearing that death might soon overtake him, Isaac wanted to pronounce a blessing on his sons. This was a common custom in their day, and it was one of the most cherished moments in any family. A father who refused to bless his son effectively disinherited the boy and made him a family outcast.

As part of his blessing, the father normally passed his role as family leader to the firstborn. Isaac planned to give the blessing of the firstborn to Esau. As a preliminary to the blessing, he asked Esau to go to the field, hunt down some wild game, cook it, and bring it to Isaac's bedside. "After I eat your food," Isaac said, "I will give you my blessing."

Esau left immediately to carry out his father's request. Rebekah, meanwhile, went to Jacob and had him retrieve two young goats from the flock. She cooked them with a flavoring Isaac liked. Then she dressed Jacob in some of Esau's clothing, glued hair from the goats on Jacob's smooth-skinned arms and hands, and told Jacob to take the food to his father, pretending to be Esau. Jacob followed his mother's instructions. And even though Isaac was wary, sensing that something was amiss, the ruse worked, for Isaac was blind from old age. Isaac enjoyed the meal, drew Jacob to him, and gave him the blessing of the firstborn.

When Esau returned from his hunt and discovered what had happened, he flew into a rage. Soon he was plotting to kill Jacob. To protect her favorite son, Rebekah hurriedly dispatched Jacob to Mesopotamia, to the home of her brother Laban. Traveling alone and with minimal provisions because of his haste, Jacob camped overnight in the open countryside.

One night, at a place called Bethel, God appeared to Jacob in a dream, saying,

> I am the Lord, the God of your father Abraham and the God of Isaac. I will give the land on which you lie to you and to your descendants. They will be as countless as the dust of the earth. And through your offspring all families of the earth will be blessed.

God concluded His appearance to Jacob by adding, "I will protect you wherever you go and will bring you back to this land; for I will not abandon you until I have done what I have promised" (Genesis 28:10-15).

These words have a familiar ring to them. They are similar to the ones God spoke to Abraham. By repeating them to Jacob, God was choosing to work through Jacob to carry out the earlier covenant with Abraham. But why Jacob? Here is a man who is a fugitive, on the run after swindling his brother and totally deceiving his father. This is hardly a man who deserves God's kindness.

Which is the very point of the story. God is not showing kindness to Jacob because Jacob deserves it.

God is simply saying that nothing Jacob has done stands in the way of what God will do with him in the future. Through the example of Jacob, God is telling us the same thing. No matter how badly we have ruined our past, God simply asks us to rise above those mistakes and become what He calls us to be. This does not mean that He approves of what we did wrong in the past any more than He approved of Jacob's lying and cheating. But God does not want the weight of our past to impede the promise of our future.

Jacob's Family (Genesis 29–37)

Quite a future lay ahead of Jacob. In Mesopotamia he met Rachel, his cousin, and fell in love immediately. But in dealing with her father Laban, Jacob came up against a man as skilled in the art of deception as Jacob himself. The young deceiver was about to learn how it feels to be tricked and cheated. Jacob asked Laban for permission to marry Rachel, and Laban consented, on one condition. Jacob would have to work Laban's flocks and herds for seven years before the marriage could take place. Jacob accepted these terms, and went to work for Laban. But at the wedding Laban gave his older daughter Leah to Jacob instead of Rachel. Jacob protested, of course, whereupon Laban offered to give him Rachel, too—but only in

<< Esau's anger

<< God's promise to Jacob

< The deceiver deceived

The name
Israel >>

exchange for an additional seven years of service.

Because he loved Rachel so much, Jacob agreed to the arrangement. And during the years he worked for her father, he managed to become quite wealthy in his own right. But his family was torn with strife, just like the one he grew up in. For one thing, Jacob never treated Leah with the tenderness and intimacy that he accorded Rachel. Perhaps he resented Leah as a symbol of her father's deception. Because of his unequal treatment, bitterness erupted between the sisters and between their children. And then, as if favoritism had not caused him enough grief already, Jacob openly displayed his fond affection for Joseph, Rachel's firstborn.

Favoritism
repeated >

Joseph sold by
his brothers >>

In the middle of this, Laban continued to find ways to cheat Jacob and leave him at a disadvantage. Jacob's frustration grew steadily, until he could bear Laban's dishonesty no longer. Without so much as a word to his father-in-law, Jacob gathered his herds, his servants, and his family and struck out for Canaan. Somehow he would try to make amends with Esau and restore his relationship with Isaac. By now Esau had become a man of considerable wealth himself. He was also a man with a forgiving spirit. Dismissing the wrongs he had suffered at Jacob's hands, he hurried to meet his returning brother and welcome him home.

Shortly after arriving in Canaan, Jacob had another encounter with God, who used the occasion to give him the name Israel, "the one who wrestles with God" (Genesis 35:9-12). This is the name that Jacob's descendants would take for themselves, down to our own day. But Canaan brought new heartaches for Jacob. Rachel, whom he loved so deeply, died while giving birth to Benjamin, her second-born and Jacob's twelfth son. Now, with Rachel gone, her two boys became especially precious to Jacob. In a blatant act of favoritism, Jacob celebrated Joseph's approaching manhood by giving him a magnificent robe that signaled the boy's singular status in his father's eyes.

The other brothers, resentful of Joseph's preferential treatment, began to plot revenge. Once more Jacob the deceiver was to be bitterly deceived. First the brothers seized Joseph and sold him to slave traders headed for Egypt. Then they took Joseph's robe, dipped it in blood, and brought it to their father. They left him with the impression that a wild beast had killed Joseph. Needless to say, Jacob was crushed. Having lost Rachel and now Joseph, he could not be consoled in his grief.

Joseph in Egypt
(Genesis 39–50)

As his father sank into sorrow, things worsened further for Joseph. Once the favorite son of a wealthy

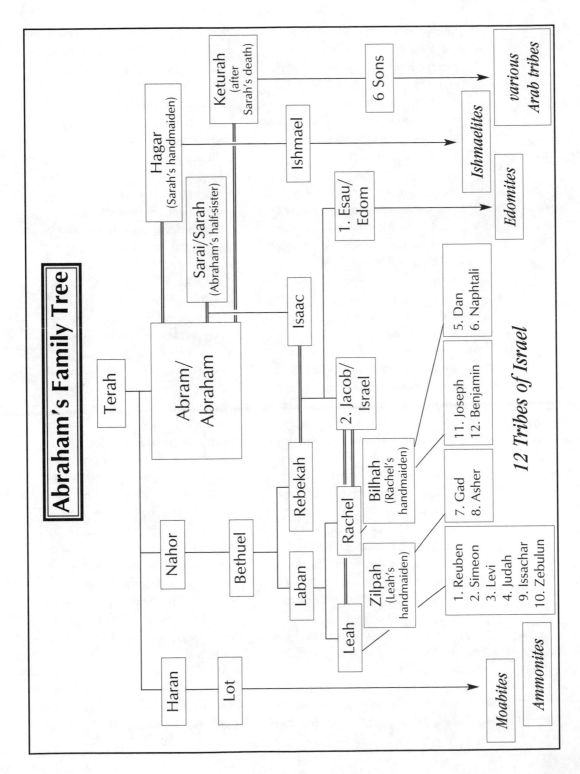

Abraham's Family Tree

Terah
- Abram/Abraham
  - (with Hagar, Sarah's handmaiden) Ishmael → Ishmaelites
  - (with Sarai/Sarah, Abraham's half-sister) Isaac
  - (with Keturah, after Sarah's death) 6 Sons → various Arab tribes
- Nahor
  - Bethuel
    - Rebekah
    - Laban
      - Rachel
      - Leah
- Haran
  - Lot → Moabites, Ammonites

Isaac — Rebekah
- 1. Esau/Edom → Edomites
- 2. Jacob/Israel

Jacob/Israel:
- (with Leah) 1. Reuben, 2. Simeon, 3. Levi, 4. Judah, 9. Issachar, 10. Zebulun
- (with Zilpah, Leah's handmaiden) 7. Gad, 8. Asher
- (with Bilhah, Rachel's handmaiden) 5. Dan, 6. Naphtali
- (with Rachel) 11. Joseph, 12. Benjamin

12 Tribes of Israel

father, he became a household slave in Egypt. But Joseph soon proved himself a person of stellar character. Unlike his father, who could be treacherous and dishonest, Joseph built a lasting reputation for impeccable integrity.

Joseph's integrity ➤

His first test of character occurred when his master's wife tried to seduce him. Knowing that it would be wrong to have sex with another man's wife, Joseph refused her advances. When she persisted, he distanced himself by running from the house. Angry at being rejected, she went to her husband and claimed that Joseph had tried to assault her.

Famine in Canaan ➤➤

Unable to exonerate himself, Joseph ended up in prison. But there he was again found so trustworthy that the jailer placed him in a position of supervision. Joseph also became known in prison for his ability to explain the meaning of dreams. Among those he befriended in prison was a former personal attendant to the pharaoh. This man was later restored to royal service and ultimately helped secure Joseph's release. The king, it seems, had a particularly disturbing dream and could find no one to interpret it. The restored attendant remembered Joseph and arranged for him to have an audience with the pharaoh.

Interpreting dreams ➤

Forgiveness ➤➤

After hearing about the dream, Joseph explained that God was using it to warn of an approaching drought, a particularly severe one.

Prior to the drought there would be seven abundant harvests. But seven years of famine would follow. Joseph advised the king to prepare Egypt for the drought by building large stockpiles of grain during the years of good harvests.

Impressed by Joseph's interpretation, the pharaoh began filling granaries with surplus. He even put Joseph over the project. And as Joseph's dependability and character became increasingly evident, the pharaoh made him the prime minister of his court.

Back in Canaan, Joseph's family knew none of this. But when the predicted seven years of famine struck, they were desperate for food. Hearing that Egypt was well supplied, Jacob dispatched his sons there to buy grain. As fate would have it, their negotiations brought them face to face with Joseph, whom they did not recognize. Nor did he reveal his identity immediately. Only at a chosen moment did he let them know who he was.

On learning that they were dealing with Joseph, his brothers had mixed emotions. Remembering what they had done to him, they worried about him using his authority to take revenge. But Joseph responded much like Esau had done with Jacob. Forgetting the wrongs they had done him, Joseph embraced them warmly and invited them to bring his now aged father, their own wives, and their children to live in Egypt.

Thus Jacob's descendants began what would become a 430-year stay in Egypt (Exodus 12:41). After Jacob died, Joseph carried his father's body back to Canaan and buried it there. Later, nearing his own death, Joseph made the Israelites pledge to take his bones with them when God returned them to Canaan. Four centuries later they honored his request (Exodus 13:19).

Lessons from Genesis

With the death of Joseph the book of Genesis closes, having introduced some of the most vital concepts in Scripture. Particularly important is what Genesis tells us about the nature of God. As we have seen, Genesis begins by affirming His unequaled power and might. Then it moves quickly to show His close involvement with the human family. In tracing that involvement we have stressed His kindness and generosity, even when people were not deserving. Later the Bible will use the word "grace" to describe this aspect of God's nature.

On the other hand, we should not let our emphasis on grace obscure another side to His nature, this one also fully disclosed in Genesis. He is a God who takes sin and immorality seriously. Genesis includes unforgettable scenes of divine judgment. He drove Adam and Eve from the Garden of Eden because of disobedience. He destroyed human society in Noah's day because of wickedness. During Abraham's lifetime He obliterated the cities of Sodom and Gomorrah because they were so shamelessly immoral (Genesis 18:16-19:29). And He vowed to punish the ones who enslaved Abraham's descendants (Genesis 15:14).

So why does God show kindness to one person who does wrong but then punish another? The difference has to do with the individual's heart. (The Bible uses the word "heart" to refer to that part of our inner being where our attitudes and decisions take shape.) So long as people are seeking God and wanting to do right, He works with them patiently, despite their mistakes. But when their hearts become calloused toward Him, or when they show continued indifference toward principles of morality and justice, He begins to warn of impending judgment. Because of His own commitment to goodness, He cannot allow evil to go unchecked forever. When people do not heed His warnings, He eventually brings punishment and destruction to bear.

◄ God knows the heart

◄◄ Genesis and the nature of God

Genesis also compels us to examine how we act toward one another. It points to the importance of

◄◄ Seriousness of sin

- ➤ treating people fairly
- ➤ practicing personal integrity and
- ➤ learning to forgive

What prolonged unhappiness settled over the families of Isaac and

Jacob simply because they were so unfair to one another. Favoritism led to lifelong resentment. Taking advantage of other family members led to lasting alienation. To be sure, some immediate advantage was gained by treating people unfairly. But in Genesis, as elsewhere in life, the price ultimately paid for being unfair often outweighed any short-term gain.

Fear as an enemy of integrity >>

When Esau came in famished, a spirit of fairness would have led Jacob to offer him food immediately. Instead, Jacob took advantage of the situation and forced Esau to barter away his birthright. Jacob no doubt thought himself quite shrewd for advancing his own self-interest at the expense of his brother. But Jacob's self-serving actions eventually made him a fugitive, cut off from his family and fleeing for his life.

Sin and family problems >

And then there is Laban. When he gave Leah to Jacob in place of Rachel, he probably congratulated himself for this crafty bit of dealing. No doubt he congratulated himself again when he grew rich by withholding wages from Jacob (Genesis 31:41-42). But in the end his self-serving ways cost him dearly. Once Jacob packed up his family and left, Laban lost the privilege of ever seeing his grandchildren again.

History repeats itself >>

These instances of treating people unfairly in Genesis went hand in hand with cheating and deception, or to put it another way, the loss of personal integrity. Genesis shows us dramatically that once integrity breaks down in a family, the impact continues for generations. Not only that, in Abraham's family, as in others since, the integrity problem grew worse in each succeeding generation.

For Abraham personally, fear served to undercut his integrity. Because Sarah was so beautiful, Abraham was always afraid some powerful figure would kill him and take her for himself. So when he was a guest of the pharaoh, he lied about who she was. "She's only my sister," he said, whereupon pharaoh felt free to bring her into his harem. When the ruse was found out, the pharaoh chided Abraham and sent him from the realm (Genesis 12:10-20). But back in Canaan, Abraham did exactly the same thing again, this time with a king by the name of Abimelech (Genesis 20:1-7).

Here he was, this great man of faith, willing to lie and put his wife in a sexually compromising position, all to keep himself out of harm's way. We can only imagine how Sarah felt about this! And then, irony of ironies, their son Isaac violated his integrity the same way. After he married Rebekah, they relocated to the area ruled by Abimelech's successor, a man also named Abimelech. Fearful of his own safety, Isaac told the men of the region, "She is my sister" (Genesis 26:1-11).

As we have seen, Rebekah had integrity problems of her own. In this regard she was like her brother

Laban, for dishonesty and deception came naturally to both of them. That probably means they learned it from their own parents. Nor is it mere coincidence that Rebekah's favorite son Jacob grew up to be a deceiver, or that one day his own sons would deceive him, just as he had deceived his father.

The person who broke this pattern was Joseph. That is why his story is so important in Genesis. Self-serving dishonesty went back three generations in his family. But Joseph chose a different standard for himself. No matter how much his father or his grandfather or his great-grandfather had forsaken a path of integrity, Joseph would prove himself a man of stalwart character.

Through Joseph's example, God calls on us to break the patterns of favoritism, dishonesty, deception, and unfair treatment that may have been in our families for generations. However corrupt our ancestry, we can choose, like Joseph, to do what is right in every circumstance.

It is interesting, indeed, that Moses structured the book of Genesis around four generations, beginning with Abraham and ending with Joseph. Through the rest of the Bible, Abraham is held up as a model of what God wants from us in terms of trusting Him and His promises. But with his moments of moral failure, Abraham is an inadequate model of personal integrity. For that we need Joseph.

He epitomizes the kind of ethical and moral behavior that God expects.

Joseph also models the essence of forgiveness. Rather than take vengeance on his brothers and add bloodshed to the wrongs already done, he opted to forgive them. Because he forgave, his children got to know their grandfather. Because he forgave, he got to see the tears of joy in his father's eyes as Jacob reunited with the son for whom he had grieved so long.

> Model of forgiveness

> Breaking the pattern

And Joseph's forgiveness was genuine, not simply a temporary postponement of revenge while his father was alive. After Jacob died, the brothers became fearful that Joseph would now strike them down. "What if Joseph should bear a grudge and pay us back in full for the wrong that we did him?" they asked (Genesis 50:15). They thus begged Joseph to forgive them. He wept when they made this entreaty and calmed their fears by assuring them that vengeance was the last thing on his mind.

In this regard Joseph was like his uncle Esau, who was cheated of his blessing by Jacob. Twenty years later, when Jacob left Laban and started tack toward Canaan, he learned that Esau was coming to meet him with a large band of men. Fearful that Esau was coming to attack him, Jacob sought to soften Esau's anger by sending servants to Esau with expensive gifts. Esau, who had come with his men to escort

Forgiveness requires forgiveness **>>**

Jacob, not to attack him, could not understand the purpose of these gifts. Esau no longer carried a grudge. He only wanted to rebuild his relationship with his brother. When the two finally came face to face, Jacob fell down before Esau to beg forgiveness, just like Joseph's brothers would do. And like Joseph, Esau assured him there was nothing to fear (Genesis 32-33).

Forgiveness destroys fear **>**

Had Esau never learned to forgive, he and Jacob would have died enemies. Instead, theirs was a story of joyous reunion. Genesis tells of the new bond of friendship they developed and how, together, they tended to the burial of their father.

In forgiving their families, neither Joseph nor Esau shrugged off the past, as though it did not matter. It did matter. They had both been hurt, and hurt deeply by what their families did to them. But both were saying that there are things in life more important than settling the score with someone who has wronged us.

When we come to the life of Jesus, we will see Him making this point. "How can we expect God to forgive us if we refuse to forgive others?" He will ask. He will also encourage his followers to learn the freedom that comes with forgiveness. So long as we fail to forgive, we poison our own spirit and attitudes through the bitterness and resentment that continue to build. We forgive, therefore, to free ourselves from the inner poison that defeats our joy.

We can sum up the message of Genesis, then, with these words: God wants us

➤ to know who He is

➤ to trust His promises

➤ to obey His instructions

➤ to treat Him with respect, and

➤ to do those things that make for integrity and harmony as we deal with other people.

In Exodus He will teach us more about each of these concepts as He enlarges His working relationship with Abraham's descendants.

Genesis = "Beginnings"

Exodus = "Going Out"

Chapter Eight

ISRAEL EMERGES AS A NATION

At some point following Joseph's death, official policy toward Jacob's family turned unfriendly. Although the Bible does not detail exactly what developed, the book of Exodus opens with the Israelites living as slaves. They are also a source of great anxiety to the Egyptians. Over four centuries, even under conditions of harsh bondage, the Israelites have grown in number to the point that Egypt fears a slave uprising.

God Calls Moses (Exodus 1–4)

To slow this growth the pharaoh ordered the murder of all newborn Hebrew boys. (As a rule the book of Exodus refers to Israelites as "Hebrews," the same name as their language.) How long this edict stayed in effect is uncertain. But it was still in force when Moses was born. In an effort to protect him, his sister Miriam hid him in a small basket that she floated among reeds in the Nile River. It was there, secreted away at the water's edge, that he was discovered by, of all people, the pharaoh's daughter.

The princess persuaded her father to let her raise the child in the palace, so that Moses was part of the royal circle the first 40 years of his life. Yet he learned early about his origins, so that despite his privileged position, he maintained a heart for his people. One day he became angry at a taskmaster who was mistreating some Hebrew slaves. Moses reacted by killing the man. When his role in the slaying was discovered, Moses fled from Egypt and took refuge in the sprawling wilderness of the Sinai peninsula. There he married and spent another 40 years living as a nomadic shepherd.

While tending sheep near Mt. Sinai, he was drawn one day to a bush on the mountainside. The bush was aflame. Yet no matter how long it burned, it remained unconsumed. As Moses approached the site, God spoke to him from the midst of the flames. He instructed Moses to return to Egypt and lead the Israelites from bondage. This was no small order, for Egypt was the most powerful nation on earth.

‹ Moses brought up in Egyptian royal family

‹‹ Pharaoh orders genocide

‹ The burning bush

Although Moses protested, insisting that he was the wrong man for the job, he finally complied with God's directive. Back in Egypt he teamed up with his older brother Aaron to ask the pharaoh to free the Israelites and let them leave the country. When the pharaoh refused, Moses warned that God would bring wholesale catastrophe on the kingdom.

The Ten Plagues (Exodus 7–10)

God punishes Egypt ➤

Over the next few months ten different natural calamities befell Egypt, each orchestrated by God.

- ➤ The Nile River turned bloody for seven days and fish died by the millions.

- ➤ Frogs overran the land and invaded the houses.

Death of the firstborn ➤➤

- ➤ Swarms of biting gnats made life miserable for man and beast.

- ➤ Armies of insects devoured the farmlands.

- ➤ Disease began decimating the Egyptian herds.

- ➤ People became covered with painful boils.

- ➤ An unprecedented hailstorm shattered the trees.

- ➤ Then locusts came in droves and continued the devastation.

- ➤ And finally a deep, impenetrable darkness settled over the land.

Prior to each disaster, Moses announced what was about to occur. He wanted to leave no doubt that God was behind these events. Even the king's sorcerers and magicians, who were legendary for their wonder-working skills, soon realized that they were dealing with a spiritual power far beyond anything they had ever seen. They told the pharaoh, "This is indeed the work of God's finger" (Exodus 8:9).

Yet none of these blows (or "plagues," as the Bible calls them) led the pharaoh to relent. On occasion he bargained with Moses, promising a concession to Israel if Moses would end a particular plague. But as soon as the crisis passed, the pharaoh reverted to his former stance and withdrew his promise.

God then told Moses to anticipate one final blow that would bring Egypt to its knees. In a single night all the firstborn of Egypt would die. This would result in the Egyptians finally allowing the Hebrews to leave. So God instructed Moses to get the people ready to depart at a moment's notice.

The Passover and Escape (Exodus 11–14)

The Lord also told Moses to have his people celebrate their anticipated departure with a special feast. Their bread for the meal was to be unleavened, signaling that God was about to act so hurriedly that they should not take time for the bread to rise (Exodus 12:39). Their preparation for the feast was to include the slaughter of a lamb, which was eaten as part of the meal. In addition, they were to smear the lamb's blood on the door frame around the entrance to their houses. God promised that no first-born would be taken in a home with blood at the doorway.

God wanted His people to remember this night forever. He therefore instructed them to establish an annual festival called the Passover (also known as the Feast of Unleavened Bread), which would commemorate the night in which death "passed over" their homes. During the Passover every family was to reenact this final meal in bondage. Through the reenactment they were to teach their children about God freeing Israel from Egypt. Jews still celebrate the Passover today, and it was during the Passover season that Jesus was killed in Jerusalem.

The Israelites carefully prepared that first Passover, ate the meal expectantly, and waited for the dawn. In keeping with God's word, death swept across Egypt that night. By the next morning all of Egypt was eager for Israel to depart. But the pharaoh had one last change of mind. Moses and his people were almost out of the country when they saw the Egyptian army in rapid pursuit. Penned in by the Red Sea and unable to retreat, the Hebrews thought their situation hopeless.

But God was still ready to work wonders on their behalf. A great wind came up, pushing back the waters just ahead of the Israelites and permitting them to cross to the other side. By the time they reached the opposite shore, the pursuing soldiers were almost upon them. But at that instant the wind stopped and the waters rushed back in, sweeping the army away.

◄ The Red Sea divided

◄◄ Sacrificial lamb

Israel at Sinai

Safe from the Egyptians at last, the Israelites continued southeastward to Mt. Sinai, the place where Moses had seen the burning bush. For several months they camped at Sinai while Moses and Aaron formed a political and social structure for the nation. More importantly, God used this time to initiate a series of covenant agreements through Moses. As part of His covenant with Israel, God outlined hundreds of regulations that would govern the life of His people. Because He used Moses to announce these regulations, we refer to these covenants collectively as the Law of Moses.

◄◄ The Passover

◄ Law of Moses

Nonetheless, God's first step was not to issue laws, but to define the type of relationship He was forging with Israel. "You have seen what I did to the Egyptians," He said. "You also know how I carried you on the wings of eagles and brought you to Myself. Thus, if you will truly obey what I say and keep My covenant, you shall be My own possession among all the people of the earth. For the earth in its entirety is Mine. And you shall be a kingdom of priests to Me and a holy nation" (Exodus 19:3-6).

When Moses relayed this message to Israel, the people responded as one, "We will do everything the Lord has spoken" (Exodus 19:7-8). And with that response the process of covenant-building began. Through His covenant God was honoring the promise to Abraham, Isaac, and Jacob to transform their descendants into a great nation. Moreover, God was taking Israel at her word. From this point forward God would expect the Israelites to repay His kindness by honoring their promise to obey Him.

The Ten Commandments (Exodus 20)

During the time at Sinai, Moses periodically retreated into the mountain to confer with God, sometimes for weeks at a time. There Moses received laws and instructions to carry back to the Israelites. This was also the setting in which God gave Moses ten basic principles, carved on two stone tablets. These principles, commonly known as the Ten Commandments, spelled out specific standards of personal conduct. They became the fundamental law governing spiritual and moral life in Israel.

Of these ten principles, four centered on what it means to respect

God. The rest had to do with respecting other people. Each command was worded succinctly, making it easy to memorize and remember. This allowed parents to teach these concepts to children at an early age.

On the other hand, the very brevity of these commands left room for people to disagree on what a particular command prohibited or allowed. Thus, God used other parts of the Law of Moses to elaborate on these commandments and how they should be understood. In fact, almost everything else the Bible says on ethics and morality is merely a commentary on these ten statements of principle. For that reason, we want to look at each commandment individually.

The First Command: You shall have no other gods before Me.

Israel was surrounded by nations who were polytheistic. That is, they believed in many gods, not just one. Due to the influence of these neighbors, polytheism often slipped into Israelite religion. Moses combated this problem for the entire 40-year period he led Israel. Later, in Canaan, there were times when paganism all but eclipsed the worship of God. The primary mission of the prophets, indeed, was calling Israel back to the worship of one true God.

Knowing the allure of false religions, God opened the Ten Commandments by reminding His

---

Margin notes:

A kingdom of priests/ a holy nation ➤

Morality in summary ➤➤

One God vs. many gods ➤➤

people that He alone was God. To modern minds this may seem an unusual way to begin a moral code. But viewed from a Biblical perspective, this starting point makes perfect sense. In the Bible, things are right or wrong based on God's nature. If God is loving, hatred is evil. If God is truthful, lying is wicked. Biblically speaking, moral wisdom begins with a clear understanding of who God is.

While disclosing His law to Moses, God offered a striking self-description of what He is like. "I am compassionate and gracious," He said, "slow to anger and abounding in loving-kindness and truth." He then pictured His loving-kindness as extending to thousands. "I am a God who forgives iniquity, transgression, and sin" (Exodus 34:6). This is a picture of a thoroughly merciful God. It is not surprising, therefore, that throughout the Bible He insists on His people treating others with mercy. Nowhere is this more apparent than in the Bible's strong admonitions to be generous in caring for the poor and to be quick to forgive those who treat us unjustly.

On the other hand, God is hardly indifferent toward those who choose to pursue evil. "I will by no means leave the guilty unpunished," He told Israel. In fact, He declared that He would visit the iniquity of people on the their children, their grandchildren, and their great-grandchildren (Exodus 34:7). In other words, the consequences of iniquity in a family has repercussions for generations.

The Second Command: You shall not create or worship idols.

As we have noted, all pagan religions in the ancient world were polytheistic. They also practiced idolatry. That is, they created statues, carvings, or paintings of their gods and then worshiped those representations. God excluded both polytheism and idolatry from the spiritual life of Israel. Not only did God forbid idolatry among the Israelites, He also ordered them to destroy the idols of any nation they conquered.

◄ No visible representations of God

For Israel this commandment was particularly timely. Moses delivered it only days after the Israelites had built an idol for themselves, a golden calf like the ones worshiped in Egypt (Exodus 32). Aaron himself fashioned the statue. This occurred while Moses was on Mount Sinai for 40 days, receiving the Ten Commandments.

When Moses returned, he was outraged to find the people bowing before the calf. Angrily he smashed the stone tablets on which the commandments were written, slamming them to the ground and shattering them. Later he went back to the mountain to obtain a second set of tablets. But not before he dealt harshly with Israel and his brother for their open rebellion against God.

Unfortunately, this was not the last time that Israel toyed with idols.

Centuries passed before the Israelites finally distanced themselves entirely from idolatry. To their credit, they never built a statue of God Himself. But whenever they turned from God to paganism, they set up idols in their places of worship, just like other nations around them.

The Third Command: You shall not take the name of the Lord your God in vain.

No misuse of God's name ➤

To understand the importance of this command, we need to look at how the Bible deals with personal names. Today we typically see names as merely a convenient way to refer to someone. But in the Bible, names often express the essence of a person's character or some vital aspect of his or her life. We have already seen this in the names God gave to key figures in the book of Genesis. Abraham means "father of nations." Isaac means "laughter," recalling the way Abraham and Sarah responded when God told them they would have a son. Israel means "the one who struggles with God," a reference to Jacob's upstart, devious nature.

Time set aside for rest and worship ➤➤

With regard to Himself, God repeatedly speaks of His "holy name." (See Leviticus 22:32 and Ezekiel 39:7, for example.) The word "holy" means to be set aside as special, to be cared for with a respect or reverence not accorded other things. Because God Himself is holy, His name is likewise holy

(Isaiah 57:15). His name expresses His essence. To treat His name with disrespect is the same as treating His holiness with disregard. Therefore, God said, "You shall not take the name of the Lord your God in vain."

This means first of all that we are not to handle His name flippantly or in a degrading fashion. Among other things, we are not to use His name in profanity or as part of a curse. We can also take God's name in vain by professing to be His followers, but behaving in ways that are totally foreign to His character. On several occasions God accused Israel of profaning His name in just this fashion. (See Leviticus 20:3 or Ezekiel 20:39.)

The Fourth Command: You shall remember the sabbath, to keep it holy.

The Israelites called the seventh day of the week "the sabbath" which means "rest." Genesis says that God created the world in six days, then rested on the seventh (Genesis 2:2-3). Moses told Israel that on the seventh day of each week they, too, should rest. "On that day you are not to do any work, you or your son or your daughter, your male or female servants, or your cattle, or anyone who happens to be staying with you" (Exodus 20:11).

The purpose of this rest, among other things, was to allow spirits and energies to be renewed. Alongside rules governing the *day* called the sabbath the Law of Moses also provided for sabbath *years*. These were again intended as a time of renewal. Farm fields were to lie idle every seventh year so the soil could rebuild its nutrients (Leviticus 25:1-7). In addition, slaves were freed in the seventh year of their service (Deuteronomy 15:12-14).

Every 50 years still another kind of sabbath was observed. The Law of Moses called it the "jubilee year." It came at the end of seven cycles of seven years. In the jubilee year all land that had been lost due to debt or financial distress was returned to the family that originally possessed it. The purpose of this action was to renew the opportunity for every family to lift itself from poverty (Leviticus 25:8-13).

Concerning the sabbath day, God told Israel to treat it with holy respect. At various intervals the Law of Moses spelled out specific activities to avoid on the sabbath. These included such things as working at one's job, gathering firewood, walking long distances, and preparing meals that required cooking. Everyone was to rest and be renewed on the sabbath.

Over the centuries sabbath-keeping has been a distinctive feature of Judaism, as it still is today. Christians observe Sunday as their holy day. This maintains a practice dating back to the first century, when the followers of Jesus began gathering on the first day of the week for worship (Acts 20:7). They chose this time because Jesus came back from the dead on the first day of the week. In recognition of that fact, early Christians referred to "the first day" as "the Lord's Day" (Revelation 1:10).

◄ The Lord's Day

The Fifth Command: Honor your father and mother.

In our review of Genesis, we saw that family life is important to God. We also noticed that family life becomes thoroughly unpleasant when people fail to treat one another fairly, honestly, and with respect. Just as God expected Israel to honor Him out of appreciation for what He had done, He calls on children to appreciate and honor their parents.

◄ Respect for parents

Throughout the ancient world a child who murdered his parents was considered the ultimate reprobate. As adults, children were also expected to provide for aging or invalid parents. But outside of Israel there was no particular stigma placed on the person who took care of his parents physically, but otherwise spoke of them disparagingly or showed them no respect. With the Israelites, God sets a higher standard of conduct. He wants His people to promote harmonious family life by actively honoring parents.

The Sixth Command: Do not murder.

The first crime mentioned in the Bible was Cain's murder of his brother. Murder is the ultimate disregard for the value of life. It strikes at the purposes of God, who is the author of life. Because God insists *Respect for life* ➤ that we hold life in high esteem, He prohibits murder in any form.

We should note, however, that God makes a distinction between murder and other acts of taking a life. Executions were allowed under the Law of Moses. The Law also allowed for killing in self-defense or to protect a friend. In addition, it made a distinction between murder and accidentally killing someone. God does not treat an accidental killing as murder.

Murder defined ➤ Murder is a calculated or premeditated slaying. It comes about *Marriage and covenant* ➤➤ when we allow anger, hatred, or envy to gain such control that we begin to plot ways to destroy another person. Or it may stem from callous indifference toward the value of someone's life. Murder thus starts in the heart, that part of our inner being where moral deliberations occur. This is why Jesus said that hatred itself is murder committed in the heart (Matthew 5:21-22).

The Seventh Command: Do not commit adultery.

Sexual purity ➤ When God created the human race, he fashioned us so that sex is both a strong and satisfying drive. But as the author of our sexual nature, God knows that sex is more than a physical act. There are also emotional, psychological, spiritual, and interpersonal dimensions to

sex. God wants all of those dimensions to be healthy, joyful, and free of regret.

Health and joy reach their greatest potential, He knows, when a man and a woman commit themselves to each other for life. Here, in their lifelong commitment, sexual intimacy takes on deeper and deeper meaning as the two lovers steadily grow closer to each other. Since God wants only the best for us, He tells us to restrict sexual intercourse to the marriage relationship, where the possibility of this deeper intimacy can mature. And then, to emphasize the importance of marriage, He refers to it as a covenant partnership (Malachi 2:14).

Nothing is more sacred in the Bible than respect for covenant commitments. In a community where we treat each other fairly, duty calls on us to respect all covenants, both the ones we make and the ones that others have made. Adultery always violates at least one covenant, if not two. For me to have sex with another person's mate is to act without respect toward their covenant with each other. And if I am married myself, I am likewise violating the integrity of my covenant commitment to my spouse.

Adultery damages covenants at several levels. This damage occurs because in true sexual intimacy, two people experience a blending of their inner beings. They are drawn closer to one another. God's phrase for this is that "the two become one" (Genesis 2:24). For me to have such intimacy with another person's mate is to set forces in motion that pull both of us toward each other and away from our own covenant partners. The resulting emotional and psychological scars can be devastating. A proverb in the Bible compares adultery to a man who tries to hold red hot coals against his chest without getting burned (Proverbs 6:27-29).

The Eighth Command: Do not steal.

Honesty and integrity are the glue of any society. Take them away, and you deprive everyone of the security and safety that makes for happiness. Only in a setting where we confidently trust everyone else do we find our greatest happiness.

Stealing undermines happiness by striking at our ability to trust. And we are stealing any time we deprive people of something that is rightfully theirs. Thus, stealing can take many forms. Cheating other people. Taking part in a fraud. Borrowing something and not returning it. These are all simply different ways to steal. So, too, is refusing to pay a debt or misguiding someone to gain financial advantage.

The Ninth Command: Do not bear false witness.

Another way of stating this commandment is, "Be honest. Don't lie about people." The specific wording, "Do not bear false witness," emphasized the importance of telling the truth in court, where honesty is absolutely essential. Since the verdict of a court can deprive another person of possessions, freedom, or even life itself, a witness has a special duty to avoid misrepresentations that could harm someone else.

But God's people are to be truthful wherever they speak, not merely in courts of law. When I make a statement about any individual, I invite others to form a judgment about that person. If their judgments are to be fair, my comments must represent that person truthfully.

◄◄ No stealing

One reason God insists on honesty and telling the truth is that He is fully given to truth Himself. God keeps His word, without fail. What He says is always reliable. There is no deception in His character. He says of Himself on one occasion, "I keep my covenant and show lovingkindness for a thousand generations" (Deuteronomy 7:9). As a truth-telling God, He demands that His people speak only words that can be trusted.

The Tenth Command: Do not covet.

To covet is to have an inordinate desire for things that belong to someone else, so much so that jealousy, envy, or bitterness develops. The opposite of living a covetous life is living a contented life. Whereas previous commandments

◄ No sinful desire

◄◄ No dishonesty

had to do with behavior that harms others — murder, stealing, lying, adultery — this one concerns our inner being and the damage we do to ourselves. No one else will be harmed if covetousness takes over my life. But I will be harmed.

Behavior starts with attitudes ➤

In this tenth command we catch an early glimpse of how the prophets and Jesus ultimately handled ethics and morality. When the prophets came on the scene, they moved the discussion of right and wrong from the realm of behavior to the realm of attitudes. Jesus then enlarged on their approach. We have already mentioned that He equated hatred with murder. He treated adultery much the same way. A man does not have to sleep with a woman to commit adultery, Jesus said. Simply fixing attention on her and stirring up inner passion for her is committing adultery in the heart (Matthew 5:27-28). The inner damage is already done.

Adultery in the heart ➤

Hatred as bad as murder ➤➤

God can never take such inner damage lightly. He made us in His image, giving us a spirit-essence like His own. While we have a body, that body will one day die and be discarded. But our spirit will live on. Damage to the spirit is thus lasting damage. God's goal for us is to develop a spiritual life that is once again pure, just as it was when He first created mankind. But we can never reach spiritual purity if we continue to flood our heart and minds with poisonous thoughts and attitudes.

Reforming the Heart

Long before Moses set forth the Ten Commandments, sin had polluted the human spirit to the point that wickedness was rampant in the earth. In giving His law to Israel, God's immediate goal was to bring this wickedness under control at the level of behavior. It is bad enough when we corrupt our spirit and harm ourselves. We compound the damage when we hurt others, as well. So God's first goal in reversing the work of evil is to curtail the damage to others. For that reason He starts off by prohibiting harmful behavior.

But to completely overcome evil, external reform is not enough. Behavior ultimately flows from thoughts, feelings, and attitudes, and those can still be immoral long after external conduct seems upright. As Jesus pointed out, I may not be murdering people. But if I am filled with hatred, I am still damaging myself. And if that hatred grows great enough, then I may end up taking the next step and actually murdering someone.

The further we go in the Bible the more God defines sin in terms of internal attitudes rather than external actions. For those who decide to follow Jesus, getting behavior under control is a prime objective. But it is never the ending point. God is also looking for a change of heart, for when our attitudes and values are right, our actions will always be proper.

In one sense the Ten Commandments all deal directly or indirectly with the outlook of our inner being, for they all relate to showing proper respect. They call on us to respect God as the only God, to respect His name, and to respect the things He calls holy. In human affairs the commands require us to respect parents, to respect life, to respect marriage covenants, to respect other people's property, to respect the reputation of others, and to respect ourselves by forgoing destructive attitudes of the heart.

With these commands in place, Moses then set out to build a nation that would embody these principles. His starting place was to establish proper worship in Israel. Again, the Bible pictures all ethical behavior as flowing from a proper understanding of God's nature and His will. Worship is one of the principal ways in which we come to understand Him. Thus, once Moses had introduced Israel to the Ten Commandments, he turned next to constructing a house of worship. We pick up that story in chapter nine.

◀◀ Morality defined by respect

Don't serve other gods

Don't make idols

Don't misuse God's name

Keep the Sabbath holy

Honor your parents

Don't murder

Don't commit adultery

Don't steal

Don't lie

Don't covet

ISRAEL MOVES TOWARD CANAAN

A tent to
worship God ➤

Apart from God giving His law to Israel, the other great event at Sinai was the building of the tabernacle. The tabernacle was a large, elaborately decorated tent that served as Israel's center of worship until the middle of the tenth century BC. It was built to be portable. The Israelites could dismantle it quickly when they moved to a new location. There they erected it again, always in the middle of the camp, with three tribes on each side of it.

Animal sacrifice ➤

The characteristic activity at the tabernacle was sacrifice. A large altar stood outside the entrance to the tent, and fire burned on this altar continuously. Here the priests sacrificed animals throughout the day.

Modern people, no longer accustomed to animal sacrifice, find the ceremonies of the tabernacle somewhat strange, or even repulsive. Yet rituals like these were altogether common in the ancient world. Israel's neighbors, watching worship at the tabernacle for the first time, would have immediately understood what was happening.

Since modern worship does not include sacrificed animals, the tabernacle and its ceremonies might seem of little value to this introduction. But to bypass this portion of the Bible would be a mistake. The New Testament tells us that God laid out the tabernacle, along with its rituals, to symbolize the work of Jesus and the purpose of His death (Hebrews 7–10). Once we understand worship at the tabernacle, Jesus takes on deeper meaning for us.

Animal Sacrifice

Behind the practice of animal sacrifice was a worldview quite different from our own, especially with regard to sin. Today we typically think of sin in judicial terms. That is, when a person does something wrong, guilt is incurred. We see sin largely as the breaking of some law, leaving us with a guilty conscience.

People in the ancient world were more likely to experience the consequence of sin as shame rather than guilt. They thought of sin as an act of disgracing their family, their people, or God. Sin was shameful behavior. And shame brings with it a feeling of being dirty or defiled. To their mind, sin literally polluted the spirit of the wrongdoer. They felt like they had died inside.

Their religion thus emphasized rituals of cleansing, purification, and renewal. Ceremonial washings were part of these efforts to cleanse themselves. So, too, were purification rituals involving blood. People of the ancient world sensed that blood carried life through the veins. They also realized that blood had a cleansing power to heal the body. In seeking to renew life and heal their inner spirit, they therefore turned to religious symbolism involving blood. Blood symbolized the life they wanted to regain.

Hence the importance of animal sacrifice. The carcass of the slain animal represented the spiritual death the worshiper felt inside. The blood of the animal connoted the life-giving power the worshiper wanted to achieve.

The animal also took on another significance in a society where sin was experienced as shame. Shame carries with it a deep sense of alienation from others, a feeling of being defiled, rejected, and worthless. People who are ashamed perceive the entire world as hostile toward them. And that hostility extends to God. Inwardly shame makes us feel like God is angry at us.

In the Bible the word for God's anger is "wrath." Numerous passages mention the wrath of God, always to portray how thoroughly He detests sin. (See Romans 1:18, for example.) When ancient people sinned, their shame left them feeling like God hated them. By sinning they had become objects of His wrath. They carried the sentence of death upon themselves.

It became common, then, to see a sacrificed animal as a substitute for the death of the worshiper. In dying, the animal absorbed God's wrath and deflected it from the sinner. The animal died to spare the worshiper, a concept we will see behind many of the rituals at the tabernacle.

<< Purification by blood

The Tabernacle's Design (Exodus 25–27)

Moses constructed the tabernacle by following explicit instructions from God. A courtyard enclosed by a curtained fence surrounded the tent. The courtyard, which contained the altar, measured 50 meters long and 25 meters wide. The tent itself was 15 meters long, 5 meters wide, and 5 meters high, a very small structure by modern standards. But again, the tabernacle was built for mobility.

The tent housed two interior compartments, unequal in size, both spanning the width of the structure. The larger chamber, the one just inside the entrance, measured five meters by ten meters. It was called the Holy Place. Beyond it was a second chamber known as

< God's design for the tent of meeting

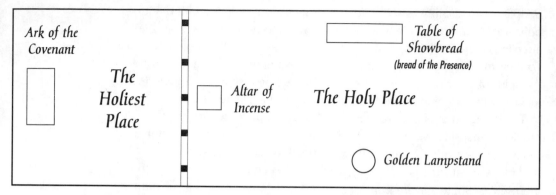

Ark of the Covenant

The Holiest Place

Altar of Incense

Table of Showbread
(bread of the Presence)

The Holy Place

Golden Lampstand

Holy Place and Holiest Place kept separate ➤

Ark of the covenant ➤

Symbolism of the tabernacle ➤➤

the Holiest Place or the Holy of Holies, laid out as a square, five meters on a side. Since the ceiling was also five meters high, the Holiest Place took the form of a cube. This was the most sacred spot in all of Israel.

A heavy curtain separated the two chambers. The only way to enter the Holiest Place was to pull back this curtain. The primary feature of the Holiest Place was a gold-covered box called the "ark of the covenant." An ark in the ancient world was a place to secure something of great value. For Moses and Israel nothing was more treasured than their covenant relationship with God. And nothing more fully symbolized that covenant than the two stone tablets engraved with the Ten Commandments. These tablets were therefore placed in the ark, which gave it the name "ark of the covenant."

On top of the ark sat a flat lid, covered in gold. From opposite ends of the lid two golden angels faced each other, perhaps in a kneeling position. Their wings were designed to draw attention to the open space immediately above the ark. This area, defined by the outstretched wings of the angels, marked the place where God promised to position His invisible presence when the high priest appeared before Him.

From this concept grew the idea, common in later Judaism, that the benchlike lid of the ark was God's throne in the midst of His people. This transformed the top of the ark into a "throne-bench," as evidenced in Israel's songs. They speak of God as enthroned on the wings of the "cherubim," the Hebrew name for the two angels on top of the ark (Psalms 80:1; 99:1).

Symbols, Priests, and God's Presence

As you can see, tabernacle ceremonies were replete with symbolism. The tabernacle itself was part of that symbolism. Its location in the middle of the camp suggested that God was nearby, in the midst of His people. But God's throne, so inaccessible in the Holiest Place, reminded Israel that the same God who is near also dwells in unapproachable holiness, transcending anything we can conceive. That is one reason God commanded the Israelites to make no representations of Him in the form of a statue or idol. He is beyond comprehension and thus beyond artistic depiction.

In the larger chamber of the tabernacle, the Holy Place, there were other symbolic furnishings. Any qualified priest could perform duties in the Holy Place, unlike the Holiest Place, which only the high priest could enter. As a priest stepped into the Holy Place, he experienced light coming from a seven-branched candlestick. Straight ahead of him was a small altar on which incense burned. Also nearby was a table containing a display of bread.

The candlestick, with its seven branches, symbolized God as the Creator, who began the process of creation by bringing light into existence. The incense altar stood for the prayers of God's people, which were to ascend constantly before Him. And the bread spoke of God's provision for His people, giving them all they needed to sustain life.

Only Levites (men from the tribe of Levi) could serve as priests. This was the same tribe that Moses came from. His older brother Aaron was the first high priest. High priests were always chosen from Aaron's descendants. The book of Leviticus details the qualifications of priests in general and the high priest in particular. It also spells out their duties and describes the various sacrifices they were to perform.

There were thousands of Levites in Israel, far more than the functions at the tabernacle required. Once Israel entered Canaan, priests not assigned to the tabernacle were dispersed among the tribes. There they were to teach God's law to the people. In addition they served as judicial advisors, offering guidance on how to apply the Law of Moses to specific cases.

It was also in Canaan that the tabernacle finally got a permanent location. After the Israelites settled there, they set it up at a place called Shiloh, where it remained for several generations. In the tenth century BC the Israelites built a great temple in Jerusalem, which then superseded the tabernacle as a place of worship.

< Looking ahead

<< God's light and provision

But that gets us ahead of our story. For now we return to Sinai, where Israel remained while constructing the tabernacle. The task took several months to complete, for the decor of the structure was richly detailed. The book of Exodus gives us the dimensions of the tabernacle, its layout, and a description of how the craftsmen went about their work.

<< Levites

Exodus concludes with the ceremony at which Moses and Aaron formally dedicated the tabernacle to the worship of God. At the height of this dedication, God filled the

< Tabernacle dedicated

Lack of faith >>

tabernacle with a great cloud of smoke. The smoke symbolized that His presence was entering the Holiest Place. This does not mean that He was taking up residence there, as though He would be present only in this tent and nowhere else. Rather, He was showing that the tabernacle would be a place were He was especially accessible to His people.

Israel Leaves Sinai (Numbers 10–14)

Years of wandering >>

A short time later, and about fifteen months after leaving Egypt, the Israelites struck camp and moved north from Sinai, setting their course toward Canaan. The book of Numbers takes up the next leg of their journey, a rather long leg to be sure, lasting some 38 years.

Originally Israel planned to move directly into Canaan and conquer it. Preparing to invade, the tribes stopped at the border of Canaan and

12 spies >

dispatched twelve spies to survey the land. Ten spies returned with a disheartening report. They had found the cities of Canaan well defended and its people of fierce stature.

Two other spies (their names were Joshua and Caleb), offered a more optimistic assessment. They admitted that Canaan was stoutly fortified and controlled by powerful people. But they argued that God would give His people victory. The Canaanites, after all, were no rival to the strength of Egypt, and Egypt had proved no match for God.

The Israelites listened to both reports and opted to discount the counsel of Joshua and Caleb. Fear took over, along with a wholesale failure of nerve. The dream of conquest quickly evaporated. Many turned against Moses for having led them from Egypt, only to leave them trapped (as they supposed) in the no-man's land of the wilderness.

In God's eyes Israel's response showed a total lack of faith in Him. He declared that He would not give Canaan to Israel until all those who doubted Joshua and Caleb had died. He told Moses to lead the people back into the heart of the wilderness, where they remained for another 38 years. This, combined with the two years that had already elapsed, extended their total stay in the wilderness to 40 years.

During that time the Israelites migrated constantly, scouring the arid Sinai peninsula for water and pasture. Because their trek took them on meandering routes that looped back on themselves, this era in Israel's history is called the Period of Wilderness Wanderings.

During this era of endless migration every person who left Egypt as an adult died. The sole exceptions were Joshua and Caleb. Yet, even while imposing this punishment on Israel, God sustained His people. He saw to it that their shoes and garments did not deteriorate. He provided water in places where previously there was nothing to drink. And at dawn each morning He

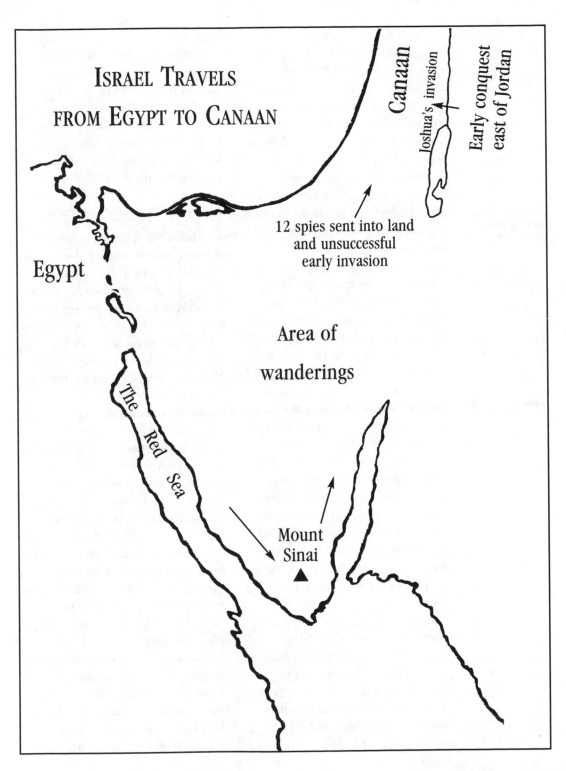

ISRAEL TRAVELS
FROM EGYPT TO CANAAN

Canaan

Joshua's invasion

Early conquest
east of Jordan

Egypt

12 spies sent into land
and unsuccessful
early invasion

Area of

wanderings

The Red Sea

Mount
Sinai
▲

Manna ▶

covered the ground with a nourishing substance called manna. The manna disappeared from the ground as the sun grew hot, and kept overnight, the manna spoiled. But families could gather a sufficient supply each morning to feed themselves all day.

The years in the wilderness served to toughen the Israelites for the conquest that lay ahead. Because the older generation died off, Israel emerged from the wilderness as a young nation, hardy and well-conditioned. As they approached Canaan, this time to seize it, their numbers struck panic in the nations that lay in their path.

Moses kept out of Promised Land ▶▶

Opposition from local kings ▶

To stop Israel's advance, various kings resorted to preemptive strikes. As a result, the Israelites were thoroughly tested in battle before they ever reached Canaan. God continually gave them victories as He positioned them for the invasion. One king, Balak by name, turned to another tactic. He hired Balaam, a man reputed to have great spiritual powers, to place a curse on Israel. But whenever Balaam opened his mouth to speak a curse, God compelled Him to pronounce a blessing instead (Numbers 23–24).

Moses' words of farewell ▶▶

Their early victories gave Israel control of the region just east of the Jordan Valley and the Dead Sea. Three tribes found this area so much to their liking that they petitioned Moses to let them settle there. He consented, but on one condition. Their fighting men would

Reasons for Israel's success ▶▶

have to cross the Jordan with the rest of Israel to help their brothers subdue the Canaanites. Everyone agreed to this, so that the tribes of Reuben, Gad, and Manasseh made lands east of the Jordan their permanent residence. (Manasseh was so large that half of the tribe also received land west of the Jordan.)

Moses Makes His Farewell

Moses himself was not to have the privilege of crossing the Jordan. He died before Israel entered Canaan. Forewarned by God that death was imminent, Moses took steps to effect a smooth transition of leadership. As his successor, Moses appointed Joshua, one of the two spies who had trusted God for victory.

Moses then gathered Israel for a series of speeches. He used this occasion to retell the story of all God had done for the nation from the time He delivered them from Egypt. "God did not choose to bless you because you were the most numerous people on earth," Moses said, "for numerically you were the least significant of nations. But because He loves you, and in order to honor His oath to your forefathers, He brought you out of Egypt" (Deuteronomy 7:7-8).

Nor was Canaan coming into Israel's possession because the Israelites were spiritually superior. Moses reminded them of their long history of stiff-necked rebellion toward God (Deuteronomy 9:6-9).

Why, then, was God driving the Canaanites from their land and giving it to Israel? For two reasons, Moses explained. First, because the nations of Canaan were so wicked. And second, because God was carrying through on His covenant promises to Abraham, Isaac, and Jacob.

In these statements Moses was laying out two principles that recur often in Scripture.

➤ First, God often chooses to work through individuals and groups that have little or no esteem in the eyes of others. He sees the potential in people that are otherwise overlooked. Israel may have been numerically smaller than any other nation, but that did not diminish her value in God's eyes.

➤ Second, those through whom God works are frequently morally or spiritually blemished, like Israel in the days of Moses. God does not require us to be perfect before He builds a relationship with us. As a result, we must never confuse God's blessings with His approval of all that we do. Frequently He blesses, not as a reward, but as an encouragement to rise above our failings.

In part this was what God was doing with Israel. He was blessing in the hope of improvement. He clearly wanted Israel to be of more noble character in Canaan than she had been in the wilderness. To this end the farewell speech of Moses reiterated the law God had given at Sinai and reminded Israel of her commitment to honor that law. Moses also warned of the punishments God would bring if the Israelites turned their back on Him.

◄ God's desire for Israel

Another Moses Is Coming

Toward the end of his address, Moses painted an ominous picture of Israel's future. He told how later generations would rebel against God. Their rebellion would become so entrenched that God would drive them off of their land. Yet, eventually God would bring His people back to Canaan and permit them to possess it once more.

In addition, Moses spoke of a great leader who would ultimately arise in Israel. A day was coming, he said, when God would appoint another spokesman, one much like Moses himself. And when this man appeared, it would be essential for Israel to follow whatever he spoke (Deuteronomy 18:18-19). Later, when Jesus appeared, God fulfilled this promise.

As one final act, Moses stored all of his writings in the Holiest Place, alongside the ark of the covenant. Included in this collection were his farewell speeches, gathered into a single manuscript known today as the book of Deuteronomy. This name literally means "the second statement of the law." It is an apt title, since the farewell speeches of

Moses repeat much of the law given at Sinai.

And so, with his work complete, Moses took his leave. He retired to a nearby mountain, whose heights gave him a panoramic but distant view of Canaan. There he died at the age of 120 years. God saw to the burial of his body so that no one in Israel would know his final resting place.

Moses buried by God ➤

Joshua Leads Israel to Canaan

In Israel, meanwhile, Joshua declared a season of national mourning that lasted for 30 days. Then he prepared Israel for the long-awaited entry into Canaan. With the ark of the covenant carried before them, Joshua formed the people into a column of march and crossed the Jordan River.

Fall of Jericho ➤➤

Joshua proved to be an extraordinary leader in his own right. The book of Joshua, obviously named for him, records his stellar exploits. His basic strategy was to prevent the kings in northern Canaan from uniting with those in the south to form a combined military front. He therefore made a rapid strike from east to west. This bisected Canaan, leaving Israel in control of a defensible corridor across the middle of the country. Next Joshua systematically conquered the regions first to the south, then to the north.

Strategy of the conquest ➤

One of his first victories, and perhaps his most notable one, came at Jericho, a fortified city in the Jordan Valley. Jericho stood in the path of Israel's planned assault on the heart of Canaan. Normally the siege of such a city would take months, permitting Jericho to secure reinforcements from elsewhere in Canaan.

But God used the siege of Jericho to demonstrate that Joshua's confidence in Him was well-founded. God told Joshua to have the people march around the perimeter of Jericho, just outside its walls, once each day for six days. Then, on the seventh day, they marched around the city seven times. As they completed the seventh circuit, they blew on horns. At that moment, whether through an earthquake or some other divinely-caused event, the walls of Jericho collapsed. Jericho's defenses were gone. Israel immediately attacked in force and quickly sacked the city. With Jericho out of the way, the hill country of Canaan lay fully exposed to Joshua's advance.

Once the Israelites dominated most of Canaan, Joshua retired from the scene. As a last act of leadership, he divided Canaan among the tribes. The tribe of Judah, named for Jacob's fourth-born son, received a sizable allotment in the hills of southern Canaan. Judah was destined to become the most influential tribe politically and militarily in Israel.

In this allotment of land, Joseph received a double portion through his sons Ephraim and Manasseh. Following the Exodus there was no tribe of Joseph. Instead, there were two tribes descended from Joseph, one named for each of his sons. Numerically Manasseh was apparently the largest tribe in Israel. And Ephraim eventually rivaled Judah in terms of influence, especially during the Period of the Divided Kingdom.

With the substitution of Ephraim and Manasseh for Joseph there are in fact thirteen tribes, not twelve in Israel. However, only twelve tribes received blocks of land. The Levites, as priests and teachers of the people, were dispersed through all the tribes. In addition, the Levites received six towns in strategic locations that were known as cities of refuge. These were places where a person could find protection and defense if he was wrongly accused of a crime or if he accidentally killed someone and had to flee from the dead man's relatives. The Levites managed the cities of refuge and heard the case of any who fled there for aid.

Cities of refuge ➤

Pledge to serve God ➤➤

With each tribe now assigned a homeland, Joshua gathered Israel's leaders for his own farewell address. He began by reminding them that God had fully honored His word to them. "You know in your heart and soul that God has not failed to carry out a single promise concerning you" (Joshua 23:14).

Pagan influences continue ➤➤

Joshua likewise challenged them to make a firmer commitment to God. Joshua knew that many families in Israel were still secretly worshiping pagan gods. In fact, because paganism was still so prevalent in Israel, God did not give Joshua victory over all the natives of Canaan. He left pockets of Canaanite power as a means of testing Israel. He wanted the Israelites to demonstrate that they would ignore the idolatry and paganism of their neighbors to stay true to Him alone.

Thus, Joshua told the assembled leaders, "Choose today whom you will serve, whether the gods our forefathers served in Mesopotamia or God Himself, who has given you this land." Then he added, "As for me and my household, we will serve the Lord" (Joshua 24:15).

The people responded, "We will serve God, too." Nevertheless, knowing their history of pagan worship, Joshua had reason to question their sincerity. "If you mean what you say," he admonished them, "then return to your tents and destroy the gods you have hidden there."

The Bible does not tell us how carefully they followed through on Joshua's instruction. But we do know that pagan influence continued to take a toll on Israel's spiritual life. As we move into the next period of Old Testament history, we will see repeated cycles of indifference toward God, not to mention a wholesale embrace of pagan gods. Even though the tabernacle continued to be a center of worship, the Israelites were by no means wholeheartedly committed to God. Several centuries would pass before they rooted out the final remnants of paganism and idolatry.

Chapter Ten

THE BOOKS OF HISTORY

With the transition to Joshua's leadership we move from the books of Moses into the books of history. The books in this section of the Old Testament are:

▽	📖 History
▷	📖 Joshua
▷	📖 Judges
▷	📖 Ruth
▷	📖 1 Samuel
▷	📖 2 Samuel
▷	📖 1 Kings
▷	📖 2 Kings
▷	📖 1 Chronicles
▷	📖 2 Chronicles
▷	📖 Ezra
▷	📖 Nehemiah
▷	📖 Esther

For the most part these books were written anonymously. It is likely that Joshua, following the example of Moses, continued to make a record of events that transpired under his leadership. If so, he probably penned most of the book that bears his name. The same is also true for Ezra and Nehemiah. Beyond that, we can only speculate who served as authors of these works.

We have already covered the material in the book of Joshua, for it describes how Israel conquered the land of Canaan. The book of Judges takes up the story of what happened between the death of Joshua and the crowning of Israel's first king. During those intervening centuries each tribe was more or less self-governed. The judges were regional leaders who provided military and sometimes judicial coordination during times of crisis.

Following the book of Judges comes the short little book of Ruth, at one time part of Judges itself. Ruth is set in the Period of the Judges and tells of a romance that developed between Boaz, a wealthy landowner, and Ruth, the woman for whom the book is named. The book is filled with tender scenes of love, devotion, and compassion. From a historical standpoint this was a truly significant romance, for both David and Jesus were direct descendents of Boaz and Ruth.

The next four books (originally one volume) record the entire history of Israel's monarchy, from the coronation of Saul until 586 BC, the year Babylon destroyed Jerusalem and the temple. Because of its length, this single volume was broken into 1 and 2 Samuel and 1 and 2 Kings, as we know them today.

Most of 1 Samuel is devoted to the reign of Saul, while 2 Samuel covers the reign of David, Israel's second king. The first eleven chapters of 1 Kings trace Solomon's rule and describe the building of the temple in Jerusalem. Following Solomon's death, the nation split into two kingdoms, the northern one known as Israel, the southern taking the name Judah. The balance of 1 Kings and 2 Kings covers the history of these two kingdoms, all the way down to the destruction of Israel by Assyria and the crushing of Judah by Babylon.

Closely paralleling 1 and 2 Kings are the books known as 1 and 2 Chronicles. They follow the history of David's dynasty, from his earliest days on the throne until the Babylonians toppled his final successor. Even though 1 and 2 Chronicles cover the entire Period of the Divided Kingdom, they look at it only from the standpoint of Judah. The book of 1 Chronicles also opens with several chapters of lengthy genealogies. Admittedly, these are not exciting reading. They nonetheless allow us to map the family tree of key figures in the Old Testament.

The historical books offer few details about Judah's experience while exiled to Babylon. Most of what we know about the exile comes from books written by prophets during those years. The historical books themselves move directly from the destruction of Jerusalem to the first efforts 50 years later to rebuild the city. Two men who spearheaded that work were Ezra and Nehemiah. The books named for them outline the obstacles they overcame and the spiritual reforms they made in order to reestablish Jerusalem.

<< Saul

<< David

<< Solomon

The last of the historical books is named for a devout Jewish woman named Esther, who became queen of the Medo-Persian Empire. (The Medes and the Persians overthrew the Babylonians during Judah's years in exile.)

<< The kingdom divides

All together the historical books encompass these periods of Bible History:

➤ The Period of Conquest

➤ The Period of the Judges

➤ The Period of the United Kingdom

➤ The Period of the Divided Kingdom

➤ The Period of Judah Alone

➤ The Period of Babylonian Exile

➤ The Period of Restoration

< Historical periods in the Books of History

The following chart lists some of the major events and personalities that we meet in these respective periods.

Period	Major Events	Key Figures
Conquest	Crossing the Jordan Conquest of Jericho Defeat of Seven Canaanite Kingdoms Division of the Land Joshua's Farewell Address	Joshua Caleb
Judges	Widespread influence of Canaanite religion on Israel Oppression by the Syrians Sisera and the Syrians defeated by Deborah and Barak Oppression by the Midianites Gideon's crushing victory over the Midianites Oppression by the Philistines Samson's harassment of the Philistines Samson's betrayal and revenge Eli and his sons destroyed for corruption Samuel's religious reforms Samuel's victory over the Philistines	 Deborah Barak Sisera Gideon Samson Delilah Eli Samuel
United Kingdom	Saul's coronation Saul's wars with the Philistines David named to succeed Saul David's defeat of Goliath Saul's efforts to destroy David Death of Saul and Jonathan David's capture of Jerusalem David's plans to build the temple David's adultery with Bathsheba Solomon's coronation Dedication of the temple Pagan religion reintroduced in Israel	Samuel Saul Jonathan David Bathsheba Solomon

Period	Major Events	Key Figures
Divided Kingdom	Rehoboam crowned	Rehoboam
	Revolt of the northern tribes	Jereboam
	Jereboam named king in the north	
	Introduction of bull-worship at Dan and Bethel	
	Introduction of Baal-worship in Samaria	Ahab
	Jezebel's persecution of God's prophets and priests	Jezebel
	Elijah's contest with the prophets of Baal	Elijah
	The death of Ahab	Elisha
	Intermarriage between Ahab's family and the royal family in Jerusalem	Amos Hosea Micah Isaiah
	Baal-worship introduced in Jerusalem	Athaliah
	Ahab's dynasty destroyed	Jehu
	Religious reforms in Jerusalem	Joash
	Assyria's growing control of the northern kingdom	Hezekiah
	Assyrian conquest of the north	
Judah Alone	Assyria turned back at the gates of Jerusalem	Isaiah Hezekiah
	The wicked reign of Manasseh	Manasseh
	Josiah's religious reforms	Josiah Habakkuk
	Babylon's invasion and destruction of Jerusalem	Jeremiah Nebuchadnezzar
Babylonian Exile	Daniel elevated to royal service	Ezekiel
	Daniel's service as governor	Daniel
	Medes and Persians overthrow Babylon	Cyrus
Restoration	The decree permitting the rebuilding of Jerusalem	
	The first parties return	Zerrubabel
	Laying the foundation of the temple	
	Esther prevents a massacre of the Jews	Esther Mordecai Haman
	Nehemiah's construction of the walls	Nehemiah
	Reinstatement of the Law of Moses and its festivals	Ezra

Babylonian exile ➤

Esther ➤➤

The historical books deal with the Babylonian exile only in passing. To know what happened to the Israelites in Babylon, we depend primarily on the books by the prophets, which we shall study later. Within the historical books themselves, the only significant events of the exile are those connected with Esther and her uncle Mordecai. They thwarted a conspiracy by a man named Haman, whose hatred for Mordecai, led him to plot a state-sponsored massacre of the Jews. Strictly speaking, the story of Esther did not occur within the 50-year time frame between the exile to Babylon and the first return to Jerusalem. Esther and Mordecai were among the Israelites who remained in Babylon after the rebuilding of Jerusalem began. Thus, the events of the book of Esther actually transpired during the Period of Restoration.

Chapter Eleven
YEARS OF UNCERTAIN LOYALTY

When Joshua stepped aside as Israel's leader, he did not appoint a successor. Instead, he allowed each tribe to set up its own local government under councils of men called elders. Elders were drawn from the heads of influential families. Certain elders governed cities, while others oversaw an entire tribe. There was also a council of elders that functioned at the national level.

So long as Joshua was alive, the elders kept Israel true to God (Judges 2:6-9). But when the next generation came along, things changed. This generation "did not know the Lord nor the work He had done for Israel" (Judges 2:10). Not everyone abandoned God, to be sure. The small book of Ruth, set in this same time period, tells of a widow from Moab who found a protector, and ultimately a husband, in the person of Boaz, a godly Israelite landowner. Yet, all too often people like Boaz and Ruth were the exceptions in Israel, not the rule.

The Worship of Baal

After Joshua's death it became common for Israelites to worship Baal and Astarte, long the principal god and goddess of Canaan. The Canaanites thought that Baal and Astarte made the land fertile, so that it produced great harvests. In Canaanite religion Baal and Astarte also controlled the reproduction of life. They determined whether a family was blessed with children or whether herds and flocks enjoyed a healthy birthrate.

‹ Baal and Astarte

Because fertility and reproduction were so important in this religion, the worship of Baal often became the worship of sex. Sexual symbols were used to mark and decorate sacred spots. Religious ceremonies degenerated into lewd celebrations of sex, with priestess and worshiper alike joining a prolonged orgy. All of this, of course, completely violated God's standards of sexual purity.

‹‹ God's care forgotten

‹ Sexual impurity

Most disturbing of all, Baal-worship sometimes included child sacrifice. Parents thought they could gain Baal's favor by offering their

Child sacrifice ➤ firstborn on his altar. They believed he would repay their devotion by granting them many more children. On other occasions families placed the body of a sacrificed child in the foundation or wall of a new house. This would secure Baal's protection, they hoped, and keep the family from harm.

God's incredible patience ➤➤

The warrior judges ➤➤

Atrocities like this prevailed as early as Abraham's day. That is why God decided to drive the Canaanites from the land and give it to Israel. God ordered the Israelites to destroy Baal-worship completely. Israel did not follow His command, however, and eventually God's own people began to worship Baal and Astarte.

So many Israelites took up the worship of Baal, indeed, that his influence often overshadowed devotion to God. When that occurred, God always made an effort to bring His people back to their senses. His usual approach was to allow some nearby nation to invade Israel. These oppressors thoroughly exploited the Israelites, often reducing entire tribes to poverty.

Such oppression consistently had the effect God desired, for once the people realized that Baal's protection had failed them, they turned back to God. They pledged that they would be faithful to Him in the future and begged Him to lift the invader's hand. In response to their pleas, God would raise up a warrior to restore His people's freedom.

Unfortunately, Israel never remained close to God once she regained independence. Instead, she drifted back into paganism within a matter of one or two generations.

Israel's Judges

Between the death of Joshua and Israel's first king, a period of about 350 years, Israel went through seven cycles of abandoning God, falling under the domination of outside powers, returning to God, and recovering freedom. Such patience on God's part was genuinely amazing. He was obviously not giving up quickly on Israel. He maintained His commitment to her, even when she ignored her commitment to Him.

We refer to this era of Israel's history as the Period of the Judges, named for the warrior-leaders who restored freedom to Israel. These were not judges in our traditional sense of the word. They were first and foremost military commanders. The Bible describes them with a Hebrew word that embraces a variety of meanings, including "deliverer," "ruler," or "savior." It could also mean "judge" in the sense of one who arbitrates disputes and settles differences. But most of them became judges in a judicial sense only after gaining public esteem by throwing off oppression.

What we know about these leaders comes largely from two books: Judges and 1 Samuel. The judges generally arose from families that

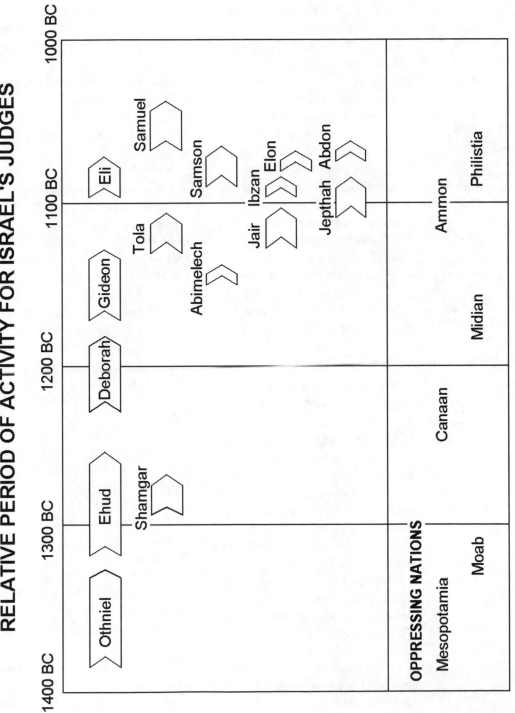

RELATIVE PERIOD OF ACTIVITY FOR ISRAEL'S JUDGES

were otherwise inconspicuous. Some, like Gideon, one of the most heroic judges, grew up in homes tainted by Baal-worship. Gideon's father maintained an altar to Baal that served the surrounding community (Judges 6:25).

Israel's most determined enemies during the Period of the Judges were the Moabites, the Midianites, and the Philistines. The Moabites and Midianites lived east of the Jordan and were themselves descendants of Abraham's family. The Philistines controlled the coastal plain that runs between modern-day Lebanon and Egypt. None of these nations overran all of Israel. Rather, they dominated the tribes closest to them.

Moabites, Midianites & Philistines ➤

Barak the wary ➤➤

Deborah (Judges 4–5)

The Bible gives only a limited account of several judges. It relates their exploits in a mere paragraph or so. Other judges are the subject of lengthy narratives. Among these are Deborah (the only woman to serve as a judge), Gideon, Samson, and Samuel. Their stories are intriguing accounts of the rewards that come from depending on God, not ourselves, for strength.

Deborah the woman judge ➤

Jael kills Sisera ➤➤

Of these four, Deborah was the first to gain prominence. Long before her military success, she was already a counselor and judicial leader in Israel. People from all the northern tribes turned to her for advice. She was also a prophetess and a mother.

Deborah would be remembered for destroying Jabin, a Canaanite king who had tormented Israel for 20 years. Jabin relied on 900 war chariots and an army under a trusted officer named Sisera. As a prophetess, Deborah told Israel's military chief (his name was Barak) that God wanted him to attack Jabin and Sisera.

Barak balked. He would go against them, he said, only if Deborah went along and stood at his side. She agreed to join the expedition. But she also warned that Barak would not get credit for the victory. Instead, the honor would go to a woman. As it turned out, the honor went to two women.

Deborah was able to muster such valor in Israel that her army struck a crippling blow against Sisera. Fleeing for his life, Sisera came to a tent that held the promise of friendly refuge. A woman by the name of Jael invited him inside to rest. Exhausted, Sisera fell into a deep sleep. Jael then slipped into the room with a mall and a tent peg. She drove the tent peg into his temple and killed him.

Meanwhile Deborah continued to pursue the remnants of Jabin's army until he was totally routed and crushed. So sweeping was her victory that the northern tribes went unmolested for another 40 years.

Gideon (Judges 6–8)

Gideon came on the scene at a time when Midianites were making life miserable for the tribes along the Jordan. Rather than chariots, the Midianites depended on camels to make rapid surprise attacks on their enemies. They would wait outside the borders of Israel until the harvest was complete, then dash in and raid new stockpiles of food.

When God chose Gideon to destroy the Midianite threat, Gideon was openly reluctant. He could not believe that he was the man for the task. "I am the least significant member of the least significant family in the least significant tribe in all of Israel," he said. So he devised a test to confirm that God had really chosen him. He put a piece of fleece on the ground and asked God for a sign the next morning. "If You truly intend for me to deliver Israel," he bargained, "let me awake to fleece that is wet with dew, while the surrounding ground is dry."

Sure enough, the next morning the fleece was soaked, the ground absolutely dry. Still unsure of himself, Gideon asked for a second sign. This time he asked that the fleece be dry and the ground soaked with dew. At dawn he found things just as he had specified.

Confident at last that God intended to use him, Gideon sent out an appeal for soldiers. To his delight, 32,000 men showed up. But God said, "This army is too large. If you prevail with such numbers, Israel will boast that it was her own power that delivered her. So announce that anyone who is afraid is free depart."

Gideon made the announcement, and 22,000 packed up and left.

Now with only 10,000 men, Gideon was clearly at a military disadvantage. But God told him that his army was still too large. God was determined that Israel would see the Lord's hand in the victory they were about to attain. So God devised another test to determine which soldiers should stay and which ones should go home.

He had Gideon take his troops to a place with an abundant supply of open water. God instructed Gideon to watch the men as they drank. He was to take note of those who dropped down on their hands and knees, to lap water like an animal. These were not to stay. Gideon issued the order to drink, and as he watched, all but 300 got on their hands and knees. These 300 were allowed to stay. The rest he dismissed.

With this tiny army Gideon slipped upon the valley where the Midianites and their allies were camped. In the middle of the night Gideon stationed his men on the surrounding mountains. He gave each one a torch, lit but hidden inside a clay pot. He also gave every man a trumpet. At a given signal each man was to let out a battle cry, blow his trumpet, smash his pot, and thrust his torch aloft.

When this happened, panic swept through the Midianite camp. As a rule, only a handful of trumpeters accompanied any army. And

<< Midianite raids

<< The reluctance of Gideon

< Army reduced to 300 men

<< Signs from God

< Torches, trumpets & clay pots

in night fighting, one man held a torch aloft to light the way for several dozen around him to fight. To the Midianites, therefore, all those torches on the mountains and the trumpets sounding on every side made it appear that an army of overwhelming size had surrounded them. In the darkness and panic, they began slaying one another and stampeding over their own people as they fled in disarray.

At that point people along the Midianite path of retreat descended on the bands of fleeing soldiers, many of whom had lost their weapons in the confusion. And to crown the victory, the Midianite commanders were captured and executed. Never again would the Midianites pose a serious military threat to Israel.

Samson (Judges 7–16)

The lot of fending off the Philistines fell to Samson, a man destined for greatness from the moment he left the womb. Before he was born, his mother had a visit from an angel. She was to dedicate her son to God's service from birth, the angel told her. As a symbol of his special status, he was never to cut his hair nor shave his beard. In fact, no razor was ever to touch his head. As a result, Samson came into adulthood with seven magnificent locks of flowing hair. So long as these remained uncut, God endowed Samson with unprecedented physical strength.

Samson evidenced his strength one night when he was trapped inside a Philistine city whose gates were barred to prevent his escape. The Philistines were lying in wait to kill him at dawn. But in the night he lifted the immense gates from their hinges and hauled them on his back to the top of a remote hill. On other occasions he single-handedly struck down and killed hundreds of Philistines who were trying to capture him.

For 20 years he served as a judge in Israel until he fell prey to the seduction of a Philistine woman named Delilah. She persuaded him to tell her the secret of his strength. She then betrayed his secret to her countrymen. One evening, while he slept in her house, she shaved his locks. Robbed of his superior power, he was quickly taken captive. The Philistines gouged out his eyes and chained him to the massive grinding stone that was part of the gristmill in a local prison. He was now forced to march long hours each day, pushing the grinding stone on its circular course.

The Philistines made a mistake, however, by failing to keep Samson's head shaved. As his locks grew out, he found his old strength returning. But crafty as always, he chose to bide his time. He was waiting for an opportune moment to take revenge on the Philistines.

That occasion presented itself during a religious festival in the temple of Dagon, the Philistines'

Samson and Deliilah ➤➤

A promise to God ➤

primary god. One purpose of this festival was to celebrate the capture and humiliation of Samson. His captors therefore decided to bring him into the temple and torment him for their entertainment.

Samson played along with this spectacle at first, until he was able to position himself between two pillars supporting the weight of the beamed ceiling. Putting an outstretched hand on each pillar, he cried out for God to give him his former strength one last time. Sensing the answer to his prayer, Samson toppled the two pillars and brought the roof crashing down on himself and the Philistines. The falling debris killed 3000 people. In death Samson killed more Philistines than he had in his entire life.

Of all the judges, Samson was least successful in permanently throwing off the enemies who afflicted his people. Even though Samson personally harassed the Philistines his entire life, we have no record of him ever leading an armed campaign against them. A number of Philistine leaders perished, no doubt, in the collapse of Dagon's temple. But that did little to deprive the Philistines of their fighting might. Nor was Eli, the next judge, any more successful at ridding himself of the Philistine menace.

Eli and Samuel (1 Samuel 1–4)

Eli was Israel's high priest. He lived in the hills of Ephraim at a place called Shiloh. This was where the Israelites placed the tabernacle once they conquered Canaan. From Shiloh Eli judged Israel for 40 years. Despite his own commitment to God, his two sons were corrupt. They stole sacrifices that people brought to the tabernacle, and they seduced women who came there to worship.

◄ Corrupt children of a good priest

When Eli allowed their behavior to continue unchecked, God declared that He was removing the high priesthood from Eli's house. God further decreed that both Eli and his sons would die on the same day. That fateful hour came during a series of battles with the Philistines. Things had not gone well for the Israelites in the initial fighting, so they sent for the ark of the covenant. The Israelite soldiers superstitiously believed that if the ark was with them, they would prevail.

◄◄ Samson kills more in death than in life

Eli's sons accompanied the ark to the battlefront. But in the next round of hostilities Israel suffered thorough defeat. The Philistines captured the ark and killed Eli's sons. A fugitive, fleeing from the battle, passed near the tabernacle, where Eli, now aged and blind, asked how the fighting had gone. When he learned that his sons were dead and the ark seized, Eli collapsed, struck his head, and died.

◄ The ark used as a talisman

In the wake of Eli's death, Israel quickly turned to a young man named Samuel as their leader. Samuel had spent his childhood with Eli's family. This was the result of a vow made by Samuel's mother, who was barren for many years. Repeatedly during those years she begged God for a son. If He granted her request, she promised, she would not keep the boy for herself. Instead, she would dedicate him to God's service at the tabernacle.

When Samuel was finally born, she honored her vow. As soon as the boy was weaned, she brought him to the tabernacle and entrusted him to Eli. The aging priest took the boy as his own and began to train him. Moreover, it was soon apparent that Samuel was an exceptional child, both in ability and character. Well before he was an adult, God confirmed him as a prophet (a person through whom God communicates special messages to others). Soon people were coming from all over Israel to benefit from his counsel.

Samuel becomes leader of Israel ➤ Once Eli died, Samuel assumed a greater leadership role. In time he was destined to serve Israel as priest, prophet, and judge. One of his first moves was to call for national spiritual renewal. He assured the Israelites that they could triumph against the Philistines, but only if they first sepa-**Perversity of the people** ➤➤ rated themselves from Baal and Astarte.

Immediately the people rose to his challenge and destroyed pagan altars in their midst. As Samuel's reforms took root, the Israelites turned back to God with singleness of heart. God rewarded their new-found commitment by giving Samuel a striking victory against the Philistines (1 Samuel 7:1-14). This offered at least a temporary respite from Philistine incursions. But it was not until the reigns of David and Solomon that the Philistines were finally and fully subdued.

God's Patience with Israel

Samuel had a long, eventful life as a leader. Among other things, he oversaw Israel's transition to monarchy. We will look at that part of his life in the next chapter. Samuel was apparently effective in restoring Israel's devotion to God, for problems with pagan religion are hardly mentioned during the first few decades of the monarchy.

Such a turnaround shows that Samuel must have been a remarkable leader. As we mentioned earlier, the Period of the Judges produced seven cycles of rising pagan influence. Morally and spiritually these cycles grew progressively more perverse, each one worse than any that preceded it (Judges 2:13-19). It was no small feat for Samuel, coming on the scene when things were at their worst, to bring Israel back to the Lord.

To stress how perverse Israel became, the book of Judges concludes with two stories that have nothing to do with a judge. The central character in both of these narratives was a Levite, a member of the priestly clan charged with keeping Israel true to God. But these two Levites had forsaken their calling. The first one was ready to sell his services to anyone who wanted to maintain a pagan shrine and would pay him enough money (Judges 17–18). The other was a heartless man who treated his concubine (i.e., a slave-wife) in an absolutely inhumane manner. Accosted by the men of a city through which he was passing, he saved himself by giving them his concubine to do with as they pleased. They assaulted her all night long until she died from their brutality (Judges 19–20).

Here is the point of these stories. If the Levites, Israel's spiritual leaders and instructors, had become men like this, imagine how corrupt the people themselves must have been!! Israel in the days of the judges was not a nation merely guilty of mild indiscretions. God's people had abandoned Him completely. His Ten Commandments meant nothing to them. Still, He wanted to find a way to make His covenant with His people succeed. So He kept working with them patiently, despite their perversity.

This is a pattern we will see throughout Scripture. God not only *makes* covenants, He also goes to great extremes to *keep* them. He is a God who keeps His word. He does not rush to cut off relationships. Instead, He waits patiently for His people to learn to honor their covenant duties to Him and to others.

His patience has its limits, however. There comes a time when He revokes or replaces covenants because of continued indifference toward Him or His will. That's what happened with Eli. You may recall from chapter six that God had made a covenant with Eli's ancestor, Phinehas, that the high priesthood would remain in his family forever (Numbers 25:10-13). But when Eli and his sons showed persistent and thorough disrespect for the tabernacle and its sacrifices, God brought their lineage to an end. And He made it quite clear that He was taking this action because they had despised Him (1 Samuel 2:30).

◄◄ Corruption of the spiritual leaders

Eventually He did the same thing with Israel and His covenant with her at Sinai. Under the monarchy Israel continued to vacillate between genuine commitment to God and wholesale involvement first with Baal, then with other pagan deities. After warning for centuries that He would punish such unfaithfulness, God finally carried out His threat. He allowed the Assyrians to obliterate the northern tribes, the Babylonians to destroy the southern ones.

◄◄ God's faithfulness and patience

But just before the Babylonian onslaught, He announced that He was planning a new covenant with Israel. It would replace the one He made at Sinai. Israel had failed to honor the Sinai covenant, He declared. But He still was not writing them off. He would create a new

◄ A new covenant predicted

covenant to redefine His relationship with them (Jeremiah 31:31-33). When we come to the New Testament we will see how He fulfilled this promise in Jesus.

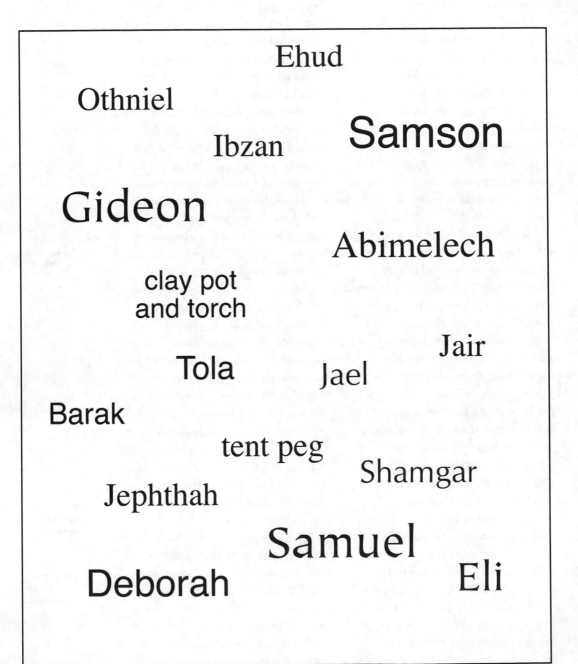

Chapter Twelve
THE UNITED KINGDOM

As Samuel's duties became too broad for him to manage alone, he appointed his sons to settle judicial disputes. But like Eli's sons, they corrupted themselves. They accepted bribes without shame and openly made a mockery of justice. As Samuel grew older, the elders of Israel could see the prospect that his sons would assert themselves as despotic leaders once their father died. The elders therefore made a special request of Samuel. They wanted him to find them a king.

At first Samuel objected, for he felt hurt by their request. He interpreted it as a rejection of what he had done for Israel. But when God told him to honor the wishes of the people, Samuel relented and began to seek an appropriate candidate.

Saul Becomes King (1 Samuel 8–15)

Samuel's search led him to a towering figure named Saul. He was from a wealthy family in Benjamin, the smallest of the tribes. Here was a man of kingly stature, who stood head and shoulders above everyone else. He also had the makings of a valiant warrior. Yet he was a man of genuine humility, at least initially.

Saul formed the first standing army in Israel and commissioned his son Jonathan to command a third of the army. Jonathan was a man of great faith, one of the most godly and upright people in all of Jewish history. In addition, he was a fearless soldier. He and his father scored a series of early victories over the Philistines, largely as a result of God's blessings and Jonathan's daring on the field of battle.

With the crowning of Saul, the Period of the Judges came to a conclusion and Israel began the Period of the United Kingdom. It lasted through the reigns of Saul, David, and Solomon. As its name implies, the United Kingdom embraced those years — basically the tenth century BC — when all of Israel, north and south, had a single ruler. The history of this period is recorded in the books of 1 and 2 Samuel, 1 Kings, and 1 and 2 Chronicles.

◄ Saul's qualifications as king

◄◄ The people request a king

Saul held the throne only a short while before he began to focus on founding a dynasty. In Jonathan he saw an able and worthy successor. Securing Jonathan's right to the crown became an obsession with him. Meanwhile, Saul himself began to change, both spiritually and psychologically. Fame and success took their toll on his character. His once godly outlook gave way to a bitter, despondent spirit. Dark moods swept over him, and he sometimes acted like a madman. As his bouts with depression grew more frequent and more severe, they gave rise to violent, unpredictable outbursts that endangered anyone nearby, including close friends and family.

Saul changes ➤

David Selected (1 Samuel 16–20)

With Saul showing such an evil nature, God opted to remove the throne from his family. Once more God dispatched Samuel to find a king for Israel. This time the choice fell on a young boy named David from the tribe of Judah. While Judah had long been one of the most prominent tribes, it was now to enjoy unrivaled prestige because of David. In fact, politically speaking, Judah would tower above the other tribes for the next thousand years.

God chooses David ➤

It was not God's intent for David to assume the throne immediately. Instead, he was to be a designated successor, standing ready whenever Saul died. As it turned out, Saul

Goliath the giant ➤➤

lived on for years, never accepting David as an heir to the crown. Saul pretended friendship with David and frequently hosted him as a guest at the royal table, but only to keep an eye on him. Saul even gave his daughter to David in marriage in hopes of having a spy in David's household. All the while Saul secretly plotted against David's life.

David Slays Goliath

Saul's misgivings toward David began early in their relationship while David was still a teen and Saul was fighting another of his wars with the Philistines. The war had not gone well. Victory seemed to elude both sides, and soon a demoralizing standoff ensued. For weeks the two armies camped within sight of each other, unable to attack, but reluctant to retreat.

In the midst of this stalemate a man named Goliath stepped out of the Philistine camp and issued a challenge to Israel. He dared Israel to send one of their own to meet him in face-to-face combat. Under other circumstances an opponent for Goliath might have come forward. But Goliath was a formidable foe. He came from a family of gigantic men, and he was the tallest of the lot, over nine feet tall. Understandably, none of Saul's men were eager to meet him, not even Jonathan. So, to taunt Israel, Goliath renewed his challenge daily.

One day as Goliath was hurling insults at Israel, David happened to be in the Israelite camp, visiting his brothers, who were soldiers. Taken aback when no one responded to Goliath's provocation, David offered to take on the giant himself.

To this point David had always been a shepherd. The youngest in his family, he was not yet old enough to be a soldier. But he was taken to Saul's tent, where he restated his willingness to battle Goliath. As a shepherd he had developed great skill in using a slingshot to fend off predators, including bears and lions. He therefore decided to take only a slingshot with him against Goliath, since swords and armor would serve to weigh him down. "God sustained me against bears and lions," he told Saul, "and He will likewise protect me from this Philistine."

With sling in hand, and armed with five stones chosen from a nearby stream, David approached Goliath. The Philistine, insulted that Saul had sent such a youth against him, began to mock and ridicule. David merely replied, "God will deliver you into my hands today, for it is His battle, and He does not need swords and spears to prevail." Then, running toward Goliath, David loosed the first stone from his sling. It struck the giant in the forehead, just above the eyes, and felled him. David rushed to the fallen figure and using Goliath's own sword, cut off the giant's head.

With their champion dead, the Philistines broke ranks and fled.

Israel took after them in hot pursuit and secured a decisive victory. Afterwards, as the Israelites celebrated victory, people began to shout that Saul had slain his thousands, but David his tens of thousands. Saul's jealousy and paranoia could not take such a comparison, and before long he was laying his first plots to destroy David.

Ironically, Jonathan did not share his father's disdain for David. Instead, he found himself drawn to David as a close friend and ally. When Jonathan learned that Samuel had anointed David to be king, he accepted that choice and became one of David's most ardent defenders. This placed Jonathan in a precarious position, for Saul never relented in his effort to kill David. When Jonathan intervened repeatedly on David's behalf, Saul became impatient with his son. In one fit of anger he even threw a spear at Jonathan.

◄ Jonathan and David

David Takes the Throne (2 Samuel 1–7)

Eventually Saul's plots intensified to the point that David could no longer stay within the king's borders. He spent the final years of Saul's reign as a fugitive, hiding in wilderness outposts or taking refuge in nearby nations. He was still a fugitive when Saul and Jonathan, in yet another battle with the Philistines, died side by side under a fierce enemy assault. Many in Israel then rallied to David, and ultimately

◄◄ David kills Goliath

◄ David becomes king

the entire nation accepted him as their ruler.

David conquers Jerusalem >

David took up his reign with vigor. Now that he was king in his own right, David moved to capture Jerusalem and make it the capital of Israel. To this point Jerusalem had never been in Israelite hands. The Jebusites, a native Canaanite nation, had controlled the city as far back as Abraham. Joshua had been unable to dislodge them. And down to David's day the Jebusites continued to hold out behind the city's seemingly impenetrable walls.

David's heart for God >>

David discovered a secret tunnel that supplied water to the city and used it to bypass the walls. Slipping into the city with an armed band and taking the Jebusites by surprise, he wrested Jerusalem from them. Then, he established his government there and launched an extensive building program. At the same time he mounted military campaigns in every direction to wipe out even the semblance of resistance to his rule. Within a few years he had created a small empire that encompassed most of Canaan. His son Solomon later expanded this empire so that its influence stretched from the Euphrates River southward to the border of Egypt.

David prepares to build the temple >>

David's military achievements alone would have assured him a glorious place in Jewish history. But his more lasting accomplishments were in the field of spirituality and literature. David was a musician, skillful on the harp and renowned

David the songwriter >

as a writer of songs. His music celebrated God's majesty, mercy, and protective presence. While living as a fugitive, David had learned to depend on God in order to survive, and much of his music reflects a confident reliance on the Lord. Dozens of David's songs eventually made their way into the Bible in the book of Psalms, a collection of 150 hymns that Israel used in her worship. Many of these songs are still sung in churches and synagogues today.

David's songs reveal the sensitive heart of a man who was always concerned about following God's will. He wanted to elevate Israel's respect for the Lord. To that end he ordered the ark of the covenant moved from its remote site to Jerusalem. He housed it in a tent he pitched in the heart of his splendid capital. Yet this left him uneasy, for he lived in a sumptuous palace, while the worship of God was relegated to a tent.

So he determined to build a great temple in Jerusalem, a structure more magnificent than any other in the city. But He never got to carry out this desire. "You are a man of war and bloodshed," God told David. "I do not want a man of war to build the house that bears my name. Instead, I want a man of peace." God therefore allowed David to stockpile the materials for the project, but postponed construction until Solomon, David's son, was on the throne.

The Forever Kingdom

In assuring David that the temple would indeed be erected, God told him, "After your death I will raise up your son after you to sit on your throne. He will construct My temple, and I will establish the throne of his kingdom forever" (2 Samuel 7:12-16). Naturally, David saw this promise as centered on Solomon, as did Solomon himself. Yet, Solomon's kingdom was not destined to last forever. It was eventually destroyed, rupturing soon after his death.

Only when we come to the New Testament do we learn the fuller meaning of this promise. There we discover that God's promise to David applied in only a limited sense to Solomon. In a far more significant way it pointed to the work of Jesus, who was a direct descendant of David (Acts 2:29-31). It was Jesus whom God had in mind when He spoke of David's son. And it was the rule of Jesus which would last forever.

David's Personal Life
(2 Samuel 11–12)

For all he achieved, David had a difficult reign. In addition to enemies along his borders, he was plagued by intrigue and treachery in his own inner circle, sometimes among his own children. As was the custom with kings of his day, David had several wives, who gave him numerous sons and daughters. Unfortunately, the rivalry and jealousies among them poisoned David's household and brought him great misery.

Many of his songs speak of the sadness and grief that he knew all too well. Yet, no matter how deep his discouragement, David never lost faith in God. His songs consistently affirm God's goodness and kindness toward him. God even referred to David as "a man after my own heart" (1 Samuel 13:14). This does not mean that David always did what was right. There were occasions when he sorely violated God's standards and law. But faced with his wrongdoing, he never hesitated to admit his sin and to turn back to God with a contrite spirit. His was truly a heart that longed for what was right.

David's most serious moral lapse involved a notorious episode with a woman named Bathsheba. Her husband Uriah was a loyal soldier in David's army. But while Uriah was away in battle, David drew her into an adulterous affair. As a result of their relationship, she became pregnant, this at a time when her husband had not been home for months.

David immediately brought her husband home under the guise of having Uriah report on the war's progress. "He will spend the night with his wife while he is in the city," David thought, "and that way Bathsheba can later act as though the child is his." But Uriah was a man of high principle. So long as his fellow soldiers were in the field and deprived of a wife's companionship, he refused to take advantage

◄ David and Bathsheba

David appoints
Solomon as
successor >>

of his visit to the city to spend time
with Bathsheba.

Now desperate to hide what had
happened, David ordered his field
commander to put Uriah in an
exposed position on the battlefront,
thus assuring his death. Once Uriah
was dead, David brought Bathsheba
into his household and made her
his wife.

After their child was born, God
sent a prophet named Nathan to
confront David with the monstrosity
of his sin. Nathan also announced

Solomon's request
for wisdom >>

that the infant was going to die. Just
as Nathan had warned, the baby
soon fell sick. David went into isola-
tion, weeping and begging God to
spare the child's life, but to no avail.
Word came after seven days that
his young son had not survived.
David, who had grieved so uncon-
trollably to this point, greeted this
sad news with a great statement of
confidence in life after death. "I
cannot bring him back to me," he
said of the child, "but I can go to
him" (2 Samuel 12:23).

Solomon's
writings >>

Because of the deep regret that
David showed for his sin, God permitted him to keep Bathsheba as
his wife. And it was to this union
that Solomon was born. Solomon's
name, strangely enough, means
"peacable," a noted contrast to the
turmoil that surrounded David and
his court.

Solomon as King (1 Kings 1–5)

On his deathbed David required
his nobles and advisors to swear

allegiance to Solomon, his son and
chosen successor. Then David
ordered them to enthrone Solomon
immediately. This was David's way
of preempting his other sons from
snatching the crown. Solomon
proved a stellar successor. Under
his extraordinary rule, Israel built a
political and commercial empire
that brought riches and glory to
Jerusalem.

Following his coronation,
Solomon had a dream in which God
asked him to name the gift he most
earnestly desired. Solomon replied
that he wanted the wisdom to rule
his people justly. God commended
him for answering this way. Moreover, because Solomon had not
requested wealth or long life, God
promised to add these things to the
gift of wisdom Solomon sought.

Indeed, both Solomon's wealth
and wisdom were legendary within
only a few years. Prominent leaders
came from great distances to see
the splendors of his capital and to
hear firsthand the wisdom for which
he was renowned. Solomon wrote
thousands of proverbs, dozens of
which weave their way through the
book of Proverbs in the Bible. He
was also credited with writing the
Song of Solomon, an erotic love
poem that celebrates the beauty of
a husband and wife who are drawn
passionately to one another.

Another book identified with
Solomon is Ecclesiastes, which
means "The Preacher." It is not
really about a preacher, but about

Solomon, now advanced in years, giving advice to his son. The book recounts how Solomon accumulated wealth, learning, and vast property holdings, thinking that these would offer happiness and security. When happiness still eluded him, he turned to all kinds of sensual pleasures and vices. But these, too, left him feeling empty. Only when he learned to respect God and keep God's commandments did he find fulfillment in life.

The Temple Is Built
(1 Kings 6–8)

Solomon's most noted achievement by far was building the temple that his father designed. It was a massive structure, sprawling across the top of Mount Zion, one of the hills on which Jerusalem rested. The main part of the temple was simply an enlarged version of the tabernacle, again with two inner chambers, the Holy Place and beyond it the Holiest Place. Surrounding these sanctuaries were extensive porticoes that allowed thousands of people to gather in the temple courts.

Not only was the temple lavish in size, its decor was resplendent. Solomon used massive marble stones in its construction. Polished cedar from Lebanon made up the woodwork. And gold was everywhere. Gold shields adorned its walls. Gold utensils and furnishings were used in its ceremonies. Even the roof itself was covered with gold leaf.

The spiritual high point of Solomon's reign was the dedication of the temple. It was a magnificent occasion, with all the pomp and ceremony befitting such an august event. At the height of this ceremony, Solomon worded a long prayer in which he asked God to bless the temple and the worship that it would foster. As you might expect, he urged God to accept the sacrifices of His people and forgive their sins. But then Solomon added,

> Hear also the prayer of the foreigner who comes to this place to worship. For those in other lands will hear of the goodness You have shown toward Israel. And they will be attracted to this temple that bears Your name. Thus, when they pray, grant them their request, so that all the people of the earth may come to know You and respect You, as Israel does this day.
> — 1 Kings 8:41-43

◀◀ Solomon's temple

This preoccupation with the foreigner provides an important insight into what Solomon thought God was doing with Israel. Why had God chosen Israel to begin with? Solomon's answer, among other things, was that God wanted to use Israel to teach the rest of the world about Himself. Later in Jewish history the prophet Isaiah picked up this theme and enlarged on it, as we shall see when we look at Isaiah's life in an upcoming chapter.

◀ Israel and other nations in God's plan

God's desire for Israel to teach other nations about Him explains the unique focus on foreigners in

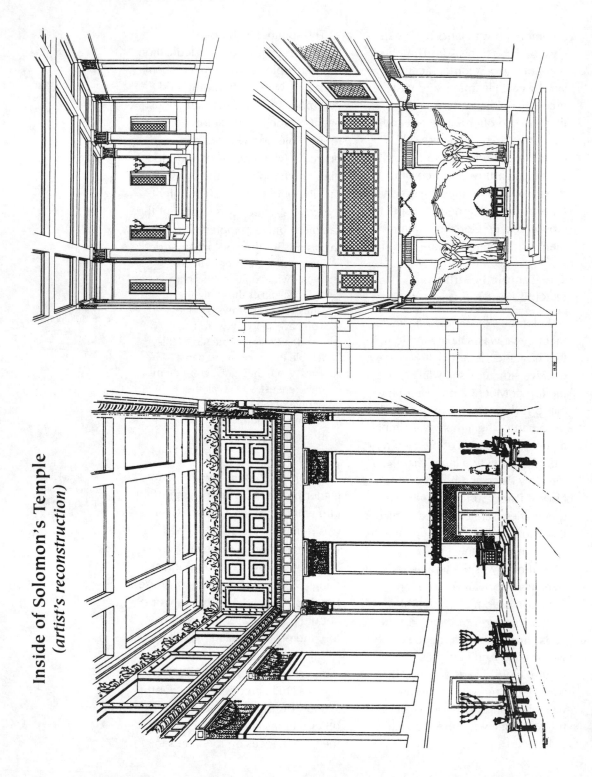

Inside of Solomon's Temple
(artist's reconstruction)

the Law of Moses. It alone, of all the ancient law codes, provides explicit protection of a foreigner's rights. It calls on Israel to treat foreigners with kindness and compassion. It also provides an established procedure by which foreigners could become citizens of Israel. God apparently intended for Israel to be a beacon to attract other people to Him. He therefore wanted Israel to make it easy for those from other nations to approach Him and His center of worship.

Pagan Religion Introduced (1 Kings 11)

Behind God's provisions for receiving outsiders was the assumption that they were seeking Him. God warned His people to take a different stance toward foreigners who threatened to bring pagan gods into Israel. In those cases both the foreigner's influence and his religion were to be suppressed.

Unfortunately, Solomon failed to heed God's counsel on this matter. As was the custom with monarchs of his day, he built a harem, marrying wives from surrounding nations. As these women came into his household, they brought their national gods with them.

To Solomon's discredit, he allowed his wives to draw him increasingly into pagan observances. He even permitted pagan altars and places of worship to be erected at state expense. In effect, he was officially endorsing paganism as an alternative to the worship of God. It would have horrified Solomon to see where his actions eventually led, for after his death the ten northern tribes abandoned temple worship altogether in favor of idolatry borrowed from Egypt. Later these same tribes aggressively curbed the worship of God and promoted the worship of Baal.

◄ Bad influence of Solomon's foreign wives

This drift into paganism served as the backdrop for the work of Israel's great prophets. Their message, through and through, was a call to purge idolatry from the land and return to a pure worship of God. When their message went unheeded, God finally destroyed Israel's independence at the hands of the Assyrians and Babylonians. In chapter thirteen we will see those events unfold.

THE KINGDOM DIVIDES, THEN FALLS

The splendor of Solomon's reign came at a high price. At first he was able to support his lavish lifestyle and huge army with the spoils of combat and by forcing conquered nations to pay him tribute. He also built a vast and prosperous commercial network that traded along the east coast of Africa and made port calls well across the Mediterranean.

But these funds could not sustain him forever, and Solomon eventually levied heavy taxes on his people. The northern tribes in particular resented his taxation, for they saw their money flowing south to enrich Jerusalem and Judah. When Solomon's son Rehoboam came to the throne (sometime between 930 and 920 BC), a delegation of national leaders asked him to relieve the tax burden borne by their citizens. Foolishly, Rehoboam treated them with contempt. He even boasted that he would be so hard on them that his father's levies would seem like nothing.

Foolish arrogance of Solomon's son ➤

10 tribes mutiny ➤

Angered at such arrogance, the ten northern tribes announced that they no longer accepted Rehoboam as their legitimate ruler. They broke from him and named Jeroboam, a longtime opponent of Solomon, as their king. Jeroboam chose the city of Samaria to be his capital. He worried, however, that his people might gradually shift their loyalty back to Rehoboam if they returned to Jerusalem regularly for religious festivals.

To offset that danger, Jeroboam set up two centers of worship, one at Dan, the other at Bethel. At both sites he erected the statue of a golden bull. He borrowed this bull worship from Egypt, where he had lived in exile during Solomon's reign. He announced that henceforth the northern tribes would worship at Dan and Bethel.

Rehoboam tried to regain the northern tribes, but failing in his effort, he grudgingly acknowledged their independence. Only Judah and the tribe of Benjamin remained subject to him. Hereafter the northern tribes referred to themselves as Israel, while the southern kingdom called itself Judah.

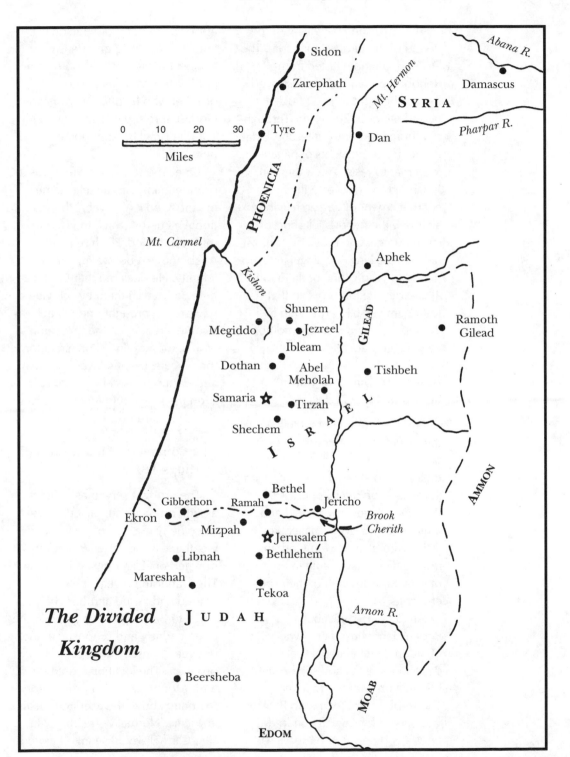

The Divided Kingdom

This marks the beginning of the Period of the Divided Kingdom. The Divided Kingdom lasted from Rehoboam until Assyria destroyed the northern tribes in 722 BC, a period of about 200 years. Throughout this period both Israel and Judah found the enticements of paganism too great to resist. A few kings in Judah did try to reverse the encroachment of foreign religions, although their efforts fell short of lasting success. In Israel, by contrast, not a single king was singularly committed to God. None of them did away with the bull worship that Jeroboam established at Dan and Bethel, and many actively promoted very degenerate religions.

Good and bad kings ➤

Elijah predicts drought ➤➤

Ahab, Jezebel, and Elijah (1 Kings 16–17)

Not everyone in Israel followed their kings into forbidden worship. There were always those who did their best to stay true to God, even in the face of official oppression. But their numbers were few and their influence even smaller. For those who aligned with God, the most difficult days came in the reign of Ahab, the seventh of the northern kings.

Ahab married Jezebel, a Phoenician whose father was king of Sidon. Jezebel had a tireless devotion to Baal, and she brought her religion with her to Samaria. There she built a temple to Baal. It was served by several hundred priests and prophets whose liveli-

Jezebel promotes Baal worship ➤

hood she underwrote personally. She also launched an offensive against the historic religion of Israel, putting to death any Levite or prophet who held to the worship of God. Before she was through, only 7000 in Israel had not bowed before Baal.

One who refused to yield was a prophet named Elijah. His name meant "God is Yahweh," the traditional name by which the Israelites referred to God. Elijah rebuked Ahab and Jezebel sternly for their iniquity. He declared that God was going to punish them by bringing a devastating drought upon Israel. Soon everyone felt the force of his words, for no rain fell on Israel for three years. Eventually every stream and pasture in Israel was bone dry. Even the king could find no place to graze his herds.

The Contest on Mount Carmel (1 Kings 18)

The drought served as a direct assault on Baal's supposed powers, since he was a god of fertility and weather. As the waterless months dragged on, Elijah stayed in hiding. Then, after three years he reappeared and raised another challenge to Baal. Elijah met Ahab in the open country and proposed a duel between himself and Jezebel's prophets. The location would be atop Mount Carmel, a promontory towering above the Mediterranean coastline. Normally a relatively lush site, Carmel would seem a favored spot for a fertility god like Baal. There had also once been an altar of God on Mount Carmel, although it was now in ruins.

Elijah suggested a contest to see which god, Baal or Yahweh, would answer his prophet's prayer. Elijah would rebuild the fallen altar of God and place a sacrifice on it. The prophets and priests of Baal would put a sacrifice on an altar of their own. The test would be to see which god sent fire from the sky to light his sacrifice.

The contest began in the early morning hours. Four hundred and fifty prophets of Baal danced around his altar, sometimes gashing themselves with knives, and calling on their god to bring fire upon their sacrifice. They continued their pleas to Baal well into the afternoon, with Elijah taunting them all the while. Finally, they danced themselves into exhaustion. Then Elijah called for twelve large jars of water, which were poured over his rebuilt altar. Not only did the water drench his sacrifice, but the firewood, as well.

Next Elijah made a simple request of God: "Let it be known today that You are God in Israel, that I am your servant, and that I have done all these things at your command" (1 Kings 18:36). Immediately fire descended on the altar, ignited the firewood, consumed the sacrifice, and evaporated every last drop of water. The people began shouting, "Yahweh is God. Yahweh is God." They then helped Elijah seize the prophets of Baal, who were slaughtered one and all.

Later in the day Elijah sent word to Ahab that the drought was about to break. A fierce storm descended on the land, and rain soaked the parched earth for the first time in years. But when word reached Jezebel that Elijah had killed her prophets, she put a price on his head. Within hours he was fleeing for his life, going all the way to Mount Sinai to hide from her wrath.

◄◄ Contest between God and Baal

Ahab's Successors (1 Kings 19–2 Kings 3)

When Elijah finally reappeared in Israel, he placed at his side a man named Elisha, who emerged as a great prophet in his own right. Shortly afterward God brought Elijah's work to a close and took him from the scene. As Elijah and Elisha were walking a remote road across the Jordan from Jericho, something that resembled a chariot of fire passed between them. Then a gigantic whirlwind swept Elijah from the earth and out of sight. His body was never found, although fifty men spent three days searching for it.

◄ Elijah's successor, Elisha

◄ Elijah carried away from the earth

Meanwhile, Ahab had launched an initiative to tie the thrones of Israel and Judah together through military alliance and marriage. He arranged for his daughter Athaliah to marry Jehoram, still a teenager, but in line to become king of Judah. Athaliah had a strong influence over

◄◄ God sends fire from heaven

Joash restores the temple >>

her husband, who died at 40 after ruling only eight years. Their young son Ahaziah succeeded him. And during Ahaziah's brief reign, Athaliah established herself as the power behind the throne. As wicked as her mother Jezebel, she aggressively advanced the cause of Baal throughout Judah.

Israel's throne usurped >

When her son met an untimely death, she snatched the throne for herself. Determined to remove all rivals, she slaughtered the entire royal household, including her grandchildren. The sole survivor of her purge was an infant named Joash. He was spirited away from the palace and hidden in the temple under the protection of Jehoiada, the high priest. For years the whereabouts of Joash remained unknown to anyone but Jehoiada's closest friends.

A godly young king crowned >

When Joash was seven years old, Jehoiada and a league of trusted soldiers and priests convened a hurried assembly at the temple to crown the lad as king. People near the temple immediately realized what was happening, and a great shout of acclamation arose from the courtyard. Athaliah heard the sound and rushed to the temple to protest. But no one came to her aid, and she was ushered to the city gates and executed.

Jehu wipes out Baal worship >

What followed next was an all-out campaign to rid the land of Baal's influence. In the north a warrior named Jehu seized the throne and wiped out Ahab's household. Jehu then slaughtered the priests of Baal. He also leveled the temple of Baal that Jezebel had built in Samaria, converting the site to a latrine.

In the south Joash directed the priests to make extensive repairs to the temple, which had suffered from years of neglect. He also did what he could to replace the once rich adornments of the temple, which various enemies of Judah had plundered. Still, Joash did not remove every remnant of paganism in his realm. During his lengthy reign people continued to perform pagan sacrifices and to burn incense to various gods atop high hills. His successors, several of them godly men, also allowed these practices to go unchecked. In this lax environment it was only a matter of time before paganism reasserted itself. Toward the end of Jerusalem's independence, even child sacrifice was being practiced in the city, on occasion by members of the royal family.

Assyria Conquers the North (2 Kings 15–19)

Beneath these efforts at reform, however, both Israel and Judah were falling apart politically. Murder and intrigue around the throne did not end with the removal of Queen Athaliah. Joash was murdered by conspirators in his own inner circle, as was his son, who followed him to the throne. A similar pattern of betrayal and assassination plagued the succession of kings in Samaria.

With so much disloyalty in their own ranks, neither Israel nor Judah was able to maintain a united front against outside aggressors. Surrounding nations began to nibble away at the territory of both thrones.

The most serious incursions came first in the north, where the Syrians brought continued pressure on Israel and snatched key cities from the king in Samaria. Weakened by Syria, Israel was no match for the rising power of Assyria. Archaeologists have recovered an Assyrian carving that shows Jehu bringing tribute payments to the Assyrian king long before Assyria reached the height of her power.

As Israel waned, her last ten kings gradually lost their independence to Assyria. First the Assyrians extracted heavy tribute payments from Samaria. Next they began to seize Israelite territory and to deport the citizens of Israel to regions beyond the Euphrates. The final chapter came when Hoshea, the last king in Samaria, refused to pay his tribute and sought an alliance with Egypt. Assyria responded with a crushing attack that brought Israel to an end in 722 BC.

For the next century and a half, Judah remained as the only surviving element of Solomon's once strong empire. The Assyrians did their utmost to subdue Jerusalem. They laid siege to the city and boasted to its defenders that God was not powerful enough to deliver Jerusalem. But God would not countenance such arrogance. He sent a plague upon the Assyrians that decimated their army, forcing them to withdraw.

Spiritual Decay in Jerusalem (2 Kings 20–25)

Unfortunately, Judah learned nothing from Israel's experience. Spared from Assyria, Jerusalem now had an opportunity to correct her ways before God turned punishment in her direction. To her advantage the man who ruled in Jerusalem when Israel fell was Hezekiah, a godly reformer who restored the temple, rebuilt respect for the Law of Moses, and destroyed pagan shrines and idols everywhere.

◄ Hezekiah's reforms

Yet, when he died, he was succeeded by Manasseh, without doubt the most wicked of all the kings in Judah. He reigned through violence and bloodshed. And he immediately overthrew Hezekiah's reforms. Not only did he reconstruct the pagan sites his father had destroyed, he even erected pagan altars and an image of Astarte in the temple in Jerusalem.

◄ Manasseh's backsliding

God therefore announced that He would bring the same fate on Judah that He had levied on Israel. Jerusalem would be utterly destroyed, its people dragged away into forced exile. God was now so determined to punish Judah that nothing could change His mind. He did not even relent when Josiah, Manasseh's grandson, set out to undo all the evil his father and

◄◄ Israel falls to Assyria

◄ Judah's fall predicted

Josiah revives
worship of God ➤

Fall of
Jerusalem ➤➤

Judah falls to
Babylon ➤

Cyrus ends
Jewish exile ➤➤

grandfather had done. The Bible says of Josiah, "Before him there was no king like him who turned to the Lord with all his heart and with all his soul and with all his might" (2 Kings 23:25). Josiah removed every taint of paganism from the temple and the lands of his realm. He republished the Law of Moses, reinstated the celebration of the Passover, and even made an expedition to Bethel, where he destroyed the golden bull that Jeroboam had built.

But when Josiah died, evil returned to the throne once more in the person of his successor. Judah's end was now in sight. She was caught in a spiraling power struggle between a resurgent Egypt to her west and the unprecedented might of Babylon to her east. She first fell under Egypt's sway. Then, as the Babylonians pushed Egypt back, she found herself at the mercy of Babylon.

Babylon was not noted for mercy, however, and Jerusalem soon came under siege. When the city could no longer hold out, the Babylonian emperor Nebuchadnezzar thoroughly pillaged Jerusalem. He cut up all the gold and silver adornments of the temple, hauled off the royal treasury, and exiled the nobles, the most valiant warriors, and all the skilled craftsmen to Babylon. He set up caretaker kings to run Jerusalem for him. But when they made a stab at regaining independence, he brought his armies

back and leveled the city completely. He flattened its walls, the temple, the houses — everything. Jerusalem was left a burning ruin.

The Return from Babylon (Ezra and Nehemiah)

The Old Testament provides only sketchy details about the years of Babylonian exile. Apart from a few passing comments, the books of history skip this period entirely. What we know about the exile comes primarily from the books of Ezekiel and Daniel, which we will review when we come to the books written by prophets. We do know, however, that the Jews returned from Babylon with the most intense dedication to God's law that they had ever demonstrated.

Jeremiah, one of the last prophets in Jerusalem, announced that the city would lie desolate for 70 years following Babylon's conquest. During those years many of the Jews deported to Babylon kept alive the dream that they could someday return and rebuild the city.

Their dream came to reality, just as Jeremiah had said, when the Medes and Persians toppled Babylon. The book of Ezra opens by telling how Cyrus, the Medo-Persian emperor, issued a decree permitting any Jew in exile to return to Judah to rebuild Jerusalem and its temple. He also agreed to restore any of the temple furnishings that still remained in his treasure house.

Several thousand took advantage of this opportunity and set out for Judah. A descendant of David named Zerubbabel and a priest named Jeshua headed the effort to reconstruct the temple. His enterprise was stoutly resisted by local warlords, who did not find it in their interest to see Jerusalem strong again. Once Cyrus was dead, these opponents managed to obtain a royal edict forbidding further work on the temple. Even though the order was eventually rescinded, work on the temple was at a standstill for years while it remained in effect.

Temple rebuilt ➤

About the time the temple was finally completed, a scribe named Ezra arrived from Babylon. (Scribes were specialists at copying and interpreting the Law of Moses.) He helped to reorganize the priesthood and to formulate worship at the temple in accordance with what Moses taught. Ezra also worked to promote a singular devotion to God in the hearts of his fellow countrymen.

Walls of Jerusalem rebuilt ➤➤

Yahweh worship restored ➤➤

Neither he nor Zerubbabel, however, succeeded at rebuilding the walls of the city. A few fitful starts were made, but enthusiasm for the project gave way to demoralization. At the height of this discouragement a new leader appeared in the person of Nehemiah, whose story is told in the book that bears his name. Nehemiah was a personal attendant to the emperor in Babylon. When Nehemiah learned that the rebuilding of Jerusalem was at a standstill, he became deeply distraught. His fallen spirit, soon apparent to everyone, caught the attention of the emperor, who asked what was disturbing him. When Nehemiah explained, the king made him governor of Jerusalem and put him in charge of reviving the city.

The imperial appointment as governor gave Nehemiah the right to draw on the emperor's forests and quarries. Under Nehemiah, the entire project got a fresh, enthusiastic start. A marvelous motivator, he inspired the populace to restore the defenses of Jerusalem as quickly as possible. Within 66 days the city wall and its gates were standing. Now, able to protect themselves, the people moved forward with their work on the temple, their homes, and businesses.

They also demonstrated an admirable heart for God. Ezra and the priests provided systematic training in the Law of Moses. And the people proved eager to hear the Law and to practice it. This signaled a remarkable turnaround in Jewish history. From this point forward the Jews would never again show the slightest tolerance for compromise with paganism. They would be known throughout the ancient world for their opposition to idolatry and the worship of multiple gods. At long last, it seemed that God's people had learned the lesson He started teaching them at Mount Sinai.

Chapter Fourteen

THE BOOKS OF POETRY AND WISDOM

Nehemiah's reconstruction of Jerusalem brings Old Testament history to a close. But while Nehemiah marks the end of the Old Testament historically, the book of Nehemiah itself comes near the middle of the Old Testament. The balance of the Old Testament pulls 22 books together in two great sections, one called the books of poetry, the other the books of prophecy.

```
▽      📖 Poetry/Wisdom
▷      📖 Job
▷      📖 Psalms
▷      📖 Proverbs
▷      📖 Ecclesiastes
▷      📖 Song of Solomon
```

There are five books of poetry, the longest written mostly by David. Three others are identified as works by Solomon, while the fifth, the book of Job, is from an unknown author. As their collective name indicates, the characteristic style of these books is poetic. But not everything in them is poetry. They are more nearly what the ancient world thought of as wisdom literature.

In Israel, as in most of the Middle East, wisdom literature was the closest thing to what we call philosophy. Writings on wisdom were found from Egypt in the west to the Tigris-Euphrates Valley in the east. Their aim was to equip the reader with the insight to make good decisions, both morally and personally. Dependent on the purpose of the author, a particular piece might take the form of extended dramatic dialogue, the recounting of life experiences, proverbs, poetry, or song. All of these styles appear in the wisdom literature of the Bible.

Job

The first book of wisdom in the Old Testament is about a godly man who suffered great reversals. His name was Job, and the book takes its name from him. This is a rather lengthy book, yet nothing in it allows us to identify exactly where or when Job lived. The setting seems to suggest a time frame prior to Moses, perhaps as early as Abraham.

God had blessed Job with a large family, immense wealth, vast herds and flocks, and scores of servants. Most importantly, Job was highly devout and morally upright. The book opens with a picture of Job offering daily sacrifices and prayers for himself and his family.

Also appearing at the first of Job is a spiritual being called Satan. The Bible never clearly explains his origin, but Satan appears in Scripture in two roles: first as one who tempts people to do evil, and second as one who slanders the reputation of individuals whom God has blessed. The name Satan, in fact, means "the accuser." This is the role he plays in Job.

When God comments on Job's exemplary character, Satan retorts that Job is hardly the godly person God makes him out to be. According to Satan, if Job were not so prosperous and privileged, he would reveal his true nature by turning his back on God. This is not the case, God insists. And to prove his point, God grants Satan permission to take anything from Job except his life.

This leads to an outpouring of tragedy for Job. Raiders steal his livestock. A great windstorm destroys the house in which his children have gathered for a feast, killing them all. And finally Job himself is stricken with disease. Covered with oozing sores, he is reduced to sitting in misery as he nurses his sick body. Yet, for all this misfortune, Job steadfastly refuses to reject God, as Satan had anticipated.

<< Job's wealth and godliness

At this point Job's friends come to sit by his side, no doubt with the hope of consoling him. But he draws little comfort from their words. They seem primarily concerned with their personal theories about why such ill has befallen him. Their basic position is that God is punishing Job for some hidden sin. When Job persists in declaring his innocence, they harden their stance. His very refusal to confess his sin, they conclude, is proof of his pride and wickedness.

<< Introducing Satan

The book thus turns out to be a philosophical examination of why people suffer. The conversations between Job and his friends are laid out like a drama, with the principal figures engaging in lengthy, poetic dialogues. As they seek a rationale for Job's suffering, both Job and his friends presume that God is just. But they also assume that death is the end of our existence. None of them has a concept of life beyond the grave where God makes right those things that are unjust in this world. In their minds God must balance all accounts prior to death. Otherwise, He would not be fair in His dealings with us. So if God is just and Job is suffering, their only explanation is that it must be Job's fault.

< Why do people suffer?

<< Tragedy strikes Job

Just when it seems that the debate between Job and his accusers will go on forever, God intervenes. He appears to them and starts firing questions rapidly. His

Hebrew poetry >>

questions center on the profound secrets behind nature and the universe. God's purpose is to let Job and his friends see how limited their knowledge is. And because of that limitation, they cannot possibly see all that is going on in Job's circumstances.

The knowledge gap between God and humanity >

Job himself finally concedes that many mysteries in life exceed human comprehension. Only God can understand them. Acknowledging that reality, Job learns to be content with his finite knowledge and the limits that come with being mortal.

Job's prosperity restored >

The book ends with God rewarding Job for his steadfastness under adversity. New children are born to him, and he recovers both his health and prosperity. At the close of his story Job has twice the wealth he enjoyed at the outset. The primary message of Job, however, is not that God blesses faithfulness with material rewards. Rather, it is about learning to be at peace with the sometimes painful limitations and unanswerable questions that are part of being human.

Psalms

From Job the Bible takes us next to the book of Psalms. This is Jewish poetry at its best. The psalms were songs written for festal occasions or worship at the temple or simply to commemorate some tragic moment. There are 150 psalms altogether, about half of them written by David.

Hebrew poetry differs from the poetic literature of other nations. It does not rhyme, as many modern poems do, nor does it maintain the careful rhythm and cadence of Greek and Latin verse. Instead, Hebrew poetry uses magnificent phraseology, the repetition of key phrases, and imaginative parallelism to create its effect.

Parallelism is the practice of wording sentences so that they place two closely related thoughts side by side. A writer may do this to draw a contrast between two ideas. Or he might use parallelism to emphasize a single idea by wording it two different ways. Psalm 78 opens with the parallelism:

> Listen, O my people, to my
> instruction.
> Incline your ears to the words of
> my mouth.

Or again, we have this example from Psalm 140:1.

> Deliver me, O Lord, from the evil
> man.
> Preserve me from the violent
> man.

On other occasions a parallelism is achieved by making the wording of two sentences very similar, with some change toward the end. We see this in the opening of Psalm 77:

> My voice rises to God, and I will
> cry aloud.
> My voice rises to God, and He
> will hear me.

This likewise illustrates the practice of using parallels to show contrasts. In this case the poet looks at two dimensions of the same outcry, first the cry as it is uttered by the worshiper, then second the cry as it is heard by God.

The New Testament treats some sections of the Psalms as having been prophecy, and even refers to David as a prophet. This passage from Psalm 2:2 is interpreted as foretelling the conspiracy between the Jewish leaders and the Roman governor to execute Jesus (Acts 4:24-28):

> The kings of the earth take their
>   stand.
> Its rulers take counsel together
> Against the Lord and against the
>   One He has anointed.

Similarly, this passage from Psalm 110:1 is taken to be a prophecy about God raising Jesus from the dead and giving Him a position of sovereignty in heaven (Acts 2:32-36):

> The Lord says to my Lord,
> "Sit here at My right hand,
> Until I make your enemies
> The footstool under your feet."

Other passages in the Psalms are seen as prefiguring the life of Jesus. Prefiguring is a special relationship in which one historical event foreshadows what will happen in another event far in the future. In prefiguring, the first event contains essential features that appear more dramatically in the one that comes later. When David wrote Psalm 2:6, for instance, he probably had his own coronation in mind. He quoted God as saying, "As for me, I have

set up My king upon Zion [the hill on which Jerusalem sits], My holy mountain." Then, addressing His king, God adds, "You are my son. Today I have begotten you." Yet, while David saw himself as the object of these words, the New Testament shows that they also depict God's relationship with Jesus (Hebrews 1:1-6).

<< Prophecy in the poetry

Another type of prefiguring in Psalms comes from statements that David made figuratively about himself, but which 1000 years later applied literally to Jesus. Psalm 22 is a striking example of this type of prefiguring. David opened the psalm with the very words Jesus would cry from the cross: "My God, my God, why have You forsaken me?" Further into the psalm, David described the agony he felt because he was surrounded by determined, cruel enemies. His description of how he felt included these words:

<< Opposition to Jesus

<< Jesus' resurrection and glorification

> A band of evildoers have encir-
>   cled me.
> They have pierced my hands and
>   my feet.
> I can count all my bones.
> They look at me and stare.
> They divide my clothes among
>   them
> And cast lots for my garments.
>   — Psalm 22:16-18

< Picture of the crucifixion

This is a precise portrayal of what happened at the crucifixion of Jesus when His executioners nailed His hands and feet to the cross but left His bones unbroken. Then they cast lots to determine which one would get his robe (John 19:17-24; 31-37).

The Psalms have been one of the world's most treasured bodies of literature for 3000 years. These songs celebrate God's grandeur, majesty, and compassion in unforgettable imagery and phrasing. Perhaps the most frequently quoted poem in the world is Psalm 23, which compares God to a caring shepherd who protects those who follow Him, nurturing them individually as members of His flock.

The "Shepherd Psalm" ➤

Wisdom of Solomon ➤➤

Other psalms celebrate the beauty and wisdom of the law God gave to Israel. Psalm 119, the longest of the Psalms, devotes 176 verses to this theme. This song is also unique in terms of design. It falls into 22 stanzas, each eight verses long. The writer chose 22 stanzas because there are 22 letters in the Hebrew alphabet. In stanza one, all eight verses begin with the first letter of the alphabet. The verses in stanza two all begin with the second letter of the alphabet, and so forth through the entire Psalm.

Source of wisdom and knowledge ➤➤

Not all of the Psalms are from David, or even from his day. A few of them were written during the Babylonian exile. In some cases we know who the author was. In other cases we do not. There is an exalted beauty to each of the Psalms, however, whoever its writer.

Proverbs

The third book of poetry is called Proverbs. As its name suggests, this volume is a collection of short, insightful pieces of advice. Most of the proverbs are attributed to Solomon, who wrote some 3000 proverbs and 1005 songs (1 Kings 4:32). You will recall that when Solomon became king of Israel, he asked God for extraordinary wisdom to rule his people well. The Bible says that God gave him a level of understanding and insight that exceeded the wisdom of all the nations around him (1 Kings 4:33).

The proverbs are themselves an appeal for the reader to hunger for wisdom, just as Solomon had done. The writer frequently commends people who are humble enough to learn from experience, contrasting them to those who are so arrogant that they continue to make foolish mistakes. Although Proverbs treats many areas of life and worship, the thrust of its advice is summed up in these words:

> Offer correction to a wise man,
>   and he will love you.
> Provide instruction to a wise
>   man, and he will be still wiser.
> Teach a righteous man, and he
>   will learn from what you say.
> Standing in awe of the Lord is the
>   beginning of wisdom
> And knowing the Holy One is
>   true knowledge.
>   — Proverbs 9:8-10

Proverbs also encourages a life of diligent work, not laziness. A life of integrity, not dishonesty. A life that is given to purity, both sexually and morally, not one spent in the mere pursuit of pleasure. Solomon spiced many of his proverbs with humor or irony. In Proverbs 25:24 he says, "It is better to live on the corner of a roof than inside a huge house with a contentious woman." Given Solomon's many misadventures in marriage, we can only wonder if he was speaking from firsthand experience.

Ecclesiastes

In the book of Ecclesiastes, often attributed to Solomon, we find that bitter experience was indeed the basis for much of his advice in Proverbs. Ecclesiastes is autobiographical and written in a tone of confession. It is cast in the form of an aged father giving advice to his son. Solomon relates how his vast wealth and unchallenged power had given him unbridled opportunities to explore every conceivable theory of happiness. He amassed huge estates. He had torrid love affairs. He dined on the finest foods and drank the finest wines. He surrounded himself with hundreds of servants to satisfy his every whim. Yet, in all of this he found that a sense of emptiness still gripped him.

The characteristic and most repeated phrase in Ecclesiastes is "Vanity of vanities. Everything is vanity." In this instance vanity means emptiness. The phrasing "vanity of vanities" was Solomon's way of saying that the emptiness inside him was the very worst kind. Only toward the end of the book does he start to find fulfillment.

Gradually he comes to realize that happiness is found, not in what we are able to acquire with our effort, but in the effort itself. The key to life, he advises, is to find what you love to do and then immerse yourself in it. He writes,

> Here is what I have found to be good and appropriate: to eat, to drink, and to enjoy oneself in all of his endeavor under the sun during the few years of his life that God gives him; for this enjoyment of endeavor is his reward.
> — Ecclesiastes 5:18

Solomon then adds that such a person "will not often fret about how old he is getting, because God keeps him preoccupied with the gladness of his heart" (Ecclesiastes 5:20).

<< Search for the best in life

Solomon also found fulfillment in coming back to what he had once moved away from — a deep respect for God and for God's law. As he closes Ecclesiastes he says, "The conclusion, when all is said and done, is this: stand in awe of God and keep His commandments, for this is what is expected of every person" (Ecclesiastes 12:13).

< God is the source

Song of Solomon

Despite his disappointment with pleasure-seeking, Solomon's intent in Ecclesiastes was not to persuade his readers to despise pleasure altogether. It was pleasure pursued as an end in itself that left him empty. In other settings pleasure was part of a fulfilling experience, as he

Marriage and
sexual love >>

makes clear in the Song of Solomon.

Of Solomon's 1005 songs, this is the only one to be preserved. Unlike David's songs, which usually contained only a few hundred words, the Song of Solomon (also known as the Song of Songs) is more like a short operatic piece. Its eight chapters are a series of musical interchanges between a beautiful young woman and her striking, handsome husband. Her every word flows from her deep love for him. He reciprocates with expressions of deep tenderness and admiration toward her.

The two lovers speak openly of their sexual, emotional, and spiritual attraction to one another. They talk of the people and circumstances that work against them. They are nonetheless determined to let nothing interfere with their love. The Song of Solomon is one of the most erotic pieces of literature to come from the ancient world. Many people are surprised that the Bible would contain a book which celebrates romance and sexuality so openly. But God never disapproves of sexuality and sensuality between husbands and wives. Indeed, he always encourages full sexual enjoyment within marriage. It is only in settings outside of marriage that God treats sex as immoral.

The Song of Solomon is the last of the books of poetry, but it is by no means the end of poetic literature in the Old Testament. The prophets, whose writings come next, frequently used poems and poetic structures to deliver their message. The books of poetry are thus stylistically a helpful introduction to the prophets, for having learned Israel's characteristic modes of poetic expression, we are better equipped to understand the words of the prophets. And it is their works that interest us next.

Chapter Fifteen

THE BOOKS OF PROPHECY

In the Bible, prophets are people who speak a message directly from God. At times this involves foretelling the future, but not always. In fact, the prophets devote far more attention to the present than the future. Their primary concern is to draw people closer to God and to lives of personal integrity. When they speak with this aim in mind, the prophets' words are called prophecy, whether they predict the future or not.

God chose prophets from all walks of life. Many were commoners. Others were highly respected leaders best remembered for military exploits or political achievement. The Bible calls Moses a prophet, for instance (Deuteronomy 18:17-18). It also refers to judges like Deborah and Samuel as prophets, along with David, the king (Judges 4:4; 1 Samuel 3:20; Acts 2:29-30).

But these are not the people we typically have in mind when we speak of the prophets. We usually reserve the word "prophet" for a group of men (and occasionally women) who began to appear in number about the time Israel established her monarchy. To a person they saw themselves as God's personal spokesmen, with a message aimed at the conscience of their nation. They attacked moral and spiritual corruption wherever they found it. This meant they were seldom popular, for they chastised kings, priests, and people alike. But the prophets did not worry about popularity. Their sole objective was truth and loyalty to God.

By the tenth century BC, prophets were making a written record of their words. Nathan, a prophet in the days of David and Solomon, wrote a book that was still known generations later. It apparently disappeared soon after the exile to Babylon, along with the writings of other early prophets (1 Chronicles 29:29; 2 Chronicles 9:29; 12:15; 13:22).

Fortunately, works by several prophets did survive and were preserved in the Bible. Beginning with Amos in the early eighth century BC, the Bible contains 17 books written

<< Prophets defined

<< Early prophets of many types

< Nathan the prophet

by 16 prophets over 350 years. The Old Testament gathers these writings together in a section that Jesus and the New Testament called, appropriately enough, the Prophets (Luke 24:44; Romans 3:21).

We usually identify books of prophecy by using their author's name as a title. The only exception is the book of Lamentations, written by Jeremiah as a postscript to the far larger work that bears his name. Unlike other sections of the Old Testament, the Prophets do not appear in chronological order. Instead, they are arranged in two groups, one called the Major Prophets, the other the Minor Prophets. In this arrangement the Major Prophets come first and consist of five books written by Isaiah, Jeremiah, Ezekiel, and Daniel. The remaining books, twelve in all, form the Minor Prophets.

Religion and ethics >>

```
▽    📖 Prophets
  ▽      📖 Major Prophets
    ▷        📖 Isaiah
    ▷        📖 Jeremiah
    ▷        📖 Lamentations
    ▷        📖 Ezekiel
    ▷        📖 Daniel
  ▽      📖 Minor Prophets
    ▷        📖 Hosea
    ▷        📖 Joel
    ▷        📖 Amos
    ▷        📖 Obadiah
    ▷        📖 Jonah
    ▷        📖 Micah
    ▷        📖 Nahum
    ▷        📖 Habakkuk
    ▷        📖 Zephaniah
    ▷        📖 Haggai
    ▷        📖 Zechariah
    ▷        📖 Malachi
```

The words "major" and "minor" refer to size, not importance. The Major Prophets contain some of the longest books in the Bible. The Minor Prophets, by contrast, are among the shortest. There is no connection between the value of what a prophet taught and the length of his writings. The Minor Prophets, despite their brevity, offer many of the most treasured concepts in Scripture. And there are great prophets who left no writings at all, including Elijah and Elisha.

What the Prophets Taught

The prophets laid out the most advanced concepts of ethics and morality to come from the ancient world. They also insisted that religion and ethics cannot be separated. The way we treat family and neighbors, they said, bears directly on God's attitude toward us.

This was an arresting idea when they advanced it. In paganism, even as late as the Greek and Roman Empires, religion and ethics were only loosely related. Religion consisted primarily of rituals and ceremonies performed at a temple or shrine. There was no necessary connection between your religious beliefs and the moral code by which you lived. To be in favor with a particular god, you only needed to worship that deity with due respect.

For your ethical code you relied on something apart from your religion. In the Middle East you might turn to wisdom literature or to local sages who preserved a tradition of helpful knowledge. In Greek and Roman settings you would probably go to some branch of philosophy, like Stoicism or Epicureanism. But philosophers — even the most devout ones — rarely tied ethical norms to one's relationship with a specific deity, or even *any* deity, for that matter. And no philosopher ever advanced the idea that ethics and morals are rooted in the very nature of God, the way Hebrew prophets did.

In contrast, the Prophets argue that God disregards the prayers and sacrifices of people who are dishonest, uncaring, and unjust. As far as God is concerned, to live that way is to be unfaithful to Him. God's primary aim in human affairs is to benefit mankind, and He wants followers who seek that same outcome. His moral code aims at promoting human health and happiness on the widest possible scale. To violate that code willfully is to work against God's own purpose and intention, which is the same as showing disrespect for Him.

Because of this close connection between God's nature and personal ethics, we encounter three recurring themes in the Prophets.

- ➤ First is a *theological* theme. The prophets' foremost goal is to clarify Israel's understanding of God and to create loyalty to Him.

- ➤ Second is a *social and ethical* theme. The prophets consistently denounce people who practice injustice or who use power abusively.

<< Greek and Roman philosophy

- ➤ Third is what we call a *"messianic* theme." This name comes from the word Messiah, meaning "the one God has anointed." The prophets often speak of a special leader that God will raise up in Israel. They also describe great blessings that God will offer through this leader. The prophets never give him a name, but the Jews chose to call him the Messiah, "God's anointed." The New Testament links these statements about the Messiah to the life and work of Jesus.

< Messianic theme

Only to the degree that we are familiar with these themes can we understand the Prophets.

The Prophets and Their Audience

Before we explore what the prophets wrote, it would be helpful to introduce these men in terms of where they worked and the people they addressed. Viewed this way, they group themselves into five classifications:

< The prophets in their setting

- ➤ Prophets sent to the northern kingdom

- ➤ Prophets sent to the southern kingdom

- ➤ International prophets

➤ Prophets during the Babylonian exile

➤ Prophets during the restoration of Jerusalem

Looking first at the Major Prophets, Isaiah and Jeremiah spoke primarily to the southern kingdom. Ezekiel and Daniel came later and served as prophets in Babylon, among captives from Jerusalem.

As for the Minor Prophets, Amos and Hosea targeted their words at the northern kingdom. Four others — Joel, Micah, Habakkuk, and Zephaniah — focused on the southern kingdom. And following the Babylonian exile, the prophets Haggai, Zechariah, and Malachi served in Jerusalem during its reconstruction. Still other prophets had a distinctly international mission. Jonah and Nahum were messengers to Nineveh, the capital of Assyria. Obadiah, another "international" prophet, prophesied to the Edomites, Israel's close relatives just south of Judah.

Classifying the prophets ➤

Thus, to expand our earlier classifications, we have this listing.

➤ Prophets to the northern kingdom
  ➤ Amos
  ➤ Hosea

➤ Prophets to the southern kingdom
  ➤ Micah
  ➤ Isaiah
  ➤ Joel
  ➤ Habakkuk
  ➤ Zephaniah
  ➤ Jeremiah

➤ International prophets
  ➤ Jonah
  ➤ Nahum
  ➤ Obadiah

➤ Prophets during the Babylonian exile
  ➤ Daniel
  ➤ Ezekiel

➤ Prophets during the restoration of Jerusalem
  ➤ Zechariah
  ➤ Haggai
  ➤ Malachi

We can also classify the prophets according to the historical period in which they served.

➤ The Period of the Divided Kingdom
  ➤ Amos
  ➤ Hosea
  ➤ Micah
  ➤ Isaiah
  ➤ Jonah

➤ The Period of Judah Alone
  ➤ Isaiah
  ➤ Nahum
  ➤ Joel
  ➤ Habakkuk
  ➤ Zephaniah
  ➤ Jeremiah

➤ The Period of Babylonian Exile
  ➤ Jeremiah
  ➤ Obadiah
  ➤ Ezekiel
  ➤ Daniel

➤ The Period of Restoration
  ➤ Zechariah
  ➤ Haggai
  ➤ Malachi

RELATIVE PERIOD OF ACTIVITY FOR THE PROPHETS

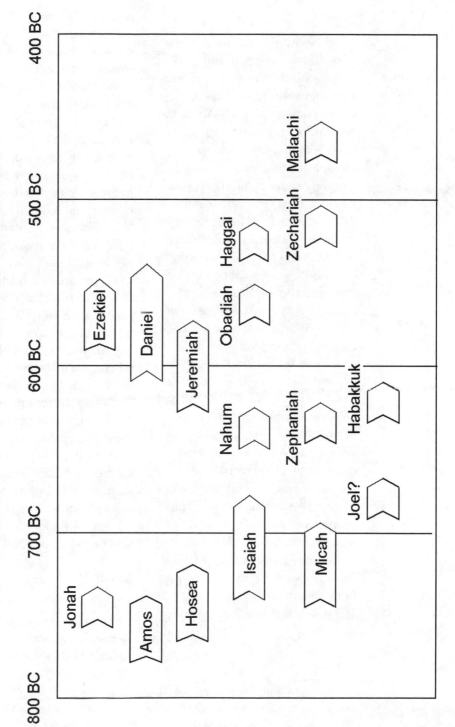

Amos

Of these prophets, five did their work during the eighth century BC. In the general order of their appearance they were Amos, Hosea, Jonah, Micah, and Isaiah. Amos, the first prophet whose writings survived, turned his attention to Samaria at a time when the city enjoyed relative comfort and luxury. Yet, at the bottom of the social ladder many gained no benefit from these blessings. Living in unbroken misery, they were victims of wealthy oppressors who exploited the poor, cheated people in business, and bribed judges. Sadly, no one in the upper class seemed to care about the misery all around them.

But God cared. And Amos warned that the Lord would punish Israel for being so callous. God had decided to make a thorough destruction of Samaria and its inhabitants (Amos 6:7-14). Amos declared that God would use Assyria as His instrument of punishment. The aristocracy greeted his pronouncement with derision, for no one in Samaria saw Assyria as a serious threat (Amos 7:10-13). The Assyrians were far away and only beginning to amass their strength. The words of Amos thus fell on deaf ears.

Hosea

Much the same thing happened when Hosea came along a few years later to challenge religious corruption in the northern kingdom. He compared Israel's spiritual condition to his own troubled marriage. Hosea had married a prostitute named Gomer, who bore him a child, then turned to adultery and had two children by other lovers. Eventually she left Hosea altogether, only to end up in slavery. Hearing of her plight, Hosea went to the slave market, bought her for himself, and brought her back to his house. He then insisted that she never go away again. He wanted her in his home forever.

Hosea used his relationship with Gomer to illustrate how Israel had treated God. Israel was like an unfaithful wife, since she was already worshiping other gods when God made His covenant with her at Sinai. Hosea compared this to Gomer's prostitution. Then, after God brought His people to Canaan, they took up pagan religions native to that land. This was equivalent to Gomer's adultery. Yet, God still wanted Israel, just as Hosea still wanted Gomer, despite her unfaithfulness. God's love for His people was deep and undying.

Micah

Meanwhile, other prophets worried that Israel's moral and spiritual decay was spreading south toward Judah. Micah, a contemporary of Amos and Hosea, joined in their protest against the northern kingdom and its vice. But Micah's greater concern was Jerusalem. He saw Judah headed down the same path that Samaria had taken. Micah cautioned that God was no more hesitant to punish Jerusalem than He was to strike Samaria (Micah 3:12). Yet, in the midst of his warnings, Micah held out a word of hope for Jerusalem that no prophet extended to Samaria. Micah foresaw a distant time when the city would rise from the ashes of destruction to be great and glorious once more (Micah 4:1-8).

Isaiah

Joining Micah in this message was Isaiah. The two of them lived in Jerusalem at the same time and developed similar prophetic themes. But Isaiah clearly overshadowed Micah and came to be considered the greatest of the prophets. Not only did Isaiah write the longest book of prophecy, he also gave us some of the most noble descriptions of God in Scripture.

Isaiah was a close advisor to the throne. He served as a counselor to four kings, the last being Hezekiah, the godly ruler who tried to reform Jerusalem's spiritual life. Isaiah had an unsurpassed vision of God's purpose for Israel. According to Isaiah, God had chosen Israel to serve as a witness to other nations (Isaiah 43:10-12). What God intended was for Israel to reveal His ways to people who knew nothing but paganism, idolatry, and immorality. Israel's role was to help a pagan world understand God more fully so that other nations, outside of Israel, would start to serve Him (Isaiah 56:6-7).

so that other nations, outside of Israel, would start to serve Him (Isaiah 56:6-7).

<< Judah and Jerusalem in Samaria's footsteps

This was not a new idea, for Solomon seems to have had the same concept. When he dedicated the temple, Solomon spoke of foreigners who would hear of God's greatness and come to Jerusalem to worship (1 Kings 8:41-43). Unfortunately, from a moral and spiritual standpoint Israel had compromised herself so thoroughly that she was no longer a credible witness. God had bestowed vast blessings on Israel, but she gave Him little credit for her pleasant condition. She acted as though her greatness came from her own ingenuity, or worse, as a benefit from serving Baal or some other god. In effect Israel had become blind and deaf, Isaiah said. She was unable to see God at work in her midst and no longer able to hear His voice (Isaiah 42:18-22).

<< Hope for the future

< Blindness to God's blessings

This presented God with a problem. What was He to do with a deaf and blind witness? How could anyone take seriously the testimony of a witness who neither hears nor sees? To make matters worse, Israel had given herself so fully to paganism that she made God look like just another ordinary deity. How could He let His witness continue to testify to her neighbors that He was no different from other gods? Although He had given His people ample warning and repeated opportunities to come back to Him, they seemed determined not to do so.

Jerusalem to be destroyed >

Jerusalem to be restored >>

Given this condition, God saw Himself as having no choice but to wipe out Israel's misleading testimony by leveling Jerusalem, the temple His people had polluted, and the dynasty that David had founded (Isaiah 29:1-6; 65:12). Yet, like Micah, Isaiah foretold a day when God would follow up His destruction of Jerusalem by restoring the city to glory (Isaiah 60:1-14). In that day of restoration Isaiah foresaw all nations making their way to Jerusalem to learn about God, just as Micah had foretold.

The Holiness of God

With Isaiah the Old Testament puts a renewed emphasis on God's holiness. Perhaps more than anyone before him, Isaiah sensed the vast gulf that separates God's holiness from human wickedness. In a particularly memorable scene, Isaiah tells of falling into a trance one day. In this trance He saw God enthroned in the temple, with angelic beings above Him. These beings hailed God as "holy, holy, holy." Isaiah immediately cried out in despair, for alongside the purity and goodness of God, his own life and the life of his nation seemed wrapped in iniquity (Isaiah 6:1-5).

God had once called Israel His holy nation (Exodus 19:6). Isaiah now realized just how much his people had failed to live holy lives. Through their conduct they had profaned the name of the God they wore. Perhaps to remind his nation that they were called to be a holy people, Isaiah often spoke of God's holy name. In Isaiah's language God was the Holy One of Israel (Isaiah 48:17; 55:5; 57:15) and the Spirit of God was the Holy Spirit (Isaiah 63:10-11). The New Testament, following Isaiah's lead, took up the custom of referring to God's Spirit as the Holy Spirit.

Isaiah thus gives us a grand, orchestrating vision of God as holy, the Lord of all people, not merely the God of a select nation or a handful of tribes. Other prophets carried his vision forward. In fact, from the first to the last, the Prophets pictured God as sovereign over all nations. That gave Him the right to judge those nations, just as He judged Israel. For example, Amos foretold judgments God would bring against Syria, the Philistines, the Phoenicians, the Edomites, the Ammonites, and the Moabites. In each of these instances, the Lord was punishing them for their injustice and immorality.

Jonah

God and the nations >

Jonah's unwelcome commission >

Nineveh's unexpected response >>

The story of Jonah is a dramatic example of God ruling over nations outside of Israel. God sent Jonah to Nineveh, the capital of Assyria, to warn the city to abandon its wickedness or face destruction. At first Jonah resisted this assignment, not wanting to go. By Jonah's day Assyria was making its weight felt on Israel. If doom was hanging over Nineveh, Jonah had no interest in helping the city avert it. But finally he went to Nineveh and did as God commanded. The response was unprecedented. The entire citizenry, from the king on down, began to seek God's favor and pledged themselves to live upright lives. As a result, God withdrew His decree of judgment and spared the city.

Nahum

Regrettably, these reforms in Nineveh did not last. She was soon back to her cruel and vicious ways. As she built her empire, conquest by conquest, Assyria subjected her captives to the most gruesome tortures imaginable. Atrocities accumulated, one on top of another. God therefore revoked His previous stay of execution against Nineveh. In the mid-seventh century BC He pronounced a new death warrant on her. This time His spokesman was a prophet named Nahum. Unlike the days of Jonah, when it was possible for Nineveh to turn back to God and escape punishment, Nahum offered the city no hope. God's decision was final, and this time He would not reverse Himself.

Zephaniah

As we move to the seventh-century prophets, the call for upright living becomes stronger. By now the Assyrians had destroyed the northern kingdom and Judah stood alone, her continued independence far from certain. For a while it appeared that the Assyrians might

◄◄ Nineveh condemned

Social Justice

The message that God is the Lord of all people, ruling over their affairs and wanting a relationship with every nation, is one of the most significant contributions from the eighth-century prophets. Another was their emphasis on social justice and personal morality. The prophets constantly warned Israel that she could not bribe God with sacrifices and religious rituals. It does no good to go through the motion of worshiping Him, the prophets insisted, if we otherwise ignore His instructions on how to treat one another.

Or to put it another way, if we cheat others, practice deceit, become sexually immoral, and show indifference toward those who are needy and poor, God completely disregards any worship we offer. Amos, speaking to people who lived like that, quoted God as saying,

I despise your religious feasts and I will not accept your sacrifices and peace offerings. Remove from My hearing the sound of your songs of worship. Instead, if you want My favor, let justice flow through your actions and let what is right stream from your life.
— Amos 5:21-24

Hosea worded the same principle this way, again quoting God: "I desired mercy, not sacrifice, and knowledge of Me rather than your burning of offerings on My altar" (Hosea 6:6). And in Jerusalem Micah continued this thought when he said,

Shall we come before the Lord with sacrifices, with thousands of rams or vast rivers of olive oil to offer Him? He has shown us what is good and what He requires of us, namely, to act justly, to love mercy, and to walk humbly with our God.
— Micah 6:6-8

In none of these statements were the prophets wanting to dismiss the importance of worship or the part that religious ritual should play in daily life. Worship and ritual have great potential for deepening our sense of personal connection with God. But no matter how meticulously we carry out such rituals, they make no impression on Him unless we back them up with lives of compassion, caring, and integrity.

Jereusalem
temporarily
spared >

devastate Jerusalem, just as they had Samaria. The Assyrians came against Jerusalem in force, but God struck their army with a deadly plague at the very gates of the city, forcing them to withdraw.

Yet Jerusalem learned nothing from Samaria's destruction and her own narrow escape. The next king in Jerusalem was Manasseh, under whose reign the southern kingdom became more immoral and ungodly than ever. Manasseh himself was evil beyond description, and his crimes were ghastly. While the impact of his wickedness was still being felt, the prophet Zephaniah began to warn Jerusalem that her own iniquity was inviting God's judgment.

What is God
doing? >>

"Day of
the Lord" >

Zephaniah, along with other prophets, described that judgment as "the day of the Lord" (Zephaniah 1:14-18). In the Bible this term refers to God manifesting His power in an extraordinary manner, often to vindicate those who suffer and to impose punishment on those who practice evil. In the case of Jerusalem, Zephaniah foresaw it as a day of gloom. It would bring destruction and desolation. "Neither their silver nor their gold will be able to deliver them," he shouted.

There was hope, however, for those who sought the Lord with humility, who kept His laws and tried to do what was right. God would purify them once His punishment of Jerusalem ran its course.

Zephaniah called them "a remnant," like a tiny piece of fabric left from a garment. From within this remnant God would eventually restore the fortunes of Jerusalem (Zephaniah 3:12-17). Jeremiah later picked up on this theme and described God as gathering the remnant of Judah from all the foreign lands to which their captors had scattered them (Jeremiah 23:3-8).

Habakkuk

Another prophet who grieved over the condition of Jerusalem was Habakkuk. He and Zephaniah were roughly contemporaries, although Habakkuk's prophecies date from a slightly later period. Habakkuk complained that God was doing nothing to stop oppression and exploitation in Jerusalem. God responded that He was indeed doing something. He was preparing to crush Jerusalem for her wrongdoing. His plan was to give the city into the hand of the Babylonians (or Chaldeans, as the Bible sometimes calls them). When Habakkuk protested that the Babylonians were even more wicked than Judah, God answered that He would also repay Babylon for her wickedness. But first He would use Babylon to punish Jerusalem.

Habakkuk received this word with mixed emotions. While glad to see iniquity destroyed, he admitted his distress over how it would happen. "My bones feel like they are decaying, and I am shaking inside because I must wait quietly for the day of disaster and for the ones who will invade" (Habakkuk 3:16). Yet, in the midst of his anguish, Habakkuk renewed his resolve to trust God, no matter what happened. He wrote a song which said,

> Even if the fig tree does not blossom
> and no fruit is on the vines;
> Even if the olives produce no yield
> and the fields produce no food;
> Even if there is no more flock in
> the sheepfold,
> nor cattle in the stalls,
> Still, I will celebrate in the Lord.
> I will rejoice in the God of my
> salvation.
> — Habakkuk 3:17-18

Earlier Habakkuk had criticized the proud, who made themselves feel secure by amassing power and wealth. In contrast to their arrogance he said, "The one who is righteous will live by being a person of faith" (Habakkuk 2:4). In his song, Habakkuk demonstrates that he was himself just such a person.

Joel

Each prophet who foretold the destruction of Jerusalem chose a set of vivid images to describe the event. For Joel it was the image of a locust plague. He pictured swarms of locusts, sweeping across the land in waves, each swarm consuming anything the previous ones left behind. When nothing else was left to eat, the locusts even gnawed the bark from the trees. Not one shred of vegetation was left. And as locusts continued to pour over the city walls and into every house, starvation set in everywhere.

Joel's words may have reminded his hearers of a recent locust invasion that was particularly destructive. But the locusts in Joel's prophecy were not insects. They were his symbolic way of showing what would happen when the Babylonian army came against Jerusalem, first starving the city into submission, then storming its walls, like locusts.

◄ Destruction by Babylon's forces

Jeremiah

The voice most often raised to warn about Babylon belonged to Jeremiah. From early manhood he walked the streets of the capital and the porticoes of the temple calling people back to God. Jerusalem had now degenerated to the point that her people were building shrines at which they sacrificed children to pagan gods. "It never entered the mind of God that you could do such a thing," Jeremiah wailed in anguish (Jeremiah 7:31).

◄◄ How the righteous live

But Jeremiah's pleas went unheeded. Of all the prophets, he was probably the least respected. Even his family turned against him. The personal circle around the king plotted constantly to humiliate him, or worse, to kill him. Still, he persisted. To his grief, he lived long enough to witness the very thing he had long dreaded. In his old age Babylon overwhelmed the city and hauled her leading citizens into exile.

◄◄ Use of vivid images in prophecy

As far as Jeremiah was concerned, his life's work had ended in failure.

Jeremiah himself was spared when Jerusalem fell. In fact, the conquerors showed him more respect than he had received from his own people. The Babylonians offered him a place of honor in their country, but Jeremiah refused. Allowed to remain in Judah, he later migrated to Egypt, where apparently he died. Sometime during this period he penned the book of Lamentations, which mourns the destruction of his city.

God protects the exiles >>

Lamentations of Jeremiah >

Obadiah

About this same time Obadiah pronounced judgment against the Edomites, cousins of Israel who lived in the wilderness regions south of the Dead Sea. (The Edomites were descendants of Esau, Jacob's brother.) When Babylon came against Jerusalem, the Edomites took advantage of Judah's weakness to join the attack. Because of this act of betrayal, Obadiah predicted the approaching ruin of Edom, which would perish, never to rise again.

God vindicates himself >>

Ezekiel

Meanwhile, other prophets were emerging among the Jews taken to Babylon. The first was Ezekiel, the son of a priestly family. As a prophet his primary mission was to lift the fallen spirits of his comrades.

He offered them a message of hope based on God's promise to restore Jerusalem at some future date. In one vision Ezekiel saw God's holiness depart from the temple in Jerusalem and move eastward, to take up residence among the exiles. In other words, God was still with His people, despite their misfortune and dislocation.

Ezekiel continued to enlarge on Isaiah's concept of God's holy name. Like others before him, Ezekiel held out the assurance that God would restore Jerusalem. But he pictured that restoration as an effort on God's part to vindicate His name. In driving His people from their land, God created a dilemma for Himself. He opened Himself to ridicule. In the eyes of Israel's unbelieving neighbors He had either violated His promise to give Canaan to Israel or He was too weak to sustain His people against their enemies. In either event, He stood discredited in the eyes of the very nations He wanted to influence (Ezekiel 36:20).

So, to save His name from further dishonor, God was preparing to gather His people back to their promised land. God was quick to add, "I am not doing this for the sake of my people, because they have continued to profane my name, even in their exile. But I am acting to vindicate the holiness of My great name" (Ezekiel 36:21-24).

Apocalyptic Imagery

In addition to his specific message, Ezekiel fostered a new style of literary expression. He wrote what is called "apocalyptic" literature, which gets its name from a Greek word meaning "an unveiling." Apocalyptic literature makes exceptional use of symbolism. It employs imagery in much the same manner as modern political cartoons. That is, it relies on exaggerated, overstated, and distorted pictures of animals, calamities, and natural events to stand for realities that have no direct connection to the symbol itself. Thus, various types of beasts may represent specific nations or empires. Or a massive storm, with its thunder and lightning, may symbolize God's power and glory.

Using an apocalyptic style, writers can wrap an idea in vivid, unforgettable word pictures. Apocalyptic descriptions also evoke a strong emotional response. It is not surprising, therefore, that other prophets followed Ezekiel's lead and chose to write this way. Daniel and Zechariah relied heavily on apocalyptic symbols, and in the days of Jesus this form of writing was highly popular. The book of Revelation in the New Testament is the most striking example of apocalyptic writing to survive from the ancient world.

Daniel

Daniel combined apocalyptic expression with a divine gift for interpreting dreams. A mere youth when exiled to Babylon, he probably came from an aristocratic family in Judah, since the Babylonians initially removed the more powerful households from Jerusalem. In Babylon he was recruited for royal service.

Like Joseph, Daniel distinguished himself early by interpreting the king's dreams. Also like Joseph, he was a man of stellar integrity. His service was so coveted that when the Medes and Persians toppled the Babylonians, they retained Daniel in their service. He rose to become high commissioner of the empire. And he died an old man, still active in government circles.

Daniel's prophecies, communicated in the form of visions, centered on events that would transpire centuries in the future. He foretold the rise of the Greek and Roman empires, destined to surpass even Babylon's power (Daniel 2:29-43). He also spoke of a kingdom that God would establish during the Roman empire, a kingdom that would spread to cover the entire earth. This kingdom would not be a political or military power, like the empires that preceded it. Instead, it was to be a spiritual kingdom whose influence would be unending (Daniel 2:44-45). We will say more about this kingdom in the next chapter and again when we look at the work of Jesus.

Through his entire life Daniel was highly devout, with a stalwart faith. He undergirded his stellar character by taking time from his busy schedule three times a day to pray. But he was not without his enemies. They did everything possible to destroy him. When they could not discredit him otherwise, they used

< Daniel foretells empires

< Daniel's character

his religion against him. They persuaded Darius, the emperor, to issue an irrevocable decree forbidding anyone to pray or make entreaty to any god or person other than himself for the next 30 days. Anyone violating the decree was to be cast into a den of hungry lions.

Daniel in the lion's den **>>**

Daniel, knowing that the measure was aimed at him, continued to pray to God, as his custom had always been. And he made no effort to hide himself while praying. His enemies went promptly to the king to report Daniel's defiance of the royal order. Realizing he had been shrewdly trapped, the emperor sought a way to avoid executing his valued deputy.

Finding no way out of the dilemma, the emperor finally consented to carry out the sentence. But knowing Daniel's faith, the king said to him, "Your God whom you constantly serve will deliver you." Which is precisely what happened. All night Daniel was left in the lion's den, its only exit sealed, while God restrained the lions from touching him.

The next morning, after spending a restless night, the king came to the den and called out to Daniel. Back came a reply from inside. Relieved, Darius released Daniel. Then the king repaid the men who entrapped Daniel by throwing them to the lions, along with their families. The lions killed them all immediately.

Rebuilding Jerusalem

In Daniel's old age the first return to Jerusalem began. Even though Daniel himself did not join the returning exiles, other prophets arose among them. With these prophets a primary objective was to sustain the builders' spirits, which often drooped. These were times of frequent discouragement. Restoring Jerusalem was no small task, and powerful enemies did everything in their power to thwart the effort.

To make matters worse, the Jews quickly lost sight of their purpose for coming back to Judah. They had returned under an imperial decree permitting reconstruction of the temple. Once in Jerusalem, however, the people became more interested in building comfortable homes than in raising a house of worship. As a result, work on the temple first slowed, then came to a complete standstill.

Haggai

A prophet of the return **>**

Among the earliest exiles to return to Jerusalem was a prophet named Haggai. As enthusiasm for rebuilding the temple grew cold, he stepped forward to urge renewed zeal for God. Haggai called attention to recent crop failures and blights of mildew that had attacked

the harvests. These reversals of fortune, he argued, were God's way of showing displeasure with a city more concerned with comfort than worship. Struck by Haggai's words, the people took his message to heart, and in a matter of days work on the temple resumed. This was not enough to satisfy Haggai, however. He also pressed them to pursue personal spiritual purity. They could not buy God's favor simply by rebuilding His house. What God wanted was their undivided and untiring devotion.

Zechariah

Meanwhile, the walls of Jerusalem were nothing but rubble, leaving the city exposed to attack. Zechariah, a young contemporary of Haggai, used his energies as a prophet to assure the people that God would be their protection. Like Ezekiel and Daniel before him, Zechariah saw visions that were God's way of relaying a message to him. In several of these visions God portrayed Himself as fully aware of what was going on everywhere on the earth. He also promised to completely destroy those nations that had scattered the people of Israel, Judah, and Jerusalem.

In other visions Zechariah saw God removing impurity from His people, their priests, and their leaders. In one of these visions, the high priest Joshua was standing before God, but robed in dirty garments. The dirt on his clothing represented his blemished character. But God replaced the filthy clothes with sparkling, festive attire (Zechariah 3:1-5). This was God's way of demonstrating that when people attune their hearts to Him, He treats them as though they are without sin. This theme will be championed time and again in the New Testament.

Malachi

The final Old Testament prophet was Malachi. About 80 years after Haggai and Zechariah, Malachi leveled charges against the priests. Despite God's continued goodness to Jerusalem (by now Nehemiah had rebuilt the walls), priests and people alike were treating Him with disrespect. Their disregard for God was easily unnoticed, for on the surface the nation seemed highly religious. The priests had meticulously restored the observance of religious festivals, as required in the Law of Moses. They had banned any semblance of idolatry from Jerusalem. And sacrifices were offered regularly in the temple.

But commitment to God was shallow, to say the least. People were finding clever ways to avoid their duties to God. The priests were interpreting the law to favor the privileged classes. Duplicity was found everywhere, for covenants were openly broken. Particularly disturbing was the casual way in which men were divorcing their wives, tossing aside their marriage vows as though such sacred promises were of no importance.

Because of such behavior, Malachi announced, God cared nothing about their holy festivals, their sacrifices, or their prayers. He was ignoring them all. As a God who Himself had gone to great lengths to maintain His covenant with Israel, He could not countenance covenant-breaking among

◄ Observance of rirtual not enough

◄◄ God's people purified

His people. To be true to Him, they had to be true to one another. Malachi thus concludes the Old Testament with a message that had been common to many prophets and will be a key concept in the New Testament. Namely, God is not impressed with external performance unless it comes from a genuine inward commitment to goodness, holiness, and purity.

God over the Nations

By directing so many of His prophets to address international affairs, God was demonstrating His sovereignty over all nations. God wanted it known that He was the Lord of all people, not just Israel. True, He had chosen to have a special relationship with the descendants of Jacob. But neither His interests nor His blessings were reserved solely for them. Nor were they the only people whom He expected to act in ways that were humane and just. Whenever God indicted other nations, it was always for the cruel and needless atrocities they committed or because of their complete disregard for justice.

With this international thrust, the prophets were providing a transition to the work of Jesus, whose message would be directed at all people in every nation. Christianity would not be the religion of the Jews only, but a faith intended for men and women of every race. Most pagan religions centered on gods whose power and domain were local in scope, extending perhaps no further than the nation's borders. But through the prophets God makes it clear that He is like no other god. His dominion is universal. Every human being is ultimately answerable to Him, the One whose presence reaches to the most remote regions of the earth. To that end, God promised that the kingdom of Jesus would encircle the globe. And today it does.

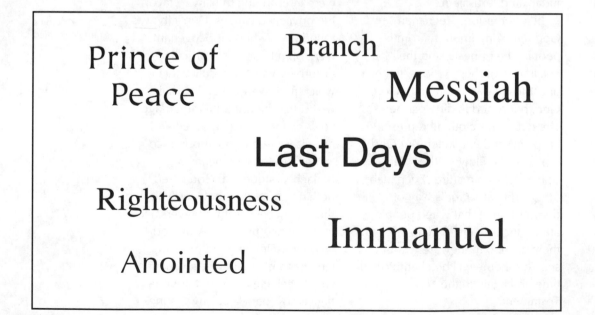

Chapter Sixteen

THE MESSIANIC MESSAGE
OF THE PROPHETS

Alongside their high ethical standards the Prophets offer the fullest anticipation of Jesus in the Old Testament. As far back as Adam, God had spoken of a great figure who would come into the world. Although the Old Testament never names this person, it associates him with a variety of promises.

➤ To Eve God held out the hope that one of her descendants would undo the damage brought on the world by her sin.

➤ God made the further commitment to Abraham that blessings would come to every family on earth through his offspring.

➤ Then Moses, bidding farewell to Israel, told his people to expect another great prophet, one like himself, sent from God. According to Moses, this was the man to whom the nations would gather.

➤ And David received the assurance that his family would give rise to a person whose throne would last forever.

Over time the Jews came to view these statements as pointing to the same individual, a man they called "the Messiah." In Hebrew this name means "the Anointed One." The blessings he would bring were referred to as "the Messianic hope."

◄ Messiah defined

Isaiah

Isaiah, who began his work about 740 BC and was the first of the Major Prophets, did more than anyone else to fashion the concept of a Messiah. It was Isaiah, in fact, who gave the Messiah his name by speaking of him as anointed by the Lord (Isaiah 61:1). He described the Messiah as a "Branch" that would grow out of David's family tree and would have the Spirit of God upon him.

◄ The Branch

Through the power of God's Spirit, the Branch would bring a kingdom of peace to the world. People would no longer hurt or destroy one another in this kingdom, for the earth would be filled with the knowledge of God. Over and above that, citizens of every nation would gather to the Branch to learn from him and to enjoy the peace he would bring (Isaiah 11:1-11).

Elsewhere Isaiah described the kingdom of the Branch as the kind of place where men would melt down swords and spears to convert them into plows and pruning tools. "Nations will not raise swords against each other," the prophet said, "And never again will they study the art of war." This would happen in an era that Isaiah called "the last days," a time when people from every nation would seek the Lord and come together to worship Him. From Mount Zion, the hill on which the temple stood in Jerusalem, God's word would radiate over the entire earth (Isaiah 2:2-4).

For Isaiah, the Branch would finally fulfill God's expectation for Israel. You will remember that Isaiah pictured God as having called Israel to make her His witness. He intended for her to show other nations who He is and what He is like. Because Israel failed to carry out that mission, Isaiah now said that the Messiah himself would become God's witness. The Messiah would have the spirit of a dedicated servant (Isaiah 42:1-7). Unlike Israel, this servant and witness would perform his duties faithfully. His lips would constantly speak of God's goodness. In a passage later applied to the work of Jesus, Isaiah said, "God's Spirit is upon me, because the Lord anointed me to bring good news to

the afflicted. He has sent me as one who binds the brokenhearted, who proclaims liberty to captives, and freedom to prisoners" (Isaiah 61:1; Luke 4:16-21).

But as Isaiah continued his description of this servant and witness, he foretold some type of tragic death the man would undergo. The servant would be rejected, beaten, and crushed. Yet his death would somehow heal the spiritual wounds of all mankind. In one of the most moving passages in Scripture, Isaiah says of him:

> He was wounded for our trans-
>   gressions.
> He was crushed for our iniquity.
> For our well-being, lashes fell
>   upon him,
> And by his scourging we are
>   healed.
> Like sheep, we have all gone
>   astray,
> Each turning to his own way.
> But the Lord has caused the iniq-
>   uity of each of us
> To be laid on him.
>   — Isaiah 53:5-6

The Kingdom of Peace

The stirring rhetoric of Isaiah's language became the centerpiece of Messianic expectations for generations to come. Other prophets seemed to take Isaiah's words as the starting point for their own pronouncements about the Messiah. For instance, Jeremiah continued the practice of referring to the Messiah as the Branch, as did Zechariah centuries later.

War replaced by peace ➤

His suffering for our salvation ➤➤

Good news ➤

For Jeremiah, the Branch would be a king whose reign was governed by wisdom. Because of the Branch, justice would prevail throughout the land and people would live in keeping with God's law (Jeremiah 23:5). Zechariah added that the Branch would be a priest upon his throne and would build a temple for God. In addition, the Branch would use his dual office of priest and king to mediate peace for his people (Zechariah 6:12-13).

Notice this recurring theme of peace. In a world such as Israel's, where warfare and invasion were a constant threat, the promise of perpetual peace was alluring indeed. As a result, many Jews came to interpret these words from the Prophets to mean that the Messiah would bring Israel newfound military and political power so that no enemy dared touch them. This was the prevailing idea of the Messiah in Jesus' day.

Jesus did not set up a physical kingdom, to the sore disappointment of many who followed Him. Yet, had they read the Prophets carefully, they would have seen that the Messiah's power was not based on military might. After all, his was to be a kingdom in which swords and spears were destroyed, not used to advance his cause. The Messiah would rely on spiritual power alone. Isaiah described him as having the Spirit of the Lord. The prophet then elaborated on what

that means: "the spirit of wisdom and understanding, the spirit of counsel and strength, the spirit of knowledge and the fear of the Lord" (Isaiah 11:2).

<< The King of justice

Not only that, the Messiah would minister to the broken spirits of people. As we have seen, he was to bring good news to the broken-hearted and to comfort those who mourn (Isaiah 61:1-2). On another occasion Isaiah says of the Messiah, "He bore our griefs and he carried our sorrows" (Isaiah 53:4). Malachi described the Messiah as like a sunrise of righteousness, "rising with healing in his wings" (Malachi 4:2).

<< The King of peace

Thus, filled with spiritual power himself and using that power to heal the broken spirits of others, the Messiah was to bring about a spiritual revolution, not a military one. His kingdom was to be spiritual in nature, not physical. He would reign as a spiritual leader, a priest, as Zechariah said (Zechariah 6:12-13). He would serve to change the hearts of people, not their political fortunes.

Jeremiah picked up this idea of changed hearts when he spoke of a new covenant that the Lord would make one day with Israel. It would not be like the covenant God made through Moses, a covenant engraved on stones. Instead, this time He would inscribe His covenant on the human spirit. "I will put my law within them," Jeremiah quoted God as saying, "and I will write it on their heart. I

< The covenant of the heart

will be their God, and they shall be My people. Nor will they teach their neighbors and brothers, saying, 'Know the Lord,' for everyone shall know me, from the least to the greatest." Then God added, "I will forgive their iniquity, and I will no longer remember their sin" (Jeremiah 31:31-34).

With our bias toward physical and material pursuits, it is easy to miss the significance of a spiritual revolution like the one Jeremiah describes. But for those who have known the liberating power of a free, unconquered spirit, even when their physical fortunes were miserable, the healing of the human spirit is the most powerful force on earth.

A Kingdom with No End

The prophets foresaw the lasting power that the Messiah's spiritual kingdom would exercise. In this regard, Daniel's description is particularly noteworthy. Early in his career, while interpreting a dream for the king of Babylon, Daniel described the coming of the Messiah's kingdom. The king's dream had centered on a huge statue made of varied materials. The head was fashioned from fine gold, the breast and arms from silver. Then, the stomach and upper legs were made of bronze, while the lower legs were iron. Finally, the feet were a mixture of iron held together by clay.

As the king stood looking at this strange object, he saw a small stone

Statue of gold, silver, bronze, iron & clay ➤

The forever kingdom ➤➤

that was carved out of a mountainside. The stone was not the product of human initiative, for no hand was used to cut it from the mountain. The king then saw this stone strike the statue and crush it. Next, the stone itself began to grow. First it became a great mountain, and in the end that mountain covered the entire earth.

Daniel explained that the various materials in the statue represented a series of political empires that would arise. The Babylonian empire was the head of gold. In just a few years it would be toppled by the Medes and Persians, whose kingdom was symbolized by the silver breast and arms. The Persians, as we know, began an ambitious program of expansion and moved westward against Greece.

Eventually the Greeks retaliated by destroying the Persian empire and building one of their own. The upper legs of bronze represented the Greeks. The Greek empire, in turn, fell to the Romans, the legs and feet of iron. As the Romans extended their rule over the entire Mediterranean and Middle Eastern world, they brought together so many diverse cultures that it proved difficult to hold their empire together. This is why the statue had a mixture of iron and clay for its feet.

But in those days of iron and clay, Daniel said, "the God of heaven will set up a kingdom that is never to be destroyed, and that kingdom will not be left to someone else," the way empires succeeded one another in the dream. In a word, Daniel said, "this kingdom will last forever" (Daniel 2:31-45).

The Messiah's Righteousness

Because the imagery of a kingdom ran through so many Messianic promises, the Jews began to focus on the indications that the Messiah would come from the family of King David. Jeremiah, speaking of "the Branch of David," said that he would execute justice and righteousness. Righteousness is a common word in the Bible, and it means to do what is right in the sight of God. Thus, in another passage about the Branch, Jeremiah said that the Messiah would wear the title "The Lord is our righteousness" (Jeremiah 23:6). This recalls the language of Isaiah, who said the Branch would wear righteousness like a belt wrapped around his body (Isaiah 11:5).

The Messiah's own righteousness, however, was destined to become the righteousness of his people. Not only the Messiah, but those who follow him bear the title, "The Lord is our righteousness" (Jeremiah 33:16). What these promises mean will become more apparent when we examine the life and work of Jesus, the one whom Malachi described as "the sun of righteousness." The message of the New Testament is that when mankind proved incapable of living

righteously, God brought a truly righteous man into the world, Jesus of Nazareth. Then God made a provision whereby those who follow Jesus are treated as though the righteous life of Jesus is their own. The New Testament phrase for this is to be "clothed with Christ," as though Jesus is a garment we wear (Galatians 3:27). Or as Isaiah worded it, "He has clothed me with garments of salvation. He has wrapped me with a robe of righteousness" (Isaiah 61:10).

◄ Clothed with salvation

Again, you will notice that the thrust of these Messianic promises is spiritual and moral renewal, not the establishment of a new military or political order. While many statements about the Messiah do borrow language from warfare and political rule, they do so as a figure of speech, not as a literal description.

On the other hand, you cannot change the hearts of people without having an impact on the society in which they live. As a result, the life-changing message of Jesus has had a profound impact on the history of governments and civilizations. In effect He has indeed toppled political regimes, not through weapons of war, but by transforming the hearts of people so that they are no longer indifferent to evil and wrongdoing. This is one reason that tyrants and dictators have historically pressed to limit the freedom of churches. Anywhere the teachings of Jesus are advanced, people gain the courage to stand for what is right and to openly oppose corruption, ruthlessness, and violence.

The Messiah as Divine

Prior existence of Messiah >>

There have been other spiritual reformers besides Jesus, of course, and they, too, have had a positive influence on human affairs. But in describing the Messiah, the Prophets anticipate a reformer unlike any other who has ever lived. In a statement with strong Messianic overtones, Isaiah speaks of a child who is born and who is given the name Immanuel, which means "God is with us." Micah, describing the birth of the Messiah, points to Bethlehem, David's hometown, as the place the Messiah will come from. Micah quotes God as saying to Bethlehem, "From you

God is with us >

one will go forth from Me to be ruler in Israel" (Micah 5:2).

But then Micah adds a striking commentary. God says of this ruler from Bethlehem, "He has been going forth from long ago, from the days of eternity." This does not sound like an ordinary mortal. Is the name Immanuel, "God is with us," to be understood literally? Is the Branch who is coming from David's family to be some type of divine being? The language of Micah and Isaiah certainly invite that interpretation. But how could the Messiah be born as a human being if he had existed ever since the beginning of time?

The Old Testament does not try to address that quandary. It simply lays out the claims of the prophets and waits for later events to make their meaning clear.

God's Secret Plans

Even the prophets themselves did not know what their statements about the Messiah pointed to. The New Testament says that they struggled to understand what God had in mind when He instructed them to foretell the sufferings of the Messiah and the great things to follow. But God did not reward the prophets' curiosity with answers. He explained that only a later generation would fully grasp what they had been saying. In the meantime God kept His plans secret from prophets and angels alike (1 Peter 1:10-12).

One purpose of the New Testament is to explain what God was planning, going all the way back to the first Messianic promises to Adam and Eve. One New Testament writer describes his role as shedding light on the plan that God had kept secret from mankind from the beginning of time (Ephesians 3:3-6). Little wonder, then, that the Old Testament concludes with a note of expectancy. The last paragraph of Malachi, the final book of the Old Testament, leaves the future open-ended. It anticipates a great day of spiritual reform that lies ahead, as "the sun of righteousness" arises with "healing in his wings." Someone special was coming. But the Jews and the world would have to wait 400 years to learn specifically who it was.

Chapter Seventeen

THE PERIOD BETWEEN THE TESTAMENTS

The centuries between the last Old Testament prophets and the opening of the New Testament brought vast change to the Middle East. When Malachi died, the Persian empire still held sway over the eastern Mediterranean and the lands of the Tigris-Euphrates Valley. But two upstart powers to the west were beginning to exert themselves.

The first to gain prominence was Greece, which swept through Canaan under its legendary leader, Alexander the Great. He subdued the entire region, including Egypt, before turning against cities east of the Euphrates. After pressing all the way to India, Alexander died suddenly and unexpectedly, throwing his kingdom into disarray. There was no plan for someone to succeed him, and his generals ended up dividing the empire among themselves.

The Jews under Greek Rule

In this division a family known as the Seleucids took over the area along the northern reaches of the Euphrates River, as well as adjoining regions such as Syria and Canaan (whose name gradually changed to Palestine). Another Greek family, the Ptolemys, established control of Egypt. Relationships between the Seleucids and the Ptolemys were often strained, which put Jerusalem and the Jews in a precarious position. Judea (as the old territory of Judah became known) was situated halfway between the center of Seleucid power and the capital from which the Ptolemys ruled. Even though they were initially under Seleucid control, the Jews were also the first to be attacked if the Ptolemys marched northward. As a consequence, the leaders in Jerusalem had to maintain a delicate balancing act in their diplomacy.

Greek rule also posed another problem for Jewish leadership. Greek dynasties always pushed Greek culture and customs on people they ruled. Many Jews, impressed with the achievements of Greek philosophy and science, found Greek ways appealing. Others saw their own Jewish her-

◄ Middle East divided

◄◄ Alexander the Great

itage at risk if they adopted Greek outlooks and manners. After all, God had destroyed the independence of Israel and Judah in the past because they indiscriminately compromised with paganism. Had the nation not learned its lesson? Was it still willing to flirt with God's displeasure by turning to pagan ways once more?

Influential families found themselves on both sides of this debate. Eventually this resulted in a divided camp in Jerusalem, with two different parties striving to control Jewish religion and politics. Those who were open to non-Jewish customs and practices were known as the Sadducees. Their opponents, the people who insisted on a strict observance of the Law of Moses and who tried to distance themselves from Greek influence, were called Pharisees.

The Jews under Roman Rule

In time the Jews were able to gain their independence by overthrowing their Greek political masters. One of the Seleucid rulers, Antiochus Epiphanes, outraged the Jews by personally sacrificing a sow on the altar at the temple in Jerusalem. Under the Law of Moses pork was forbidden as a food for the Jews. To slay a pig on the altar was therefore an act of absolute sacrilege. Under a family called the Maccabees, the Jews rose up in revolt. Spurred on by their fury at Antiochus, they equipped them-

selves well as warriors and won a hard-fought freedom.

Still, their independence remained threatened so long as they stood between the warring Seleucids and Ptolemys. Looking for allies, they turned to a new emerging power in the Mediterranean, the Romans. Battle by battle the Romans were unseating the Greeks and taking over their dominions. Rome's protection had a price, however, and the Jews eventually lost their freedom in the bargain.

Now a new balancing act confronted Jewish leaders. As with the Greeks, power struggles were constantly underway among the Romans. The Jews had to be adroit in deciding which Roman leaders to align with, which ones to resist. Fortunately, they chose the winning side when they allied themselves with Julius Caesar as he moved to solidify his position. Once he prevailed, Caesar rewarded the Jews by granting them special privileges, including the right to exempt themselves from pagan festivals and activities that might violate their conscience. But the Romans exercised an ironclad political control of Jerusalem, and Jewish freedom was a thing of the past.

While the Jews retained control of the temple and their religion, the Romans parceled out Jewish lands to various kings and governors. Many of these rulers were cruel, if not insane. One of the most notorious was a king named Herod the

Rise of Roman power >>

Sadducees and Pharisees >

Antiochus >

Maccabees >

Great, who ruled toward the end of the first century BC. Knowing that the people hated him, he set out to win them over by enlarging the temple in Jerusalem. Poverty and lack of leadership had prevented the Jews from restoring the temple to the splendor it had known under Solomon. But Herod announced plans to expand and enhance the temple so that it would overshadow even Solomon's splendid structure.

Temple and Synagogue

It took 46 years to accomplish this ambitious undertaking, but in its final form the temple was one of the most impressive buildings in the ancient world. It contained so much glistening marble that travelers, approaching Jerusalem from a distance, sometimes mistook it for snow covering the top of the hills. Sadly, the completed temple stood only a few years before the Romans leveled it, along with the rest of Jerusalem. The temple was in its moments of greatest glory during the years that Jesus walked its courts. And the earliest Christians gathered in the porticoes of this temple for worship and prayer.

Yet, for all its importance, the temple was no longer the most common center of Jewish worship. On a weekly basis, or even more frequently, Jewish families met in a building called a synagogue, which closely resembled a small modern church. Synagogues first appeared in the lands to which the Assyrians

and Babylonians relocated the Jews. With the temple no longer available to them, these exiled Jews sought an alternate place at which they could worship and preserve their Hebrew heritage.

Meanwhile other Jewish families left Judea at their own initiative, and they, too, built synagogues. They typically moved to Asia Minor, Egypt, and elsewhere, sometimes to escape an invading army, on other occasions to pursue trade and business. By the time of Jesus millions of Jews lived outside of Palestine. The Jews in a given locale gathered at a synagogue every Sabbath day to hear instruction from Scripture. The leaders of the synagogue, usually known as elders, also served as overseers who watched out for the well-being and needs of the local Jewish community.

So successful were these synagogues that Jews in Palestine began to build synagogues of their own. There were dozens of them in any city of significance, some identified with the Sadducees, others with the Pharisees. The teacher in a synagogue was known as a rabbi, and he went through extensive schooling to master the Law of Moses.

Scribes and Pharisees

Working closely with the rabbis were specially trained men called scribes. Their job was originally to make transcriptions of the Bible by hand. Each synagogue needed a copy of the works of Moses, a pro-

<< Herod the Great

<< Herod's temple

<< Synagogues

ject that might take months or even years for a scribe to complete. Because they spent so much time copying the Bible, scribes also became experts in what it said.

Politics of first-century Palestine >>

This led people to view the scribes as legal specialists. Whenever a judicial decision turned on a fine point of Jewish law, the elders of the synagogues and the courts in Jerusalem asked respected scribes for their opinion. Gradually the scribes came to be as highly regarded for their knowledge of the law as for their dedication to copying Scripture. In time the scribes moved beyond merely explaining the law and began issuing decrees about how to apply it.

Legalism >

For example, Moses had said that no one was to work or to carry a burden on the Sabbath. The scribes interpreted this to mean that no one with a wooden leg could wear it on the Sabbath. Nor could a doctor call on sick patients during the Sabbath hours. Of course, neither of those provisions are found in the Law of Moses. But the scribes made such regulations just as binding as the words of Moses himself.

Messianic expectations >>

The Pharisees, with their deep concern about keeping the Law carefully, were especially inclined to accept such binding regulations. They associated themselves closely with the scribes, and in the New Testament we see them working together. Jesus Himself was often the target of attack by the scribes and Pharisees, for he disagreed with many of their regulations.

Political Climate

Thus, as we move to the New Testament the social, political, and religious landscape of Israel is quite different from what it had been near the end of the Old Testament. Jerusalem is under Roman rule. The broader region of Judea (the name now given to the area once controlled by Judah) is the domain of Herod the Great. Jerusalem is prosperous and filled with splendid structures, the temple sitting among them like a crown jewel. There is a high priest, an appointee of the Romans, who is as much a political leader as a spiritual one. And synagogues are everywhere, with rabbis and scribes among the most highly respected people in the community.

At the same time there is a deep spirit of unrest beneath this splendor and prosperity. Roman rule is not popular, and Herod and his kind are detested. Interest in the Messianic promises is running high. People are longing for the Messiah to appear, set up his kingdom, and throw the Romans out. Both Herod and the Romans know about this Messianic fervor, and at times it makes them nervous. They watch every political movement with a wary eye. They cannot take a chance that someone might appear, claiming to be the Messiah, and seize a large enough following to mount a serious military revolt.

Geographically there are new names to contend with as we open

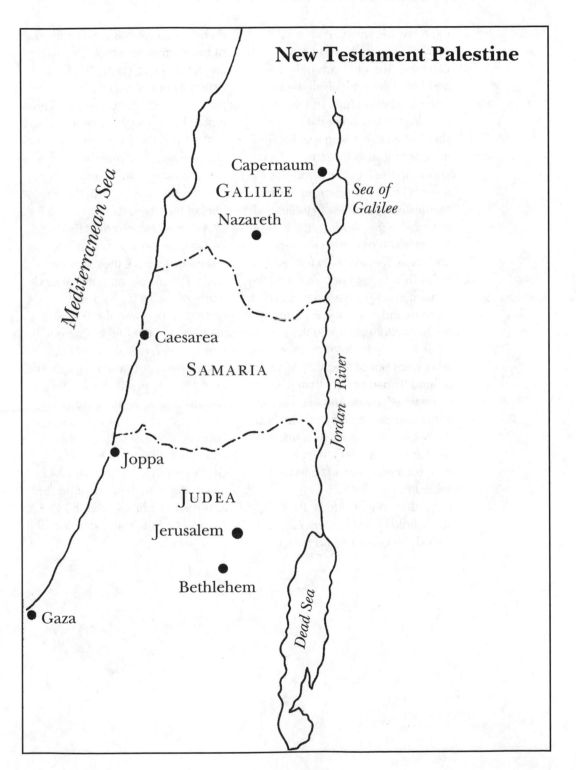

New Testament Palestine

the New Testament. As we have seen, Canaan has become Palestine. The old lands of Israel and Judah are now divided into three distinct sectors. To the north is Galilee. It lies along the western shore of a large inland sea. Fed by the upper Jordan River, this lake is known in the New Testament as the Sea of Galilee. It is here, in Galilee, that Jesus lived most of His life and did most of His work.

Sanhedrin >>

Samaritans >

Just south of Galilee is a region known as Samaria, held for centuries by a foreign people called the Samaritans. They were transplanted there by the Assyrians. Even though the Samaritans accepted the Law of Moses, the Jews detested them. The Jews went out of their way to walk around Samaria rather than pass through its towns. And the Samaritans were denied the right to worship in Jerusalem. As a result, the Samaritans built a temple of their own near Samaria and worshiped there.

Further south is Judea, the stronghold of first century Judaism. Herod the Great had his palace there. Judea was also the residence of the Roman governor. Day-to-day life in Israel was controlled by a national council called the Sanhedrin, which doubled as a governing body and the supreme court of the land. The Sanhedrin traditionally had about 70 members, who had the same respect and esteem that the Romans accorded members of their Senate.

As we move into the New Testament, all these places and institutions weave their way into the story. The social and political landscape of the New Testament is quite different from the one we have seen in the Old Testament. In terms of literary style, the New Testament is also a sharp departure from the way in which the Old Testament was written. From its opening pages, however, the New Testament stresses that its themes and events build and enlarge on God's promises to Abraham and Israel. The New Testament presents itself, not as a break with the Old Testament, but as an extension of it.

Chapter Eighteen

THE LIFE OF JESUS

The New Testament takes us through the last two periods of Bible history: the Period of the Life of Jesus and the Period of the Early Church. Together these periods encompass about 100 years, although most of the New Testament is devoted to about a 30-year period. Listed on the next page are some of the events and personalities we will encounter in the New Testament.

```
▽  ▤  New Testament
   ▷      ▤  Gospels
   ▷      ▤  History
   ▷      ▤  Letters
   ▷      ▤  Prophecy
```

The New Testament opens with four biographies of Jesus, each named for its author. These books (Matthew, Mark, Luke, and John) are called Gospels, from a word meaning "good news." In the New Testament the concept of "good news" always centers in Jesus of Nazareth — who He was, what He did, and the hope He brought to mankind. The Bible describes anyone who tells that story as proclaiming "good news." Thus, early Christians also gave these biographies the name "Good News," or Gospels.

```
▽      ▤  Gospels
   ▷          ▤  Matthew
   ▷          ▤  Mark
   ▷          ▤  Luke
   ▷          ▤  John
```

The individual Gospels portray Jesus from unique perspectives, so that each account provides different details about Him. Mark, the shortest of the four, concerns itself primarily with what Jesus did, offering only brief accounts of the things He said. Matthew, Luke, and John, by contrast, highlight His role as a teacher. Yet, none of them attempts to capture everything He taught.

What these authors offer is a selection of events and sayings from His life. The individual authors base their selection on the topics that relate directly to their audience.

◄◄ Biographies of Jesus

➤ For Matthew that audience is Jewish.

➤ For Luke it is non-Jews who are learning about Jesus for the first time.

➤ Mark seems to have written for non-Jewish readers, too, perhaps Christians in Rome.

➤ And John writes for those who already follow Jesus, but whose trust in Him needs deeper roots. John also devotes most of his Gospel to the days immediately surrounding the death of Jesus.

Period	Major Events	Key Figures
Life of Jesus	The birth of Jesus	Jesus Joseph Mary
	The baptism of Jesus	John the Baptist
	Selecting and training the Apostles	
	The teachings of Jesus	
	The miracles performed by Jesus	
	The Sermon on the Mount	
	The transfiguration	Peter James John
	The Lord's Supper established	
	The betrayal and trial of Jesus	Pilate
	The crucifixion	
	The resurrection	
	The ascension	
Early Church	The church begins on the Day of Pentecost	Peter
	Stephen is martyred	Stephen
	Philip brings Samaritans into the church	Philip
	Peter baptizes Cornelius, the first Gentile Christian	Cornelius
	Saul of Tarsus converted	Paul
	Paul plants churches in Asia Minor and Greece	Barnabas Silas Timothy Titus
	Paul arrested and sent to Rome	
	Persecution breaks out against churches across the empire	

The Birth of Jesus

None of the Gospels traces the entire life of Jesus. Instead, they focus on His public career, which lasted about three years before He was executed. Apart from those three years, the only things we know about Him come from Matthew and Luke, who begin their Gospels by recounting the extraordinary events of His birth. Matthew looks at these initial years through the eyes of Joseph, the father of Jesus. Luke tells the story from the vantage point of Mary, His mother.

According to Luke, an angel appeared to Mary after she and Joseph were engaged, but before they were married, to announce that she would have an unusual son. The angel said that she would conceive a child miraculously, even though she was a virgin. This would come about through the agency of God's Spirit, more commonly called the Holy Spirit in the New Testament (Luke 1:26-35).

When Joseph learned that Mary was pregnant, he naturally thought that she had been unfaithful to him. Initially he decided to withdraw from his commitment to marry her. But God warned Joseph in a dream not to act hastily. He told Joseph that the child in Mary's womb had been implanted by the Holy Spirit. As difficult as it must have been for Joseph to believe such a report, he accepted God's message as true. Rather than abandon Mary, he moved immediately to marry her (Matthew 1:18-25).

About this same time a royal decree required all Jews to return to their town of origin to register for a census. For Joseph and Mary this meant traveling to Bethlehem, the city where David had lived. Mary's pregnancy was now quite advanced, and while they were in Bethlehem, she gave birth to Jesus. Luke tells of angels appearing in the night skies and announcing the birth to shepherds in nearby fields. "We bring you good news," they said. "This day, in the city of David, a Savior has been born for you, who is Christ the Lord" (Luke 2:11).

These words highlight three decisive roles the newborn child would fulfill.

➤ He was to be a *Savior*.

➤ He was to be recognized as *Christ*.

➤ And He was to be respected as *Lord*.

These names had special meaning to the shepherds.

➤ In their language a savior was someone who rescued others from imminent danger.

➤ The second title, Christ, was the Greek form of the Hebrew word Messiah. The angels were confirming that the long-promised Messiah had arrived.

➤ Further, they added that the Messiah was Lord, a title ascribed to rulers. But in the first century it was also a name for God.

◄ Census for taxation

◄◄ The story of Christ's birth

◄ Shepherds hear the news

◄◄ A surprising pregnancy

Told by the angels how to find the baby, the shepherds hurried to the city. Once they had seen the infant, the shepherds went out excitedly and spread the news of what they had witnessed. Others also came to Bethlehem to find the child. Among these visitors were several magi (or wise men) from east of the Euphrates. They had seen a sign in the night sky. They interpreted this sign to mean that an exceptional child had been born to become king of the Jews.

The wise men ➤

In searching for this child, they went first to the palace of Herod the Great in Jerusalem. A deeply suspicious man, Herod was ever fearful of plots to overthrow him or create rivals for his throne. After hearing the wise men, he concluded that they had seen a sign marking the birth of the Messiah. Learning from his counselors that the Messiah would come from Bethlehem, he instructed the wise men to go there, then report back to him once they located the child (Matthew 2:1-8).

Herod's jealousy ➤

The wise men did succeed at locating Jesus, but choosing to disobey Herod, they slipped out of the country without notifying him. Furious, Herod ordered the murder of all male children in Bethlehem under two years of age. Joseph, warned in a dream of what Herod planned, fled with his family to Egypt just ahead of the massacre. There he remained until Herod died a short time later. Then Joseph

Flight to Egypt ➤

returned with Mary and Jesus to the small town of Nazareth in Galilee, about 70 miles north of Jerusalem. Jesus grew to manhood in Nazareth, working as an apprentice to Joseph, who was a carpenter.

John the Baptist

Beyond the narratives surrounding His birth, the Gospels say little about the early life of Jesus. They pick up His story as He nears 30 years of age. It was about this time that John, a cousin of Jesus, gained fame in Judea for teaching with the fervor of a prophet. (This John is not the same one who wrote a Gospel.) John lived in the wilderness along the lower Jordan River, and people went out by the hundreds to hear him. Like the prophets, he insisted that people change their lives and conform to God's standards.

The New Testament calls this kind of change "repentance." The prophets, too, had pleaded with their hearers to repent. But in addition to repentance, John urged people to take a step that no prophet had previously required. John told his hearers to be baptized. Baptism was a ceremonial washing in which John immersed people completely under water, then raised them back up. This act, he said, served to cleanse from sin. Or to put it in his own words, it was "a baptism of repentance for the forgiveness of sins" (Luke 3:3). Baptism was so vital to his message that history remembers him as John the Baptist.

John claimed that God had sent him to baptize in order to prepare Israel for a great figure who was soon to appear (John 1:26-27). John never specified who this person would be, because John himself did not know (John 1:30-33). That changed one day when Jesus came to John and asked to be baptized. As John carried out the request, he saw a sign that God had told him to watch for. When Jesus came out of the water, the Spirit of God descended on Him, the descent becoming visible so John could see it. John also heard a voice from heaven saying, "This is my beloved Son, in whom I am well pleased" (Mark 1:9-11; Luke 3:21-22).

The Temptation in the Wilderness

From this point forward John redirected his followers to Jesus, even though Jesus was not yet ready to start a public career. First He needed to strengthen His mind and spirit for the demands of what lay ahead. To that end, He withdrew further into the wilderness to fast for 40 days while praying. Fasting was a common religious practice in the first century, although few people extended a fast for 40 days. During a fast no food was eaten, allowing large blocks of time for prayer and meditation. Those who practiced this discipline often found that it gave them a clearer, more focused mind.

As the 40 days drew to a close, Satan made an appearance. While we have seen Satan only occasionally in the Old Testament, in the Gospels he is always lurking just behind the scene. His goal is to defeat Jesus and destroy the work that God sent Jesus to do. When Satan showed up in the wilderness, he threw a series of temptations at Jesus. They were all designed to lure Jesus away from a singular trust in God. But Jesus withstood each temptation, and Satan withdrew, looking for a more opportune way to attack (Luke 4:1-13).

<< Forerunner of the Messiah

< Jesus tempted by Satan

Training the Apostles

Now, ready to begin His public career, Jesus returned to Galilee. There He recruited twelve men to travel and work with Him and to continue His work once He was gone. They joined a group around Jesus known as His disciples. A disciple is a learner who builds a close relationship with a master teacher. In addition to being disciples, the Twelve were called "apostles," from a word meaning "to be an ambassador." Jesus would send them out as His personal representatives to the world.

The twelve apostles included two sets of brothers, Peter and Andrew, along with James and John. Three of them — Peter, James, and John — had a unique relationship with Jesus that set them apart even from other apostles. Jesus took these three with Him on occasions when no one else

< Jesus' closest friends

was present. And after His death, they emerged as the most prominent leaders of the early Christian community.

From the outset Jesus planned to send the apostles abroad as His personal spokesmen. Yet their backgrounds hardly commended them for such work. Several were fishermen. One was a tax collector. Another was a political activist associated with a group known for promoting insurrection. Still, Jesus was convinced that they were the raw material from which He could fashion effective teachers. The Twelve, as they were known, went with Him everywhere, and often He took them aside privately to give them special training.

Miracles bring popularity >>

Bringing the dead back to life >>

Crowds Grow around Jesus

Death of John >

Early in their training, John the Baptist was arrested, imprisoned, and beheaded (Mark 6:17-29). He had alienated the throne by accusing the king of immorality. John's death brought deep grief to Jesus, who admired John greatly. In John's death, moreover, Jesus could foresee what would happen to Him once the rulers turned against Him.

And by now the governing authorities were beginning to take note of Jesus. Teaching from city to city, He was attracting huge crowds. Except in His own hometown, He received an enthusiastic welcome everywhere. Two things drew people to Him. First was the forceful way in which He taught.

His hearers were amazed that a carpenter's son, with no formal schooling, gave them more insight and understanding than professional teachers like the scribes and rabbis (Matthew 7:28-29).

Second was the extraordinary power He displayed. Wherever He went, Jesus healed all types of crippling illnesses and handicaps with only a spoken word or a touch. He regularly restored health to people who were lame, blind, deaf, and epileptic, along with those who suffered other maladies like leprosy. On three occasions He brought a dead person back to life.

➤ One was the son of a widow in the little village of Nain (Luke 7:11-17).

➤ Another was the young daughter of a synagogue official (Luke 8:49-56).

➤ And the other was a close friend named Lazarus, who lived near Jerusalem (John 11:1-46).

Jesus claimed that such demonstrations of power (or "miracles," as the Bible calls them) verified that He was speaking a message from God (John 5:36).

One group of miracles drew particular attention. On numerous occasions He came upon people under the influence of some type of evil spirit. It was as though these invading spirits had taken over the bodies of their victims and compelled them to behave in ways that were harmful and self-destructive.

> **"God's Spirit is upon me, because the Lord anointed me to bring good news to the afflicted. He has sent me as one who binds the brokenhearted, who proclaims liberty to captives, and freedom to prisoners" (Isaiah 61:1).**

When Jesus spoke to these spirits, He addressed them as though they were a different being from the person whose body they controlled. The controlling spirits not only responded to Him, they called Him the Holy One of God (Mark 1:23-24) and the Son of the Most High God (Luke 8:26-28). Without exception Jesus confronted these spirits harshly. And with a single command, He was able to drive them out of the bodies they had invaded.

Jesus treated the presence of these evil spirits as evidence of Satan's work in the world. By casting out evil spirits (more commonly known as "demons"), He claimed to be declaring war on Satan. He was driving Satan from a position of domination (Luke 11:15-20). Word quickly spread that Jesus had the power to force demons to obey Him. And later, when His critics tried to discredit Him, they were compelled to concede His extraordinary power over evil spirits.

Opposition Begins to Mount

Constantly amazed at His miracles and what He taught, the masses began to speculate that Jesus must be the Messiah. But now their first disappointments with Him began. Popular expectations held that the Messiah would set up a political kingdom with the specific intent of throwing out the Romans and giving Israel her freedom once more. Not only did Jesus show no interest in political aspirations, He resisted any effort to give Him a crown (John 6:15). He talked about God's kingdom, to be sure. But He never described it as a political or military enterprise. "The kingdom of God is within you," He told the crowds (Luke 17:20-21). And when He pictured the kingdom for them, He spoke in terms of having a heart that maintained a godly outlook and attitude.

But the crowd never fully appreciated the meaning of these words.

◄◄ Evil spirits

◄ Military expectations of the Messiah

Enemies among the elite >>

Nor, for that matter, did those in His inner circle. To the very end of His life, His own apostles were confused about the nature of what Jesus increasingly called "My kingdom." They argued among themselves as to which ones would have the most prominent positions in the kingdom. In response Jesus scolded them for failing to understand that His kingdom had nothing to do with prestige and greatness, at least in the ordinary sense of greatness. Instead, His kingdom was about learning to serve others with a selfless heart. "The one who will be great in the kingdom of God," He told them repeatedly, "is the one who learns to be the servant of everyone else" (Luke 22:24-26). Sometimes He would state this principle in the form of a paradox, "The one who would become great should become the least of all" (Luke 9:48).

Jesus the humble servant >

Jesus Himself demonstrated this servant outlook in all that He undertook. He never asked for special treatment. He was as happy to have a humble meal in a poor home as to be the guest of honor at a wealthy citizen's dinner. Indeed, His critics often belittled Him for spending so much time with poor, sometimes immoral people. Jesus always replied to such criticism by saying, "It is people who are sick, not the ones who are well, that need a physician" (Matthew 9:11-12).

Moses and Elijah appear >>

But criticism of Jesus was mounting rapidly. His teachings often contradicted the cherished ideas of the scribes and rabbis. He aimed stinging words at religious leaders who gave the appearance of being committed to God, but whose hearts were filled with deceit and selfishness. And in the temple in Jerusalem, He openly attacked those who were using religion to make a lucrative living, often at the expense of the poor (Mark 11:15-18). Needless to say, such actions only multiplied His enemies in high places.

The Transfiguration

Knowing that opposition was building, Jesus began to warn His apostles that death awaited Him in Jerusalem. He gave Peter, James, and John a special insight into what was coming. He asked them to join Him one day on a mountainside to pray. As He was praying, His physical appearance went through a striking change, as if it were shedding its physical nature. The Bible calls this a "transfiguration."

Suddenly the three disciples recognized that Jesus was talking with two other figures, Moses and Elijah, reappearing after all these centuries. They were talking with Jesus about the death that lay ahead in Jerusalem. Then, just as suddenly, Moses and Elijah were gone. Stunned by these events, Peter blurted out, "Let's build three shrines on this mountain, one for Jesus, one for Moses, and one for Elijah." But immediately a cloud surrounded them and from its darkness came a voice saying, "This is My beloved

Son, the One I have chosen. Listen to Him" (Luke 9:28-36).

Coming down the mountain Jesus told them that they should say nothing about this episode until He was raised from the dead. The three apostles were not certain what He meant about rising from the dead (Mark 9:9-10). Yet, He had told them only days before that the Jewish leadership would mistreat Him, abuse Him, and put Him to death. He also declared that having died, He would return to life and carry on the work God had assigned Him to do (Matthew 16:21).

The Final Journey to Jerusalem

The disciples basically dismissed such talk. They could not comprehend the significance of what Jesus was saying. They had been to Jerusalem with Him several times during holy festivals. In their minds Jesus would use one of those holy seasons, with thousands thronged around Him in the temple, to seize the throne and set up His kingdom. So they treated His talk of being killed as merely a statement with some kind of obscure meaning.

When the Passover season came, Jesus and His disciples set out once more for Jerusalem. As they neared the city, mobs of people poured out to greet Him. They cheered continuously as He made His way toward Jerusalem. And they chanted phrases that hailed Him as the long-awaited descendant of David whom the

Prophets had foretold (Mark 11:9-10). This all seemed to confirm the apostles' expectations.

Little did they know that elsewhere the high priest and others were plotting to destroy Jesus. He had attacked the religious leadership of Israel all too often. And now it seemed that the entire populace was ready to follow Him. Powerful figures in Israel were eager to rid themselves of Him, if only they could find a way. With so many people around Jesus, seizing Him would be difficult.

As it turned out, one of the apostles provided Jewish leaders the opportunity they needed. The man's name was Judas. For reasons never made clear, Judas became disillusioned with Jesus. Satan played on that disillusionment. The Gospel of John says that Satan planted the idea in the mind of Judas to betray Jesus (John 13:2,27). On his own initiative, Judas approached the Jewish leadership with an offer to deliver Jesus into their hands for the right sum of money. They agreed to give him 30 pieces of silver if he succeeded in what he promised (Matthew 26:14-16).

Judas carried out the betrayal on the night of the Passover. That evening Jesus had gathered with His disciples in a private home to eat the Passover meal. Jesus, knowing what Judas had done, dipped a piece of bread in a spicy sauce. Holding it up, He said, "The one with whom I share this morsel is the one who will

◄◄ Jesus predicts his suffering and death

◄ Judas plans a betrayal

◄◄ Jesus greeted with joy and celebration

betray Me." With that, He handed the bread to Judas, who took it and departed hurriedly (John 13:21-30).

The Lord's Supper

Meanwhile, Jesus continued to talk ominously of an eminent departure that would take Him from His apostles. He called their attention to the unleavened bread that was part of the Passover meal. Taking the bread in His hands, He said, "This bread is My body, which is given for you" (Luke 22:19). He encouraged each person to take the bread in turn, break off a portion, and eat it. Then He lifted a cup of wine and told them, "This is My blood by which I am making a new covenant. And I am shedding My blood on behalf of many so that they can have forgiveness of sins" (Matthew 26:27-28). Again He had each of them drink from the cup.

All this talk of giving His body and shedding His blood must have struck the disciples as strange language. But Jesus was preparing them for the death that awaited Him within hours. And with the symbols of the bread and wine, He instituted a ceremonial meal that was destined to become the central act of Christian worship. This meal is most commonly known as the Lord's Supper. In some circles Christians call it the Eucharist, from a Greek word meaning "to give thanks." It is a rather simple ceremony, in which each participant eats a bit of unleavened bread, usu-

The Last Supper ➤

Jesus arrested and put on trial ➤➤

ally preceded by prayer. Then after another prayer, the worshipers take a sip of wine together.

Using these symbols of bread and wine, the Supper serves to recall the terrible death that Jesus died. As He instituted the Supper, Jesus told the disciples, "Whenever you eat this meal, do it in My memory" (1 Corinthians 11:23-25). It also is a reminder that those who take part in the Lord's Supper are in a special covenant relationship with Jesus and with one another. Jesus called the wine "the new covenant in My blood." And the New Testament says that in eating the bread, Christians are drawn together as one (1 Corinthians 10:16-17).

The Betrayal and Trial

When Jesus and the disciples had completed the Passover, they slipped out of the city to a private garden beyond the walls. Jesus withdrew from His men and began to pray fervently about what was soon to transpire. All the while Judas was organizing an armed band. He knew that Jesus and the apostles would be in the garden, so he descended on the site with a troop of men carrying torches, clubs, and swords.

Jesus was taken by force to a late night meeting of the Sanhedrin, the 70-member supreme court of the Jews. False witnesses were already lined up to offer evidence that would result in His being condemned to death. The trial continued into the early morning hours, and Jesus was struck and beaten repeatedly during the ordeal.

At dawn the Sanhedrin hauled Jesus to the palace of Pilate, the Roman governor for the region. They asked the governor to give the order to crucify their prisoner. When Pilate asked about the charges against Jesus, nothing he heard seemed deserving of death. Pilate was ready to free Jesus, when the mob outside his court turned threatening. "This man has been claiming to be a king," the Jewish leaders said. "If you let Him go, you will be no friend to Caesar" (John 19:12).

Fearful of how Rome would react if he somehow assisted a man who claimed to be setting up a new kingdom, Pilate reconsidered his decision. He had Jesus flogged, then brought beaten and bleeding before the crowd. Pilate tried to arouse the mob's sympathy for Jesus. But they shouted loudly, "Away with this man. Crucify Him!" (John 19:15.)

The Death and Resurrection

In the end, Pilate consented to the death decree. And his soldiers, responding to the talk of Jesus being a king, wove thorn branches together to make a crown, which they forced on His head. Next they marched Him out of the city to the place of execution, forcing Him to carry the cross on which they would nail Him. By midmorning He was suspended on the cross, nails driven through His wrists and feet to hold Him in place.

Some time later, about three in the afternoon, He said, "It is finished." Bowing His head, He breathed His last and died (John 19:30).

Late that afternoon Pilate permitted family and friends to take His body from the cross for burial. To be certain that He was dead, the Roman soldiers thrust a spear into His side, piercing the heart cavity. A wealthy man named Joseph offered to let Jesus be buried in a nearby cave that Joseph had carved from a hillside to serve as his own tomb.

<< The crowd turns against Jesus

Since the next day was the Sabbath and it was already late in the afternoon, those who buried Jesus had to wrap His body hurriedly in the strips of linen with which Jews bound their dead. Burial customs called for other preparations for the body, but those details would have to wait until the Sabbath was over. (Jewish regulations prevented anyone from performing physical labor on the Sabbath, including the preparation of bodies for burial.) In the meantime, Jesus was laid in the tomb and a massive stone was put in place to cover the mouth of the cave.

< Jesus buried

Pilate posted an armed guard on the tomb to be sure that no one stole the body or created a disturbance at the site. But on Sunday morning, just before dawn, an angel appeared and pushed the huge stone aside. In panic, the guards fled the scene. A few moments later several women who were close to Jesus approached the tomb to continue preparing His

<< A crown of thorns

An open and empty tomb ➤

body. Concerned that they would be unable to remove the stone from the mouth of the cave, they were surprised to see it rolled away already. To their further amazement they looked inside, only to find the body gone. Neatly folded in the tomb, however, were the wrappings they had put around Jesus.

Jesus is alive! ➤

What they soon learned was that Jesus had returned to life. The Bible calls such a return from death a resurrection. As the day progressed, Jesus confirmed His resurrection to those who had accompanied Him from Galilee. They encountered Him at various places and conversed with Him at length. The Gospels record several occasions on which people saw Jesus over the next 40 days. The New Testament says that about 500 people were eye-witnesses of His resurrection (1 Corinthians 15:6).

In the weeks following the Passover, the apostles were with Jesus repeatedly. They briefly went back to Galilee, but returned to Jerusalem after only a few days. By now the Feast of Pentecost was approaching. It was a harvest festival that always came 50 days after

Jesus commissions messengers ➤➤

Passover. Just before Pentecost, Jesus took His apostles to a hill outside Jerusalem. There, as He conversed with Him, Jesus began to rise

Jesus ascends to heaven ➤

into the air. Continuing to ascend, He disappeared from their sight.

As the stunned disciples looked on, two angels suddenly stood at their side. They announced that God had taken Jesus into heaven.

He would remain there, they said, until some future date, at which time He would return (Acts 1:9-11). Now the apostles began to understand what Jesus had meant the night before His betrayal when He said, "I am going to a place you cannot go now. But you will follow Me there later. And just as I am going away, I will also return, so that where I am, you can be there also" (John 14:3-6).

Jesus had used the time since His resurrection to give His apostles a fuller understanding of why it had been necessary for Him to suffer and die (Luke 24:44-48). After all, with the great power He had so frequently displayed, why had Jesus not used His might to resist arrest, overwhelm His enemies, and walk out of Jerusalem unharmed? The rest of the New Testament serves to answer that question. What God was accomplishing through the death and resurrection of Jesus transcended anything the apostles had ever imagined. Now they were being entrusted with the responsibility of announcing what God had done.

In fact, just before He ascended into heaven, Jesus gave one final command to His apostles. He charged them to take His story to every nation on earth (Matthew 28:18-20). The New Testament tells us in the book of Acts how they fulfilled this commandment. But before we turn to that phase of the story, we need to explore more fully the things that Jesus taught.

Chapter Nineteen

PARABLES ABOUT THE KINGDOM

Jesus used a style of teaching that was altogether unique. He taught in stories called "parables." Parables were stories about one thing that illustrated the truth about something else. Hidden within the parable was a particular principle that Jesus wanted His followers to embrace.

Matthew 13 offers a striking example of how Jesus used this approach. The chapter builds around eight parables that describe some aspect of the kingdom of God (or the kingdom of heaven, as the Gospels sometimes call it). Six of the parables begin with the words, "The kingdom of heaven may be compared to . . ." They then draw parallels between the kingdom and

➤ a man whose enemy sowed weeds in his wheat

➤ a mustard seed

➤ a lump of leaven mixed with dough

➤ a man plowing a field

➤ a merchant in search of exquisite pearls

➤ a fishing net

As you can see, these subjects have little in common with the kingdom of God. Nor do the details in the parables themselves have an immediate connection to the kingdom. But Jesus is making comparisons at the level of principles, not details. Behind each story awaits one or more principles that Jesus wants us to discover, because these principles illustrate a truth about the kingdom.

Jesus typically told a parable, then left it to His hearers to derive its meaning. In Matthew 13, however, He thoroughly explains what two of the parables mean. By looking at His explanations, we gain a clearer understanding of how to interpret other parables, both here and elsewhere.

The Parable of the Sower

The chapter opens with one of the best known stories Jesus ever told. Commonly called the parable of the sower, it is also known as the parable of the soils. The story tells of a farmer sowing a field. Some of the seed fell alongside a nearby footpath, where the ground was packed

◄ Four soils contrasted

hard. Birds quickly devoured these exposed seeds. Others fell on soil that had not been prepared for planting. Here there were large rocks in the topsoil. As a result, these seeds were never able to develop deep roots, and when days grew hot, they quickly withered in the scorching sun.

Other seed fell in an area where the soil was rich and deep, but where thorns had already established themselves. These seeds sprouted and thrived for a while, only to be choked out by the thorns. Finally, much of the seed fell on fertile soil, grew to maturity, and brought forth an abundant harvest. Jesus concluded the parable by saying, "He who has ears, let him hear" (Matthew 13:1-9). This was His way of saying, "Listen carefully. Don't miss what I'm telling you."

Later Jesus explained that the parable was about the "word of the kingdom" and how different people receive it. Perhaps this accounts for His closing appeal to listen carefully. The seeds eaten by the birds represent people who never really absorb God's word because they fall under the influence of "the evil one," a name Jesus frequently ascribed to Satan. The seeds in the rocky places stand for people who initially receive God's word with joy. Lacking deep roots, however, they fall away from God when affliction or persecution comes along.

As for the seeds among the thorns, they symbolize individuals who receive God's word joyfully at first, but become distracted by day-to-day worries or by the pursuit of wealth. As a consequence, their lives never prove fruitful in God's service. Finally, the seeds falling on good soil represent those who hear God's word, understand it, and allow its influence to mature within them (Matthew 13:18-23). This is the kind of hearer Jesus obviously wanted His disciples to be.

The Parable of the Weeds

Now, having urged them to listen carefully to "the word of the kingdom," Jesus moved to the six parables that begin, "The kingdom of heaven may be compared to . . ." We can group these parables into three pairs, each pair developing a common theme. The parable of the weeds and the parable of the net form the first pair. They are about counterfeit Christians in the kingdom of God. Such people are like weeds that a man discovered when his wheat began to mature. The weeds were the work of an enemy who intentionally sowed them in the field.

These particular weeds were called tares. In their early stages of growth, tares look very much alike wheat. That makes it difficult to tell them apart. Knowing he could damage the wheat by uprooting the tares, the landowner in this story decided to let the wheat and weeds grow together. At harvest time he ordered his reapers to gather the tares first, bundle them, and burn

Parables of common themes >>

Different responses to the word of God >

them. After that they brought the wheat into his barn (Matthew 13:24-30).

The parable of the net ends in a similar fashion. The net was cast into the sea and towed toward shore. Dragged along, it hauled in many good fish. But it drew in worthless fish as well. Once ashore the workers had to divide the good fish from the bad, like the reapers removing tares from the wheat (Matthew 13:47-50).

In explaining the parable of the weeds, Jesus identified Himself as the one who planted the good seed. The field represented the world, He said, and the wheat was a symbol for the "sons of the kingdom." Conversely, the tares were "sons of the evil one," planted by the enemy, who was Satan. The harvest stood for a moment that Jesus often foretold, a time when God will end the world and judge all mankind. On that day the angels will serve as His reapers (Matthew 13:36-43). Having offered this explanation of the parable, Jesus counseled once more, "He who has ears, let him hear."

For Jesus to interpret a parable in such detail is unusual, as we noted above. Yet, even here Jesus gives only a partial explanation of His story. He indicates what the narrative elements stand for, but leaves it to us to isolate the principles behind the parable. In this case there are at least three principles to recognize.

➤ First, the kingdom of God will attract some who are not honest and sincere in their commitment. Initially they will look like Christians. But the passage of time will reveal their true nature, just as it did with the tares.

> ◄ Attitude of the heart not always obvious

➤ Second, God knows genuine disciples from those who merely pretend to serve Him. He sees the weeds from the start.

> ◄◄ Dividing the good from the bad

➤ And third, God will ultimately remove pretenders from His kingdom.

Other principles may also strike you in this parable, for Jesus often told stories with multiple layers of meaning. But the major principles behind a parable are usually obvious after only brief reflection. This is especially true with the remaining parables in Matthew 13. The parable of the mustard seed and the parable of the leaven are about small beginnings that lead to great outcomes. The tiny mustard seed, once planted, turns into a plant so large that birds build nests in it. So it is with God's kingdom. Its influence may seem insignificant at first, but wherever it takes root, the kingdom branches out to have an ever-increasing impact. Likewise, a pinch of leaven kneaded into a mound of dough has an influence far beyond what its size suggests. As the yeast goes quietly about its work, it causes the entire lump of dough to rise (Matthew 13:31-35).

> ◄ Great outcomes from small beginnings

Other Parables of the Kingdom

In the next two parables Jesus deals with priorities. One tells of a man who unearthed a hidden treasure while he was plowing. Since he was working a field that belonged to someone else, the treasure was not legally his. He therefore placed the treasure back in the earth, hurried off to sell everything he owned, and bought the land. In the second story a pearl merchant happened upon an exquisite pearl. He, too, sold all his possessions to acquire this newfound treasure (Matthew 13:44-46). Here again the principle is obvious. These parables are stressing the value of the kingdom. It is so valuable that we should prize it above anything else in life.

Unmatchable value of the kingdom ➤

Which brings us to the primary reason Jesus used parables. He never told a parable merely to illustrate a principle. His greater goal was for the principle to anchor itself in our lives. Parables, in other words, always had practical implications. We can see this in both the parable of the weeds and the parable of the net.

➤ At a practical level they warn that God will not be fooled if we pretend to be Christians. He knows our true disposition and will deal with us accordingly.

➤ For those genuinely committed to God, these parables also serve notice that pretenders exist. True followers of Jesus must be prepared for the counterfeits, since the conduct of false Christians is sure to disappoint true followers of Jesus. But it would be a mistake to become disillusioned because some are insincere. After all, we are called to be part of the kingdom because of what we believe about God, not because of what we believe about people.

At this point in Matthew 13 Jesus asked His disciples, "Do you understand what I've been saying?" They answered that they did. Jesus then offered one last parable, a parable about a scribe. In this case the scribe represents any person who knows God's law. Jesus said that when a scribe becomes a disciple of the kingdom, He is like a man who has a vast array of household wares and valuables, some of them old, some of them new. This permits him to bring out what is most appropriate, whether old or new, according to the needs of the moment (Matthew 13:51-52).

Scribes were, of course, specialists in the language of Moses and the Prophets. They understood the truth that God had given Israel in earlier centuries — what we might call the "old" truth. Now Jesus was setting forth "new" truth, the word of the kingdom. Thus, when the scribe became a disciple of the kingdom, He had a command of all truth, both old and new, and could draw on the most appropriate truth for a given circumstance.

Not everyone who heard the parables would gain such skill in using truth. Jesus made Himself very clear on that point (Mark 4:10-12). Many would see His parables as nothing more than interesting little stories. Others would miss the point of His parables altogether. Only those with hearts attuned to the kingdom would hear the deeper meaning in His teaching.

Such hearts were always few in number, at least during His lifetime. Interestingly, on those few occasions when Jesus explained the meaning of a parable, it was never with His larger audience, but with His closest disciples, usually in private. He considered these disciples more serious about learning than the crowds who came to hear Him. What He observed in the crowds led Him to describe them with words from Isaiah: "You keep on hearing, but do not understand. You keep on seeing but do not perceive. For you are a people whose hearts are dull, who can barely hear with their ears, and who have shut their eyes" (Matthew 13:13-15).

For the disciples of Jesus, this quote from Isaiah was rich in implications. It came from the setting in which Isaiah accused Israel of being a witness who had failed in her duty. In Isaiah's words, God had called Israel to be His witness to the nations nearby, but Israel had turned a deaf ear and a blind eye toward God. Isaiah then foretold the day when God would raise up a faithful witness who would be His true messenger to the nations.

Jesus was Himself that witness. And in His work with His apostles, He was preparing them to be witnesses, too. He therefore contrasted them to the masses in the crowds by saying, "Your eyes are blessed, because they see. And your ears are blessed, because they hear" (Matthew 13:16). These words would have immediately taken them back to the witness themes in Isaiah. And this would have deepened their understanding of why Jesus kept saying, "He who has ears, let him hear." What they were learning from Jesus they would one day tell to others. Indeed, His very last words to them were, "You will be my witnesses in Jerusalem, Judea, and Samaria, even to the most remote regions of the earth" (Acts 1:8).

As witnesses themselves, they developed their own personal styles of teaching. None of them would use parables the way Jesus did. But His parables continued to resonate in what they taught and the way they lived. His parables were unforgettable stories wrapped around timeless principles. And over the centuries they have had as much life-changing impact as any portion of Scripture.

◄◄ Parables unclear to some

◄ Disciples to be witnesses

The kingdom of God is like . . .

Chapter Twenty

THE TEACHINGS OF JESUS

Kingdom within
you >>

When Jesus taught, His constant theme was the kingdom of God. He never nailed down a definition of the kingdom, and He used the word in a host of ways. But day after day He talked about life in terms of the kingdom. The closest He came to a definition may have been in the Sermon on the Mount, His longest and most famous speech. As part of that sermon He gave instructions on prayer. He told His disciples, "When you pray, speak like this: 'Our Father in heaven, how holy is your name! May Your kingdom come. May Your will be done on earth, as it is in heaven'" (Matthew 6:9-10).

May Your kingdom come. May Your will be done. In other words, God's kingdom prevails in any age and in any place where people gladly do His will. The kingdom is not place on a map. It is not an imperial power with standing armies and centers of government. Instead, the kingdom is found wherever people eagerly submit themselves to God.

Thus, Jesus would say on another

God's measure of
righteousness >>

Righteousness
defined >>

occasion, "The kingdom of God is within you" (Luke 17:21). The kingdom grows only to the extent that individuals yield their hearts to God and live by His commands. By choosing that path, they invite God to reign within their spirits, within their souls. He truly becomes their Lord, enthroned in their lives. One New Testament writer, emphasizing the inner nature of the kingdom, described it as "righteousness and peace and joy in the Holy Spirit" (Romans 14:17).

The Kingdom and Righteousness

Jesus talked about the kingdom in terms of righteousness. In the Sermon on the Mount He told His followers, "Unless your righteousness exceeds what you see in the scribes and Pharisees, you shall not enter the kingdom of heaven" (Matthew 5:20). Given that warning, we would do well to become more familiar with what it means to be truly righteous.

In the Bible, righteousness centers on treating people properly.

Strictly speaking, to be righteous is to measure up to God's expectation, both in attitude and action. Noah was the only man in his generation that God considered righteous (Genesis 7:1). Others described as righteous include Abraham, Job, and David. David, indeed, captured the essence of righteousness when he wrote, "The Lord has rewarded me in keeping with my righteousness. In accordance with the cleanness of my hands He has recompensed me. For I have kept the Lord's ways and have not acted wickedly against my God" (2 Samuel 22:21-22).

Being righteous most commonly means having appropriate attitudes towards others and treating them properly. David referred to this when he described his hands as clean. He had not defiled them by acting wickedly. From David's psalms we know that his conduct was merely an extension of his heart. He was righteous inwardly and outwardly. The Bible describes him as "a man after God's own heart," which means that his heart was attuned to God (1 Samuel 13:14).

By contrast, the righteousness of the scribes and Pharisees was often superficial. It was outward only. The people of Israel, turning to the scribes for instruction, had learned to keep the letter of God's law, not the spirit of it. They had failed to see (because the scribes had failed to teach) that righteousness is first

and foremost a matter of the heart. For that reason, Jesus used the Sermon on the Mount to reinterpret the Law of Moses. He explained that the Law was about attitudes as much as actions.

For example, the Ten Commandments said, "You shall not murder." This means more than simply not killing, Jesus said. It also means not hating people or calling them fools (Matthew 5:21-22). Hatred poisons our inner spirit — the domain of the kingdom — just as surely as taking someone's life. Next Jesus expanded on the commandment, "You shall not commit adultery." Again He showed that we can violate this commandment as fully with our thoughts as with our actions. To focus sexual desire on someone who is not our husband or wife shows that we are not singularly devoted to our mate. Inside our heart we have already committed adultery, corrupting our inner spirit in the process (Matthew 5:27-28).

◄ Thoughts as important as actions

The Visible Kingdom

With examples such as these, Jesus not only taught a deeper sense of righteousness. He also placed the realm of the kingdom within our inner spirit. The kingdom is about reforming our attitudes and desires, the habits of our heart. Yet there is also an external aspect of the kingdom. The kingdom is something that can be seen. It takes on this quality when people who have

◄◄ An appearance of righteousness

The kingdom of eterenal life >>

the kingdom inside them band together. The society they create is unlike any other on earth, for it is a community where God's will prevails. In this sense Jesus intended the church (the community of people who follow Him) to be an expression of the kingdom.

That is why Jesus spoke of the kingdom not only as something within us, but also as something that we are inside. "The kingdom has been announced since the days of John the Baptist," He said, "and people are shouldering their way into it" (Luke 16:16). In the parable of the man who found tares in his wheat Jesus pictured God as removing wrongdoers from the kingdom (Matthew 13:41). And a later writer credited God with transferring us from the dominion of spiritual darkness into His kingdom (Colossians 1:13). These are all statements that view the kingdom as something visible and observable.

Our presence in the kingdom >

The ultimate form of this visible kingdom is yet to be experienced. Jesus looked to its appearance when He spoke of people from every point on the compass joining Abraham, Isaac, and Jacob in the kingdom of God (Matthew 8:11). He also was looking to a final phase of the kingdom when He taught about God's final judgment of mankind. He said that God will tell those who are faithful to Him, "Come, inherit the kingdom prepared for you since the creation of the world" (Matthew 25:34).

Viewed this way, the kingdom is an existence we enter following death. The New Testament describes it as an eternal life in the presence of God. Christians usually refer to it simply as heaven. The New Testament equates the kingdom with heaven on several occasions. One of the apostles, imprisoned and facing possible death, wrote a friend to say, "The Lord will deliver me from everything evil and will bring me in safety to His heavenly kingdom" (2 Timothy 4:18). And another New Testament writer told early Christians that they were "heirs of the kingdom," again referring to a reward which God reserves in heaven for those who love Him (James 2:5).

It was this external form of the kingdom that caught the attention of the prophets. Centuries in advance they foresaw the collective influence of the thousands who would follow Jesus. What they saw seemed to resemble the emergence of a new kingdom, and the language of the Prophets reflects that vision. Because the prophets focused on the kingdom as a visible, world-changing reality, people around Jesus believed that the Messiah would be a political and military champion. As a result, Jesus found it difficult to explain the true essence of the kingdom to them.

Inner Contentment and Joy

To offset their preoccupation with external interests, Jesus kept asking His listeners to examine the inner self. He challenged them to start building the kingdom on the inside. His goal was for the kingdom to become manifest externally by first taking root internally. For that reason He taught His disciples to pursue a path of inner joy and peace.

Among other things, this meant freeing themselves from anxiety and worry. He told His listeners to trust God to provide what they needed. "Which of you can lengthen your life by even half a step, no matter how much you worry?" He asked. "So why worry about what you will eat or drink or what you will wear? Your Heavenly Father knows you need these things. So seek His kingdom first, and He will add these things to your life" (Matthew 6:31-34).

Inner well-being also meant learning to forgo material attachments, selfish pursuits, and personal vengeance. In making this point, Jesus often resorted to unforgettable imagery. The Sermon on the Mount includes this admonition: "If someone snatches your tunic, give him your coat also. If you are struck on the cheek, don't strike back; turn your other cheek. And if a person compels you to go with him a mile, go two miles" (Matthew 5:38-41). On the surface this seems like foolish counsel. After all, common sense says, "If someone takes advantage of you, fight back or they will do it again. Don't let anyone run over you."

But Jesus understood that thoughts of striking back only stir up resentment, frustration, and anger, the very emotions that choke out personal happiness and tranquility. By harboring bitterness and animosity, we continue to damage our innermost being. The kingdom cannot thrive in such poisoned soil. Thus, the sooner we learn to live without letting people provoke and agitate us, the sooner we will enjoy the true peace of the kingdom.

◄ Revenge is negative

Nevertheless, is it really possible to remain unperturbed if someone takes our possessions, slaps us on the cheek, or makes selfish demands on us? Jesus believed it was. He modeled that life Himself, choosing to remain nonviolent even in the face of betrayal and death. Yet He knew that such responses do not come naturally for us. If we are to achieve such inner strength, one thing is essential. We must be absolutely confident that life continues beyond death. If we only exist in the present world, with no sense of security except for what we possess, we will always be drawn to self-interest and material interests.

◄◄ Worry

Therefore Jesus regularly assured His disciples of a world beyond this one. And He always promised His followers an inheritance in that future world. When Peter said to Him, "We have left everything to follow You," Jesus responded, "Anyone who has left homes or family or farms for Me or for the gospel will receive a hundred times

◄ Life after death necessary

as much in this age, and in the world to come, eternal life" (Mark 10:28-30). If life goes on beyond death, we can dislodge ourselves from undue attachments to physical and material concerns. And with that freedom comes the strength to be robbed and mistreated without it shaking our inner peace.

In the interest of such freedom, Jesus regularly warned about damaging our inner spirit by making material possessions the object of life. The Gospel of Luke recounts an episode in which someone called out to Jesus, "Tell my brother to divide our family's inheritance with me." Jesus answered, "Keep your guard up against every type of greed, for even when a person has abundant possessions, his life does not consist of what he owns" (Luke 12:13-15). Jesus then told a parable about a man who made the mistake of trusting in his riches, only to die unexpectedly, having made no preparation for life beyond the grave (Luke 2:16-21). On the other side of death the man's material possessions were of no value whatsoever.

What does matter on the far side of death is whether we lived righteously in this world (Matthew 25:31-45). According to Jesus, all who die must stand before God to account for their conduct on earth (John 5:28-29). Heaven is the reward for those whose deeds were righteous. For the unrighteous a far different fate awaits. They will suffer

eternal banishment from God's presence in an existence known as hell (Matthew 25:46).

The Son of God

Jesus claimed that He Himself would be the judge who determines where people spend eternity (Matthew 16:27-28; John 5:26-29). It was claims like this that angered His enemies. But He never backed down from them. Instead, He insisted that He was entitled to judge humanity, because He had a relationship with God that no one else enjoyed (John 5:21-23). To be specific, He was the Son of God (Luke 1:25; John 20:30). This title closely resembled another name He was happy to wear, the Son of Man (Matthew 8:20; 9:6; 12:8; 17:9).

In first-century Judaism the titles "Son of God" and "Son of Man" had far greater significance than we might recognize initially. People of that day often used the phrase "son of" to mean "having the essence of." The early Christians gave the name "son of encouragement" to one of their leaders, because he excelled at encouraging (Acts 4:36). Jesus called James and John "sons of thunder," referring to their blustery personalities (Mark 3:17).

Thus, when the Bible describes Jesus as the Son of Man, it means that He was fully human. He was not an apparition who only looked like a man (as some claimed late in the first century). No, His essence was fully that of a human being.

Jesus is God ▶▶

Material possessions unimportant ▶

Heaven is our reward ▶

Similarly, when He is called the Son of God, the Bible is affirming that His essence is fully divine. The New Testament never explains exactly how He and God can be alike, yet distinct Beings. But the Bible consistently portrays them that way.

The concept that Jesus is God in human form is pivotal to the New Testament. In fact, Jesus called it the truth on which He would establish His church. (This was the name He gave to the community of believers who follow Him.) Jesus made this statement while conversing one day with the apostles. He asked them who they thought Him to be. Peter answered, "You are the Christ [i.e., the Messiah], the Son of the living God." Jesus commended him for this answer. Referring to Peter's words as a rock, Jesus said, "Upon this rock I will build My church" (Matthew 16:13-19). Thus, the foundation for the Christian community is the deity of Christ.

The Gospel which argues most fully for the deity of Jesus is the Gospel of John. John opened his Gospel by equating Jesus with the Logos, a first-century word for the binding force that gives unity and predictability to the universe. We normally translate Logos as Word. John said that in the beginning, at the very moment of creation, Jesus as the Logos was with God and was Himself God. It was through this Logos (hence, through Jesus) that everything was created. Then John noted, "The Logos became flesh and dwelled among us " (John 1:1-14).

In His role as Son, Jesus promoted the practice of addressing God as Father. Only about ten times in the entire Old Testament is God called Father. Most of these instances occur in the Prophets, particularly Isaiah and Jeremiah. In the New Testament, on the other hand, references to God the Father are found everywhere. When Jesus taught His followers to pray, He instructed them to begin with the words, "Our Father in heaven, how holy is Your name!" (Matthew 6:9). He also encouraged them to approach God with the confidence of a child putting a request to a loving parent. "Your Father knows what you need even before You ask Him," Jesus assured the disciples (Matthew 6:8).

◄ God is our Father

When Jesus talked about the Father, He always suggested an intimate relationship, even an identity between Himself and God. Near the end of His life the apostles asked what the Father was like. Jesus answered, "Have I been with you all this time and you have not seen the Father? He who has seen me has seen the Father" (John 14:8-9). These words merely enlarged on what they had heard from Jesus before. He once told a crowd in the temple, "I and the Father are one" (John 10:30). And in another setting, "I am in the Father, and the Father in Me" (John 14:11).

◄◄ LOGOS

The Jewish leaders reacted to

such statements with shock and dismay. To them Jesus was guilty of absolute sacrilege by suggesting that He was divine. They considered it their duty to destroy anyone who advanced such claims. Otherwise, they would not be defending God's honor and integrity. To put it in their own words, "By our law He ought to die because He made Himself out to be the Son of God" (John 19:7).

Persecution of Disciples

Eventually the Jewish leadership got its way. But their anger was not finished. Jesus knew that His disciples would also engender opposition by teaching that He was God's Son. It was necessary, therefore, to prepare them for persecution. In the opening remarks of the Sermon on the Mount, He tied faithfulness under persecution to eternal reward. "Consider yourself blessed when people mock you and persecute you and say all kinds of false, evil things about you because of your association with Me. Rejoice and be glad, for you will have a great reward in heaven. After all, this is exactly how the prophets were persecuted before you" (Matthew 5:11-12).

Shortly before His betrayal Jesus alerted His apostles once more to looming persecutions. "They will deliver you up to the courts and flog you in the synagogues," He predicted, "and you will be hauled before governors and kings on My

Forewarned is forearmed ➤

What it means to be saved ➤➤

behalf." He then added, "You will be hated by all on account of My name, but the one who endures to the end will be saved" (Mark 13:9-13).

In a word, opposition and difficulties were inevitable. But through them all the apostles were to pursue one goal above all others. They were to endure, keeping their eyes on being saved. (More about "being saved" in a moment.) Just as Jesus predicted, the early church did experience fierce persecution. Peter and John underwent their first of many imprisonments only weeks after Jesus died. And most of the Twelve suffered violent deaths at the hands of Jewish or Roman authorities. Still, apart from Judas, the apostles all persevered in their loyalty to Him.

And what did Jesus mean when He spoke of being saved? What would they be saved from? Overall they were being saved from eternal separation from God in the world that lies beyond death. Being saved, in other words, was another way of saying that they would go to heaven. This is what Jesus had in mind when He told the apostles to go throughout the world proclaiming the gospel, noting, "The person who believes and is baptized will be saved" (Mark 16:16).

Parables of the Lost

Since those who are saved live forever, Jesus spoke of heaven as "eternal life." On one occasion He told the crowd, "The one who hears

My words and puts his trust in the One Who sent Me has *eternal* life. He does not come under condemnation [at God's judgment], but has passed from death into life" (John 5:24). Strikingly, Jesus did not say, "Such a person *will receive* eternal life." Instead, that person *has* eternal life. He already possesses it. Jesus wanted eternal life to be so real to His disciples that death became transparent. They would look right through it to eternity with God. In that context Jesus could say, "If anyone keeps My word, he shall never see death" (John 8:51).

Because nothing is more tragic than the loss of eternal life, the New Testament pictures those who are not saved as lost. In describing His mission on earth, Jesus said He came to "seek and save the lost" (Luke 19:10). In that regard He told three parables in Luke 15 to illustrate the depth of God's desire to reach the lost. The parables are about a lost sheep, a lost coin, and a lost son. The first parable portrays a shepherd searching diligently for a sheep that has strayed from the flock. The second concerns a woman looking everywhere for a misplaced coin. In both cases there is great rejoicing when the lost possession is found.

In the third parable, the longest we have from Jesus, a young man entreats his father to give him his inheritance so he can start to enjoy it. When the father grants the request, the son leaves home and travels to a distant land. There he gives himself to unprincipled, hedonistic living. He wastes his money until none is left. Hungry and brokenhearted, he decides to return home and offer himself to his father as a hired servant. But when he arrives, the father refuses to treat him as a servant. Instead, his father throws a banquet to celebrate his return. "This son who was lost," the father says, "has now been found."

≪ Eternal life a present possession

The father does not chastise the boy or reject him because of the fortune he has squandered. The father loves him so much that he is simply thrilled to have the boy home. With this parable Jesus is making the point that God the Father feels the same way about us. He wants His lost children to come back to Him. For that reason, God sends messengers into the world seeking the lost, like the shepherd searching for his lost sheep and the woman looking everywhere for her lost coin.

≪ God searches for us

In giving these parables, Jesus used things that were lost to symbolize people whose lives are corrupted by sin (Luke 15:6-7; 9-10). What these particular parables do not address is the barrier that sin creates between the sinner and God. While God is always eager for the lost to return to Him, their sin stands as an obstacle between themselves and His own inner nature. God has always and consistently condemned sin and held those who sinned personally accountable. So how can we

≪ Sin separates

return to Him, yet avoid His condemnation?

Salvation from Sin

The answer to that question takes us to a second sense of what it means to be saved. In many settings the Gospels equate being saved with not having to experience personal punishment for sin. At the birth of Jesus angels announced that a Savior had been born (Luke 2:11). A savior brings salvation. The salvation the angels had in mind was a rescue from sin and its punishment.

Zechariah, the father of John the Baptist, foretold his son's work in those very terms. John, he said, was to prepare the way for one who would "give His people the knowledge of salvation through the forgiveness of their sins" (Luke 1:77). Some thirty years later John described Jesus as "the Lamb of God who takes away the sin of the world" (John 1:29).

How are sins forgiven? ➤

So how would Jesus accomplish this salvation, this forgiveness of sins? He addressed that subject only indirectly in what He taught. But John the Baptist pointed toward the answer when He spoke of Jesus as "the Lamb of God." His phrase recalled Isaiah's language about the Messiah: "He was oppressed and afflicted, yet He did not open His mouth, like a lamb led to slaughter." Isaiah then added, "He was cut off from among the living because of the transgression of my people,

who deserved the blow he took" (Isaiah 53:7-8).

In the Old Testament, lambs were offered as a sacrifice for sin. Isaiah foresaw another lamb, distant from his own day, who would also be a sacrifice for sin. To quote the prophet once more, "He was pierced through for our transgressions and crushed for our iniquities." Or as Isaiah went on to say, "The Lord caused our iniquity to fall upon him" (Isaiah 53:5-6).

The New Testament draws on the imagery of Isaiah 53 to explain the death of Jesus (Romans 4:25; 1 Corinthians 15:3; 1 Peter 2:24-25). God had ordained that He would accept the death of Jesus as a substitute for the punishment deserved by anyone who sins. Jesus would serve as an ultimate and universal sacrifice to replace the constant sacrifice of animals that had been part of Jewish worship (Hebrews 10:9-12; 13:11-12).

In this way, the two concepts of "being saved" in the New Testament merge as one.

➤ First, we are saved from condemnation because the death of Jesus gives us forgiveness of sin.

➤ Second, because there is no sin on our record, we are spared eternal separation from God.

We can confidently anticipate a resurrection, like the resurrection of Jesus, that ushers us into an unending existence with God. As Jesus told a close friend, "I am the resurrection and life. He who believes in Me shall live even though he dies" (John 11:25).

Jesus therefore presented Himself as the gateway to eternal life. On more than one occasion He spoke as though He personified every person's resurrection. "This is My Father's will, that everyone who sees the Son and believes in Him should live eternally. I Myself will raise that person up on the last day" (John 6:40). In passages such as this Jesus pictured the resurrection as occurring on one final great day when all who have died will come to life. "An hour is coming," He assured His disciples, "when everyone in the grave will hear My voice and come forth. Those who pursue what is good in this world will come forth to a resurrection of life. But those who do evil will face a resurrection of condemnation" (John 5:28-29).

Love

Since the resurrection of life is for those who pursue what is good, Jesus spent much of His time explaining what doing good means. To Him the one word that expressed the highest good was love. When asked to name the greatest commandment in the Law of Moses, He responded by citing two commandments, both having to do with love. The first is to love God with your complete being. The second is to love your neighbor as yourself (Matthew 22:35-39). Jesus once expressed His hope that the

world would know His followers by the depth of love they showed for one another (John 13:35). And He summed up what it means to act lovingly when He taught, "Always treat others the way you want them to treat you" (Luke 6:31).

>> *Jesus is the door into life*

One of His most striking statements about love centered on how we react to enemies. It is somewhat natural to live by the adage, "Love your friends and hate your enemies." Jesus rejected that value system by telling his disciples to love their enemies and to pray for those who persecuted them. If they were to think of themselves as God's children, Jesus observed, they needed to notice the breadth of God's kindness. He gives rain and sunshine even to those who reject Him. Thus, to be like Him it is necessary to treat everyone kindly, including people who would do us harm (Matthew 5:43-48).

< *Love your enemies*

Jesus saw His entire life as offering a model of genuine love. Even His death was motivated by love. "No one can have a greater love than to lay down his life for His friends," He explained to the disciples (John 15:13). When they heard these words, they no doubt thought of someone stepping into harm's way to protect a friend in imminent danger. But as was often the case, there was deeper meaning to His statement than the disciples realized. Jesus was laying down His life so that His disciples, and all others who follow Him, could be saved.

< *Jesus the example of love*

>> *Love God totally*

Moreover, in giving up His life He was demonstrating the Father's love as well as His own. Jesus once told a prominent Jewish leader, "God loved the world so much that He gave His only begotten Son, so that anyone who trusts in Him will not perish, but have eternal life" (John 3:16). To perish, in this context, means to lose eternal life. Later the New Testament says, "This is genuine love, not that we love God, but that He loved us and sent His Son to be a sacrifice for our sins" (1 John 4:8).

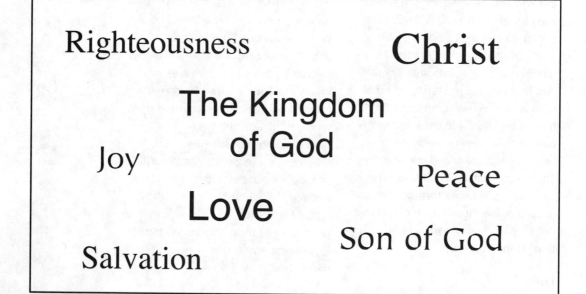

Chapter Twenty-One

THE FIRST CHRISTIAN COMMUNITIES

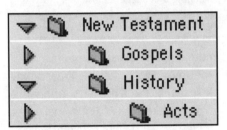

The Gospels conclude their narrative with the death and resurrection of Jesus. To trace what happened next, we turn to the book of Acts. Written by Luke, Acts is more or less a second volume designed to accompany his Gospel. The only book of history in the New Testament, Acts covers the birth of Christian communities across the Roman Empire in the decades immediately following the death of Jesus.

Acts is actually a shortened name for this book. The early church called it the Acts of the Apostles, for it shows how they carried forward the work that Jesus began. Some have suggested that a more appropriate name would be the Acts of the Holy Spirit. Through this entire account, Luke emphasizes how the Holy Spirit was working through the apostles. This was in keeping with

something Jesus promised on the night of His betrayal. "The Father will send the Holy Spirit in My name," Jesus told them. "He will be your Helper who will teach you everything you need to know and bring to your mind all that I have said to you" (John 14:26).

The Holy Spirit

Nowhere else in the Bible is the Holy Spirit so prominent as here in the book of Acts. Within these pages the Spirit functions in four capacities.

< What the Holy Spirit does

➤ He reveals truths which the apostles are to proclaim.

➤ He endows the apostles with the power to perform miracles.

➤ He bolsters the disciples' spirits, giving them courage to speak boldly in the presence of intimidation.

➤ He serves as God's personal gift to all who accept Jesus. What this means for Christians is developed more fully in later books of the New Testament.

The Person of the Holy Spirit

You will notice that we have referred to the Holy Spirit on the previous page as "He," not "it." Whereas we normally think of a spirit as a thing, the New Testament describes the Holy Spirit in terms of personality. In this regard, Jesus always used personal pronouns to refer to the Holy Spirit. Speaking about the Spirit with His disciples, Jesus said, "The world cannot receive Him because it does not behold Him or know Him. But you know Him, because He abides with you, and will be with you" (John 14:17).

A few moments later, Jesus added these words about the Spirit. "When He comes, He will guide you into all truth, for He will not speak from His own initiative. Instead, what He hears, He will speak, disclosing to you what is to come. He shall glorify Me, for He will take things pertaining to Me and disclose them to you" (John 16:13-14).

The gospel message ➤

Since the Spirit was to guide the apostles into all truth, it is not surprising that the book of Acts emphasizes what these men taught. Just as the Gospels record sermons from Jesus, the book of Acts includes speeches from His apostles. These speeches proclaim Jesus as one

➤ who has been raised from the dead

➤ who has ascended to the throne room of heaven

➤ and who now sits enthroned as Lord of the universe

The apostles portray themselves as messengers, sent by Jesus, to announce His Lordship to the world.

The Resurrected Christ

Christ = Messiah = Anointed One ➤

In recording these speeches, Acts elevates the practice of using "Christ" as a name for Jesus. "Christ" is a Greek form of the word "Messiah." The Gospels used the word "Christ" originally as a title, not a personal name. In Matthew 16:16, Peter affirmed that Jesus was "the Christ." And those who mocked Jesus at His trial asked if He was "the Christ" (Matthew 26:63).

Over time, however, the disciples of Jesus transformed the title into a name. Rather than referring to their Master as "Jesus the Christ," they simplified the phrase to "Jesus Christ." That, in turn, paved the way for followers of Jesus to be known as Christians (Acts 11:26). And when they proclaimed the story of Jesus, they described themselves as "preaching Christ" (Acts 8:5; 9:22).

In their speeches the apostles always place the death and resurrection of Christ on center stage. They make a point of saying that God anticipated the crucifixion and foretold it through the Prophets. They also insist that the resurrection vindicates Jesus and the claims He made about Himself. He was not a false Messiah, but a Messenger truly sent from God.

The apostles staked everything on the truth of the resurrection. Jesus made bold and startling claims about Himself. If those claims were mere talk, He was nothing more than an imposter, more of a madman than the Messiah. On the other hand, if God indeed raised Him from the dead, what striking evidence that heaven endorsed what Jesus said.

Over the centuries opponents of Christianity have attacked the credibility of the apostles and their eye-witness accounts of the resurrection. Skeptics have accused the disciples of making up the resurrection story then shrewdly convincing people to believe it. But several factors argue against this claim.

➤ First, the apostles pointed doubters in their own day to some 500 people who had seen Jesus alive after His crucifixion (1 Corinthians 15:3-8).

➤ Second, to a person the apostles went to their death insisting that the resurrection was true.

➤ Third, the apostles had nothing to gain by perpetuating a hoax about the resurrection. They underwent brutal persecution, imprisonment, and finally execution because of what they taught about Jesus. If the story of His resurrection was simply something they made up, at least one of them would surely have admitted the hoax. Instead, they accepted severe deprivation and miserable

deaths to defend the resurrection as true.

Other skeptics, impressed that 500 witnesses saw Jesus alive after the crucifixion, have explained these appearances by saying that Jesus never died. They assert that He recovered from His wounds while lying in the tomb. Again, this contention overlooks some critical details.

First, the Romans crucified thousands of people. It was an excruciating, bloody way to die, and the maddening pain began immediately. Roman records indicate a few rare occasions when someone was crucified, but later removed from the cross because of a reprieve. Almost no one taken from a cross under these conditions ever survived. Yet these victims were suspended on a cross only a few minutes. Jesus was on the cross for hours, far too long to survive.

◄◄ Reasons to believe in the resurrection

Second, Romans frequently left bodies on a cross until the flesh rotted away and only a skeleton remained. Granting someone the right to bury the corpse (as was the case with Jesus), while not unusual, was not necessarily routine. In such instances, Roman law required a spear to be thrust into the heart to assure death occurred before the body was removed. That is why the Roman soldiers pierced the chest of Jesus with a spear. Jesus clearly did not come from the cross alive.

◄ Certainty of death in Roman executions

To summarize what we have said, none of the apostles became rich or powerful because he advanced the story of the resurrection. And given their perpetual hardships for proclaiming Christ, we must presume that their motivations were pure and their testimony truthful.

The Day of Pentecost (Acts 1–2)

Acts opens with Jesus' preparing His apostles for the teaching that will now become their primary task. About six weeks after His resurrection, Jesus gathered His apostles on a hillside near Jerusalem to give them final instructions. He was about to return to the Father, and this was the moment of His departure. The apostles, still not clear in their thinking about the kingdom, asked if Jesus was about to restore the splendor of Israel's kingdom. Jesus did not answer that question directly. Instead, He told them to go back to Jerusalem and wait until they received special power that God would impart to them. When that occurred, they were to begin telling His story far and wide, beginning in Jerusalem, Judea, and Samaria, but ultimately going to the entire world (Acts 1:1-8).

As He was speaking those words, Jesus rose into the air, steadily slipping from their sight. He was being taken from them to rejoin the Father in the throne room of heaven. Stunned by this turn of events, the apostles made their way back to Jerusalem, where 120 disciples were spending time in prayer.

For the next few days they continued together, waiting for what Jesus had promised. During that time they selected a man named Matthias to replace Judas as an apostle. Judas, realizing the terrible mistake he had made, committed suicide shortly after the death of Jesus (Matthew 27:3-10).

On the Day of Pentecost, the Jewish harvest festival, this group was together in a portico of the temple when the sound of a mighty wind swept through the building. At the same time something akin to tongues of fire appeared in the air above the apostles' heads. A crowd of several thousand quickly gathered, people from all over the Roman Empire who had come to Jerusalem for Pentecost. The apostles began to address this throng of people, with the Holy Spirit giving them the words to say. And to everyone's amazement, the apostles spoke to each person in the language of that person's native land (Acts 2:1-11).

The most memorable remarks came that day from Peter. He announced that Joel, the Old Testament prophet, had foretold what was happening. Joel had foreseen a day when God would pour out His Spirit on all mankind (Joel 2:28-29). And now, in the presence of those who were witnessing this event, God was carrying out what Joel talked about, Peter said (Acts 2:16-21). The rushing wind, the tongues of fire, and the ability for

Anointing by the Holy Spirit ▶▶

Waiting in Jerusalem ▶

Fulfillment of prophecy ▶▶

unlearned fishermen to speak languages from around the world — these were all signs that the Holy Spirit was behind this moment.

Peter then called his audience's attention to other signs, the ones that Jesus had performed. God used miracles, wonders, and signs, Peter explained, to attest to Jesus. Yet, some in this very crowd had been part of the mob that urged Pilate to crucify Him. Then to the astonishment of his hearers, Peter announced that Jesus was no longer dead. God had brought Him back to life, and the apostles and others standing before the crowd were eyewitnesses to His resurrection.

Peter then showed how the resurrection of Jesus conformed with Old Testament statements about the Messiah. Moreover, God had now exalted Jesus by seating Him at God's own right hand on the throne in heaven. "God has made this Jesus whom you crucified both Lord and Christ," Peter concluded (Acts 2:32-36). Many in the crowd were taken aback by these words.

Asking for guidance on what they should do, they heard Peter reply, "Repent and be baptized, every one of you, in the name of the Lord Jesus Christ for the remission of your sins. And you shall receive God's Holy Spirit as a gift" (Acts 2:38). Not only that, Peter added, this same promise was true for people anywhere and everywhere who feel called to God (Acts 2:39).

◀◀ Miracles as God's signs

That day about 3000 people were baptized. Within a matter of weeks their number grew to 5000. One thing that accounted for this success was the extraordinary power that the apostles displayed. Aided by the Holy Spirit, they were performing the same kinds of miracles that Jesus had been known for (Acts 5:12-16). This drew throngs of people to the apostles. As with Jesus, the purpose of these miracles was to demonstrate that God had truly endorsed the apostles (Hebrews 2:2-4). They were speaking a message from God Himself, communicated to them through the Holy Spirit.

◀ 3,000 baptized

◀◀ You crucified Him; God made Him Lord

The Church

The Day of Pentecost marks the formal beginning of the church, a word that has two related but distinct meanings in the New Testament. In its broadest sense "the church" refers collectively to all followers of Jesus. Thought of this way, there is only one church. From another perspective there are many churches, because the Bible calls every local community of Christians a church. Accordingly, the New Testament refers to the church in Jerusalem, the churches in Asia Minor, and the church in Rome, just to name a few.

Persecution and Expansion

Given what had happened to Jesus, it is not surprising that persecution set in immediately after Pentecost. Within days Peter and John were jailed, beaten, and released. On another occasion all of the apostles were thrown in prison, but made their escape with God's aid. Stephen, a prominent leader in the young Christian community, was tried before the Sanhedrin. When the court became angry at his defense, they dragged him outside, threw him in a pit, and pounded him with large stones until he died (Acts 7). At a later date James, the brother of John, was executed (Acts 12:2). Yet it seemed that such fierce opposition only caused the Christian community in Jerusalem to grow larger.

Persecution forced many Christians to leave Jerusalem. Wherever they went, they shared the story of Jesus. As the prophets had foretold, God's word was going out from Jerusalem. Philip, a co-worker with Stephen, proclaimed the message of Jesus in Samaria and found a receptive hearing in that region. The church had now shed its distinctively Jewish character. Peter carried that process a step further when he baptized Cornelius, a Roman military commander, along with his family and servants.

This began the transition that transformed Christianity into a movement which embraced both Jews and non-Jews. The principal force in effecting this change was a man who at one time fiercely fought the church. His name was Saul.

Saul of Tarsus (Acts 8–9)

When Stephen was killed, Saul was one of the primary participants.

A native of Tarsus in Asia Minor, he developed a reputation for ruthlessly persecuting Christians, men and women alike (Acts 8:1-3). Expanding the scope of his persecution, he obtained authorization from the Sanhedrin court to go to Damascus and arrest followers of Jesus in that city (Acts 9:1-2).

As he approached Damascus at midday he was suddenly blinded by a bright light. Cowering in his blindness, he heard a voice saying, "Saul, why are you persecuting me?" He asked, "Who are you?" Back came the reply, "I am Jesus, the one you are persecuting" (Acts 9:3-5). Jesus then instructed Saul to go into Damascus and await word as to what he should do.

Saul entered the city, where he began an extended time of prayer, still blind from the incident on the road. Meanwhile God used a vision to communicate with a man named Ananias, a disciple of Jesus who lived in Damascus. God indicated that Ananias should go to Saul and explain Christ to him. Knowing Saul's purpose in coming to Damascus, Ananias was reluctant to accept this assignment. But God reassured him, saying, "I have chosen this man as my instrument to carry my name to the non-Jewish world and to kings, as well as to the people of Israel" (Acts 9:10-16).

Ananias found Saul and announced his reason for coming. Saul's blindness immediately reversed itself, and he turned

---

Stephen ➤

Saul on the Damascus Road ➤➤

James ➤

Philip ➤

Ananias ➤➤

Peter and Cornelius ➤

eagerly to see what Ananias had to say. Ananias related what God had revealed about His plans for Saul (Acts 22:12-15). "So why delay?" Ananias asked him. "Rise from where you are, be baptized, and wash away your sins" (Acts 22:16). Little did Ananias know that he was baptizing the man who would become more influential in Christianity than any person besides Jesus Himself.

Once a Christian, Saul began to use the name Paul. Jesus also made Him an apostle. Paul became known as the apostle to the Gentiles, the name the Jews used for all non-Jews. Raised in a Greek city and highly educated, he was an ideal choice to take the message of Jesus to a culture that did not know Moses and the Prophets.

Paul and Barnabas (Acts 13–14)

Paul first teamed up with a man named Barnabas. Together they traveled through the heart of Asia Minor, planting new communities of "believers," a common name in the Bible for those who follow Jesus. As we noted earlier, the Bible calls each community of believers a church, which originally meant "the ones called out." A church was a gathering of people who had each responded to God's call to leave a life of sin and to live in keeping with His will. New Testament writers, especially Paul, liked to refer to Christians as "called" and to their

life in Christ as their "calling" (Romans 8:28-30; 2 Timothy 1:9).

To lead these churches Paul appointed groups of men known as elders (Acts 14:23). Each church had several elders, who constituted a council that guided the life of the local community of believers. This form of leadership was patterned on the role that elders played in the villages of Israel and in Jewish synagogues. Paul compared their duties to those of shepherds who tend a flock. In this case, the flock was the church entrusted to their oversight (Acts 10:28-30).

◄ Elders

◄◄ Saul = Paul

During his travels Paul began to recruit young men who could learn from him and become teachers in their own right. At least two of these men, Timothy and Titus, went on to distinguished careers in Christian leadership. Meanwhile, Paul and Barnabas ended their work together, and Paul took on a new coworker named Silas. The two of them pushed beyond Asia Minor to Macedonia and Greece. There they planted churches in Philippi, Thessalonica, Berea, and Corinth.

◄ Timothy and Titus

◄ Silas
◄◄ Barnabas

Controversies over Circumcision (Acts 15)

Because of his tireless endeavors, Paul brought thousands of Gentiles into the kingdom of God. Their numbers, in fact, created a special challenge for Christian leaders in Jerusalem. The church in Judea was now quite large, but its members were drawn entirely from Jewish backgrounds. Paul's success raised the question of what requirements to place on Gentiles who wanted to become Christians. Should they have to keep the Law of Moses the way Christians in Jerusalem did?

Circumcision and the Gentile Christian ➤

The thorniest question had to do with circumcision. The Jews had practiced circumcision ever since the days of Abraham. The Law of Moses required that every male child be circumcised on the eighth day after birth. Historically the Jews had treated anyone who was uncircumcised as not having a covenant relationship with God. When a Gentile took up the practice of Judaism, he was never fully a part of the Jewish synagogue until he was circumcised. Did that mean that Gentiles would have to be circumcised before they could be accepted fully as Christians?

Paul appeals to Caesar ➤➤

Paul's answer was, "No!" But others disagreed, and they stirred up trouble for him everywhere. This controversy grew so intense that a conference was finally called in Jerusalem to settle it. Paul and Barnabas attended, along with all the other apostles. After days of careful deliberation, prayer, and study of Scripture, the conference concluded that circumcision had been part of God's covenant with Israel at Sinai, not a universal requirement to be levied on all people. The conclave ended, therefore, with a letter sent to Greek

The Jerusalem Council ➤

churches telling them that circumcision was not required of Gentiles who became Christians (Acts 15:22-29).

This only triggered additional controversy. Now the Jews themselves stepped up their opposition to Paul. The Sanhedrin viewed his rejection of circumcision as contemptuous disregard for God's law. They therefore set out to destroy Paul. While he was visiting Jerusalem, they managed to have the Romans arrest him (Acts 21:27-36). But Roman courts were frustrated by the religious charges that his accusers brought against Paul. These were not matters that the Romans took seriously, much less considered punishable by death.

To put distance between himself and his adversaries, Paul appealed for a hearing before Caesar in Rome. As a Roman citizen, he was entitled to that privilege. (Only a fraction of the people who lived in the Roman Empire were actually citizens, so this was an option denied to most prisoners.) The Romans agreed to his appeal and after a lengthy imprisonment in Palestine, he went under armed guard to Rome. The Book of Acts ends with him under house arrest in Rome, awaiting his day in court.

The Bible does not relate the outcome of his trial. Other historical records indicate that he was exonerated and set free. According to these sources he resumed his travels on behalf of Jesus and eventually returned to Rome. Ancient traditions hold that he was beheaded in Rome under the emperor Nero, who blamed the Christians for the great fire that destroyed a third of the city in AD 64. Tradition also says that Peter died by crucifixion in Rome during the same persecution.

Letters to Gentile Churches

By the time Paul and Peter died, the impetus of Christianity was changing rapidly. Gentile Christianity was steadily eclipsing Jewish Christianity. The basic difference was that Gentile Christians did not keep all the feast days and holy seasons from the Law of Moses, while Jewish Christians usually did. After AD 69, when the Romans leveled Jerusalem, Jewish Christianity went into decline. There were still churches with a strong Jewish core in Asia Minor and around Alexandria in Egypt. But churches made up solely of Gentiles became increasingly common.

Not having a heritage in which they learned Moses and the Prophets from childhood, Gentile churches needed considerable guidance. Unlike the Jews, they were not clear in their thinking about the dangers of paganism, the nature of God, and what God expects of His people morally and ethically. During his travels Paul frequently wrote letters to churches he had established, showing them how to deal with moral issues and spiritual problems. These letters, comprising thirteen books of the New Testament, provide keen insight into the message that the apostles carried to the cities of the Roman Empire.

Like the prophets, the apostles summoned people initially to repent. In the book of Acts, which records several sermons by Peter, Stephen, and Paul, we see a continuation of the call for repentance and baptism that began with John the Baptist. Once people were baptized, the apostles then urged a commitment to godly conduct. Many of Paul's letters focus on what it means to live as a godly person. This is also true of other books in the New Testament, including letters from Peter, James, and John.

◄ Godly conduct

These letters also developed the teachings and vocabulary that have characterized Christianity over the centuries. Jesus left the earth with many questions about Himself and about His message still unanswered, even in the minds of His apostles. He told them on the eve of His death that after He was gone, He would send the Holy Spirit, who would guide them into all truth. The sermons in the book of Acts and the letters that form the balance of the New Testament capture the truths imparted by the Holy Spirit.

◄◄ Guidance for Gentile Christians

The Spread of Christianity

We should note that Christianity had a much broader expanse in the first century than the history detailed in the Bible. The book of Acts and the letters in the New Testament focus on churches in the northeastern part of the Mediterranean. Nothing is said of the major inroads Christianity made in Egypt, especially in Alexandria, and in cities of the Tigris-Euphrates Valley. From Alexandria the message of Christ spread westward across the Mediterranean states of Africa. Prior to the rise of Islam, towering thinkers and leaders in Christianity frequently came from this part of Africa.

Further spread of Christianity ➤

By the close of the book of Acts the most significant Christian centers outside of Jerusalem were at Antioch in Syria, Ephesus in Asia Minor, Corinth in Greece, and Rome. Antioch was the first church that thoroughly integrated Jews and Gentiles into one body (Acts 11:19-21). This was also the place that believers were first called Christians (Acts 11:26). And it was the church in Antioch that sent Paul and Barnabas to Asia Minor to build a Christian presence there (Acts 13:1-3).

Corinth ➤➤

Antioch ➤

Rome ➤➤

Of the many churches that flourished in Asia Minor, none was more significant than the one in Ephesus. A great university town, Ephesus was a cultural and political center for the entire region. Paul made several visits to Ephesus, including one that lasted for more than two years (Acts 19:8-10). During this time people turned from paganism

Ephesus ➤

and black magic in such numbers that it damaged trades that profited from those forms of spiritualism. As people became Christians, they brought their books on magic and sorcery to a common site and burned them, so many books that the value totaled 50,000 pieces of silver (Acts 19:11-19).

Corinth was another city in which Paul made an extended stay. He spent 18 months establishing the church there. And he came back to Corinth on at least one or two other occasions. Corinth was a bawdy commercial city, situated on one of the most lucrative trade routes in the Mediterranean. The city's lifestyle was so sensual that even the Romans shook their heads in disbelief at the shamelessness of the Corinthians. After he left there, Paul wrote two letters to this church. As you might imagine, a major theme in those letters was the need to maintain separation from the immorality all around them.

The New Testament does not tell us much about the church at Rome. It is first mentioned in Acts as a church that already exists and is doing well. Paul had a long-held dream of visiting that church, and in anticipation of his visit he wrote them what turned out to be his most influential letter. From the language of his letter it is apparent that the church in Rome had large numbers of both Jews and Gentiles. And he speaks of the Christians in Rome as having a reputation for faithfulness to Jesus that is known throughout the entire Empire.

By coincidence, our most treasured letters from Paul were written to three of the four churches we have just described: Ephesus,

Corinth, and Rome. Together they provide the fullest development of Christian teachings to come from his pen. As a result we will have an opportunity to visit these churches again as we examine the letters in the New Testament.

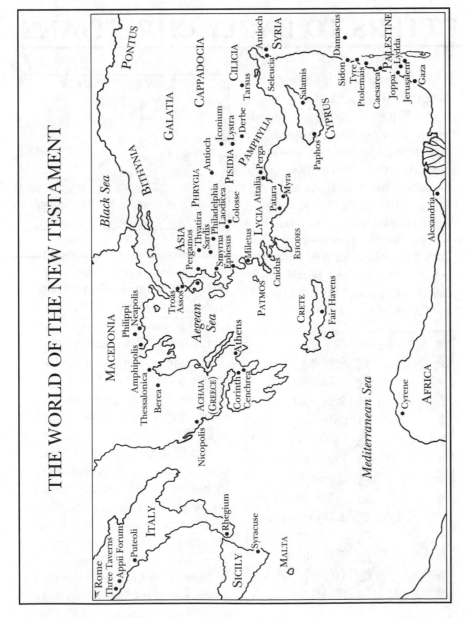

THE WORLD OF THE NEW TESTAMENT

Chapter Twenty-Two

LETTERS TO EARLY CHRISTIANS

As you have seen, the four Gospels and the book of Acts were written in the form of biography and history. Together they constitute more than half of the New Testament. At the end of Acts, however, the style of the New Testament changes. The next 21 books were written originally as correspondence. Not surprisingly, then, we refer to this section of the Bible as "the Letters." (You may also hear them called "the Epistles," from the Latin and Greek words for "letters.")

Epistles ➤

▽	📖 Letters
▷	📖 Romans
▷	📖 1 Corinthians
▷	📖 2 Corinthians
▷	📖 Galatians
▷	📖 Ephesians
▷	📖 Philippians
▷	📖 Colossians
▷	📖 1 Thessalonians
▷	📖 2 Thessalonians
▷	📖 1 Timothy
▷	📖 2 Timothy
▷	📖 Titus
▷	📖 Philemon

▷	📖 Hebrews
▷	📖 James
▷	📖 1 Peter
▷	📖 2 Peter
▷	📖 1 John
▷	📖 2 John
▷	📖 3 John
▷	📖 Jude

Unlike modern correspondence, the New Testament Letters do not include the date on which they were composed. As a result, we cannot arrange them in strict chronological order. Instead, the Bible groups them by author, placing the books by Paul first. There are thirteen Letters from him, which means that he gave us more books of the Bible than anyone else.

In addition, Paul's books are unique in the way they received their names. His letters are named for the people who *received* them, while other New Testament letters (except for Hebrews) are named for the person who *wrote* them.

Nine of Paul's letters went to young churches. Four others were sent to individuals. The Bible organizes his books so that the letters to churches come first, then his letters to individuals. They appear in this order.

Letters to Churches

➤ Romans (to the church in Rome)

➤ 1 & 2 Corinthians (to the church in Corinth in the heart of Greece)

➤ Galatians (to the churches in the region of Galatia in Asia Minor)

➤ Ephesians (to the church in Ephesus, probably the largest church in Asia Minor)

➤ Philippians (to the church in Philippi in the Macedonian area of Greece)

➤ Colossians (to the church in Colossae, another city in Asia Minor)

➤ 1 & 2 Thessalonians (to the church in Thessalonica in northern Greece)

Letters to Individuals

➤ 1 & 2 Timothy (Paul's younger coworker who remained in Ephesus to help that church mature)

➤ Titus (another coworker whom Paul left on the island of Crete to strengthen churches there)

➤ Philemon (a personal friend of Paul and a man of considerable influence in the church at Colossae)

Notice that Paul's letters went to a thin band of cities stretching from Asia Minor to Italy. This was a predominantly Greek area, where problems often arose when Biblical principles were blended with Greek culture. These problems come up frequently in Paul's letters. Except for Romans and Colossians, he wrote exclusively to churches that he personally established.

Of the remaining eight Letters, we have

➤ two from Peter

➤ three from John

➤ one apiece from two church leaders named James and Jude

➤ one book (Hebrews) from an unknown author

Whereas Paul wrote to specific churches, these writers usually aimed at a broader audience, intending their letters to circulate from one congregation to another. As a result, the letters themselves usually do not identify the church or individual who first received them. However, their language permits us to isolate the general audience for which they were intended.

➤ Hebrews — to Jewish Christians

➤ James — to Jewish Christians living outside of Judea

➤ 1 Peter — to both Gentile and Jewish Christians in Asia Minor

➤ 2 Peter — probably to Christians in Asia Minor

➤ 1 John — to an unspecified group of Christians

➤ 2 John — to a woman identified only as "the elect lady"

➤ 3 John — to a man named Gaius, otherwise unknown to us

➤ Jude — to an unspecified group of Christians

Answers to questions ➤➤

Because these books were intended for such a generalized audience, they are sometimes referred to as "the General Letters."

Collectively the books of Paul and the General Letters provide our most valuable guide to what the early church taught. We will begin to examine those teachings in the next chapter. But first, it would be helpful to introduce each of the 21 Letters individually. And to do so, we will take them in the order in which they appear in the New Testament.

Paul's Letters to Churches

Romans

Doctrine ➤

Of all the books in the Bible, Romans offers the most systematic statement of Christian doctrine. ("Doctrine" is another word for "core teachings and concepts.") As a consequence, we will mention Romans often in the chapters ahead. Paul writes this letter in part to introduce himself to the Christians in Rome, where most know him only by name. Hoping to come their way in the near future, he uses this letter to acquaint them with what he teaches as he travels the Empire.

1 Corinthians

In contrast to his relationship with the Romans, Paul is well known to the Christians in Corinth. He writes 1 Corinthians in response to a list of questions that they have sent him. The questions touch on a wide range of issues, from marriage to the resurrection to a special fund they are gathering to help impoverished churches in Judea. Paul has also learned (perhaps from the messengers who brought the questions) that major divisions are upsetting the unity of the Corinthian church. This disturbs him greatly. He responds by weaving warnings about division through the entire letter.

2 Corinthians

Paul's anxieties about the church in Corinth are greatly allayed by the time we come to 2 Corinthians. He has received word that the Corinthians have graciously accepted the counsel in his first letter and have taken steps to correct problems in their midst. Paul now calls on them to develop godly character, to anchor their hope more deeply in the resurrection, and to view themselves as God's messengers to the world.

Galatians

As with 1 Corinthians, Paul writes Galatians after hearing of troubles in the churches there. Jewish teachers have moved into the region, discrediting Paul and claiming that Gentiles can become Christians only if they are circumcised and keep the Law of Moses. Paul answers by denouncing these teachers and the ideas they espouse. He shows that God always intended for the message of Christ — the gospel — to replace the sacrifices and rituals established by Moses.

Ephesians

Ephesians, the next letter in the New Testament, is like a crowning jewel in Paul's writings. While not as lengthy as Romans, Ephesians is every bit its equal in terms of offering an exalted view of God and His purposes. More than any other book, Ephesians lays out God's ideals for the church. In the imagery of Ephesians, the church is the bride of Christ, adorned in splendor. As such she is to keep herself pure. For that reason, Paul devotes much of this letter to the subject of personal morality and integrity.

Philippians

If one church in Paul's day approached his ideal, it was the congregation in Philippi. He always speaks of this church in the most endearing terms. The Philippians formed a partnership with Paul to underwrite his expenses as he traveled proclaiming the gospel. He writes the book of Philippians to acknowledge a recent gift from them. He uses the occasion to point them to the selflessness and self-sacrifice that marked the life of Jesus. They should model their own lives, he says, on that example.

‹‹ Circumcision

Colossians

Within Paul's letters, the two with the greatest similarities are Ephesians and Colossians. They may have been written at the same time and dispatched by the same courier. Yet, Colossians is far more than a copy of Ephesians. Even when it repeats a theme from Ephesians, Colossians has a style and content of its own. Colossians is especially noted for the way in which it celebrates the deity of Jesus. "In Christ," Paul writes, "the fullness of deity dwells in bodily form" (Colossians 2:9).

‹ Deity of Christ

‹‹ God's ideals

1 & 2 Thessalonians

Paul's last two letters to churches are addressed to Thessalonica. These are among the earliest works from his pen. Paul started the church in Thessalonica after leaving Philippi under heavy duress. Now the Thessalonians themselves are facing persecution and entrenched opposition. This obviously raises the constant threat of discouragement. For that reason Paul thinks it essential to remind them of the resurrection and the return of Jesus from heaven, what these letters call "the day of the Lord."

It seems that a document has begun to circulate under Paul's

‹ Hope in persecution

‹‹ Partnership

name reporting that the day of the Lord has already come. In 2 Thessalonians he declares the document a forgery and insists that there is no

Fighting heresy >>

need for alarm. The Thessalonians can be absolutely confident that they will share in Christ's glory when He appears.

Paul's Letters to Individuals

1 & 2 Timothy

When Paul departed for Macedonia from Ephesus, he left Timothy behind to strengthen the Ephesian church (1 Timothy 1:3).

Governing the church >

Later Paul sends him further instructions in the form of a letter that we know as 1 Timothy. Paul uses this correspondence to outline the pri-

Slave and slave owner >>

orities that should govern Timothy's leadership of the church. Of special concern is the need for healthy teaching, the kind that promotes spiritual and congregational health. Equally important, Timothy is to be forceful in opposing those who teach doctrines that are untrue.

Paul continues this subject in his second letter to Timothy, which repeats many themes from the first letter. By now Timothy is no longer at Ephesus, although his precise location is not clear. Paul once more impresses on him the urgency of teaching only those things that will make the church healthy.

Titus

Paul's letter to Titus closely parallels his counsel in 1 and 2 Timothy.

Titus was another traveling companion of Paul and a trusted colleague. Paul left Titus on the populous island of Crete to strengthen new churches there (Titus 1:5). These churches were being hurt by men — Paul calls them "rebellious deceivers" — who were advancing concepts foreign to true Christianity. As with Timothy, Paul gives specific guidance on the kinds of things that Titus should teach and what he should do to offset the influence of the "deceivers."

Philemon

Paul's last book in the New Testament is addressed to a close friend named Philemon. A man of wealth, Philemon had a slave named Onesimus who ran away. As a fugitive, Onesimus sought out Paul, who was imprisoned in some unnamed city. Paul persuaded Onesimus to become a Christian and to return home. As Onesimus prepares to return, Paul writes the letter of Philemon to go with him. The letter begs Philemon to treat his returning slave kindly, even to consider giving him his freedom.

The General Letters

Hebrews

As we have noted, Hebrews was written anonymously. Some have suggested that it was not originally a letter, but a sermon delivered to Jewish Christians. It does not open with the salutations or greetings

that are characteristic of most letters. Rather it moves directly into its
subject matter with no preliminaries
or introduction.

What becomes immediately
apparent is that its author assumes
that he is speaking to an audience
that is well versed in the Old
Testament. Almost every paragraph
draws on stories, examples, and
statements from Hebrew history,
which gives the book its name.

The primary purpose in Hebrews
is to show that the blessings
enjoyed in Christ far exceed the
blessings that came with the Law of
Moses. Although Hebrews is quite
different from Galatians stylistically,
both books argue the same conclusion, namely, that the death of Jesus
replaces the covenant of Moses
with a new covenant between God
and mankind.

James

Like Hebrews, James was written
to Jewish Christians. Its author was
one of the brothers of Jesus. James
rose to leadership in the church in
Jerusalem following the resurrection
of Jesus. The book that bears his
name is highly practical in tone,
urging a life of peaceful conduct,
sensitivity to others, compassion,
and prayer.

1 & 2 Peter

The practical tone in James continues unbroken in the next two
books of the New Testament, the

letters we know as 1 and 2 Peter.
Where James seems to have been
written to Jewish Christians, Peter
addresses those with Gentile backgrounds. In times past, he says, they
have embraced the full range of
pagan vices, from drunkenness to
orgies to idolatry (1 Peter 4:3). Now
he urges them to turn their backs
on such things.

<< A Jewish
perspective

Written to Christians in Asia
Minor, 1 Peter preoccupies itself
with an imminent persecution faced
by those who received this letter.
On five different occasions in this
relatively short book Peter speaks of
suffering that they will endure. His
anticipations would prove correct,
for some of the harshest persecution
of early Christians broke out in Asia
Minor during the first century.

< Stand firm
through suffering

Interestingly, when we move to
2 Peter there is no further mention
of the suffering that looms so large
in Peter's first letter. Perhaps this is
because his second letter goes to a
slightly different group of churches.
Who these churches may be, we do
not know. The letter gives no clear
indication. It is apparent, however,
that what worries Peter this time is
not so much external opposition,
but voices within the church who
are teaching ideas that contradict
Christian truth. Peter calls them
"false teachers" (2 Peter 1:1).

1, 2, & 3 John

In John's letters we also find a
focus on the damaging work of
false teachers. John refers to

Antichrists ➤

"antichrists" (people who oppose Jesus) who have come on the scene. It seems that these teachers have undermined confidence that Christians will receive eternal life. The purpose of 1 John is to restore that assurance. "I have written these things," he says, "so you can know that you have eternal life" (1 John 5:13). Along the way he assures his readers that their prayers are heard and their sins are forgiven, for they are indeed the children of God.

Walking in the truth ➤

In 2 and 3 John he writes proudly of friends who have rejected false teaching and continue to "walk in the truth." These two letters are little more than short notes, jotted down hurriedly to personal friends. But they demonstrate the tenderness and affection John has for other members of the church.

Jude

The final letter of the New Testament was penned by a man who identifies himself only as "Jude, a bondservant of Jesus Christ, and brother of James." There were two prominent men named James in the history of the early church. One was an apostle, the brother of John. He was executed by Herod soon after the church started (Acts 12:2). The other was the brother of Jesus,

the one who wrote the book of James.

Jude appears to be the brother of this second James, which would also make Jude a brother of Jesus. But he does not claim that title. He calls himself merely the bondservant of Jesus. Perhaps he viewed himself as an unworthy brother, since he and others in his family were slow to believe in Jesus (John 7:5).

The message of Jude is quite similar to the one in 2 Peter, which may suggest that Peter and Jude worked closely together. Like Peter, Jude writes to combat the problem of false teachers. In this case these teachers are denying the truth about Jesus and are dismissing the need for high moral standards among Christians.

Looking Ahead

With this brief introduction, you are now ready to delve into the message of the New Testament Letters. In the next four chapters we will survey what the Letters teach. Rather than examine the Letters individually, we will review the major themes that are found throughout this section of the Bible. After you become familiar with these themes, you will want to read each of the Letters and acquaint yourself more fully with what they say.

Chapter Twenty-Three

THE THEOLOGY OF THE LETTERS

The word "theology" means "the study of things pertaining to God." The entire Bible is therefore about theology. The Letters of the New Testament, however, give us an understanding of Biblical theology that transcends anything we find in the Prophets or even the Gospels.

We rely on the Letters, for instance, to understand the full significance of Christ and what He accomplished. The Gospels tell us how He lived and what He taught. The Letters explain the *meaning* of His life and especially His death. They also give us a fuller perspective of His deity.

The Letters likewise enlarge our understanding of the Holy Spirit. Always identified with God in the Old Testament, the Holy Spirit emerges in the New Testament as a distinct divine personality. The Letters treat Him as a coequal with God and Jesus Christ. This resulted in the early church speaking of God the Father, God the Son, and God the Holy Spirit.

God the Father

Interestingly, the Letters do not preoccupy themselves with examining the nature of God the Father. The Letters presume that the reader already knows the Old Testament, with its extensive revelation of God's character. The New Testament is far more concerned with explaining the person of Jesus and His divine nature.

Still, the Letters do add valuable information to what the Old Testament tells us about the Father. In particular, the Letters show us the design that God used to guide human history ever since the creation. Paul's name for this design is "the eternal purpose." He says that God framed this plan before the creation of the world (Ephesians 1:3-11; 3:11). What motivated the plan was God's desire to have an intimate, eternal relationship with every man and woman. Paul captures the essence of that intimacy when he says that God wants us to call Him "Abba," the most tender word a Hebrew child had for his father (Romans 8:15; Galatians 4:6-7).

◄◄ Theology defined

◄ God's overall plan

Yet, at the beginning of time, as God looked into the future, sin loomed on the horizon as an ominous threat to His relationship with mankind. Sin, He knew, would erect a barrier between Himself and humanity, for God's very nature is incompatible with wrongdoing. As James reminds us, "God cannot be tempted by evil, nor does He Himself tempt anyone" (James 1:13). This is an echo of Habakkuk's words when he wrote, "Your eyes are too pure to approve evil, and You cannot look on wickedness with favor" (Habakkuk 1:13).

God understood how we would react deep inside once sin corrupted us. Standing before Him would no longer be a joy, for guilt and condemnation would cause us to wither in His presence. To overcome that situation and assure Himself a lasting relationship with us, God had to find a remedy for sin. In the eternal purpose He set forth that remedy. He chose to send Jesus into the world as a human being, to die on the cross, and to allow that death to annul the consequences of sin.

This means that God foresaw the death of Jesus from the very moment of creation. On the Day of Pentecost, Peter described Jesus as having been delivered to death "according to God's definite plan and foreknowledge" (Acts 2:23). And later, in his first letter, Peter said that Christ's death was decreed before the earth came into existence (1 Peter 1:19-20).

Why God chose this course of action is never revealed in the Bible. Could He have resolved the problem of sin some other way? Perhaps. The Bible simply says that He decided to accept the death of Jesus as a substitute for the punishment we all deserve because of our sin (1 Peter 2:21-25). This is what Isaiah foresaw when he declared,

> He was wounded for our transgressions.
> He was crushed for our iniquity.
> For our well-being, lashes fell upon him,
> And by his scourging we are healed.
> Like sheep, we have all gone astray,
> Each turning to his own way.
> But the Lord has caused the iniquity of each of us
> To be laid on Him.
> — Isaiah 53:5-6

Since God made this decision about Jesus before time began, we might have expected Jesus to appear immediately once sin worked its way into the human community. Yet, for reasons known only to Himself, God delayed Christ's birth for centuries. During that time God kept the details of His plan to Himself. He gave His Old Testament prophets only the faintest outline of what He had in mind. Even His angels were denied access to His specific intentions (1 Peter 1:10-12). It was only to the apostles and prophets in the early church that He revealed the full scope of His long-secret purpose (Ephesians 3:4-5).

Sin separates from God ➤

Jesus pays for the remedy ➤➤

God plans ahead ➤

Meanwhile, He used His covenants with Israel to prepare for Christ's appearance. The Law of Moses was thus a temporary measure, serving to set the stage for Jesus. Galatians compares the Law of Moses to a special kind of slave, well-known in Greek households, who took care of children until they were adults. The slave controlled every movement of the child's day. But once the father proclaimed the child an adult, the slave lost his authority. He no longer had control. The same thing happened with the Law of Moses, Paul says, when Jesus came on the scene (Galatians 3:23–4:4). The message of Jesus replaced the regulations and rituals handed down from Moses.

The purpose for the Law of Moses, according to Galatians, was to lead mankind to Christ. The Law and its related covenants prepared for Jesus in several specific ways.

➤ First, through His dealings with the Israelites, God was able to teach them about His true nature. This helps us delineate Him from pagan concepts of deity.

➤ Second, through His laws and the prophets' words, God gave us a deeper sense of right and wrong.

➤ Third, through the sacrifices and rituals in Israel, God dramatized the seriousness of sin. The constant sacrifice of animals was a daily reminder that sin has deadly spiritual consequences.

God also used physical features of Jewish worship to teach lessons about spiritual realities. The book of Hebrews indicates that God even designed the tabernacle and its rituals of worship to symbolize deeper spiritual truth (Hebrews 9:8-9). The high priest, offering sacrifices for sin, prefigured the work of Jesus (Hebrews 8:1-3). The Holiest Place, the most inaccessible portion of the tabernacle, symbolized heaven and our ultimate destiny (Hebrews 8:1-2; 9:24).

◀◀ Law of Moses only temporary

◀ Old Testament symbols

This identification of the Holiest Place with heaven was only natural since the Old Testament alludes to God as enthroning Himself in the Holiest Place, above the ark of the covenant, while the New Testament pictures Him enthroned in heaven. The curtain that guarded entrance to the Holiest Place also had symbolic importance, Hebrews tells us. It foreshadowed our entrance into the throne room of God, made possible through the death of Jesus (Hebrews 10:19-20).

God the Son

In essence, everything God did in the Old Testament pointed toward Jesus and His work. Through promises, prophecies, and symbolism God used Old Testament events to foreshadow what Jesus would accomplish. The task of the New Testament, therefore, is to help us understand who Jesus is. It approaches its task in two ways.

➤ First, it explains the significance of Jesus by showing all the ways in which the Old Testament anticipated Him.

➤ Second, the New Testament unfolds truths about Him that God revealed only after Jesus appeared.

Jesus' role as Creator ➤➤

This second approach is especially prominent in the Letters. Like the Gospel of John, the Letters declare Jesus as originally divine. Philippians says that He was once an equal with God the Father (Philippians 2:5-6). But Jesus did not cling to His privileged position. Instead, He took on human form and assumed the role of a servant among men. Beyond that, He was obedient in all that God called on Him to do, even to the point of dying on the cross (Philippians 2:7-8).

In return, God raised Him from the dead and restored the full majesty of His divinity. God also exalted Him to have rule over the entire created order, so that ultimately every being will bow before Him, compelled to recognize Jesus as Lord (Philippians 2:9-11). That is why in Acts the apostles go everywhere proclaiming Jesus to be the resurrected Lord.

Jesus greater than the angels ➤➤

What Jesus did for us ➤➤

Two books, Colossians and Hebrews, depict the deity of Christ in magnificent imagery. Colossians celebrates Jesus as the visible expression of an invisible God, preeminent over every part of creation (Colossians 1:15).

➤ In Jesus all the fullness of deity took bodily form (Colossians 2:9). That is why Jesus could say to His disciples, "He who has seen me Has seen the Father" (John 14:9).

➤ In addition, He transcends all rulers and authorities in power (Colossians 2:10,15).

➤ Everything that was created, whether in heaven or earth, is the product of His initiative. And the entire creation holds together only because of His power (Colossians 1:16-18).

In similar language the first chapter of Hebrews portrays Jesus as:

➤ God's Son

➤ the one who created the world

➤ the radiance of God's glory

➤ an exact representation of God's nature

➤ seated at the right hand of God's majesty

➤ superior to the angels in every regard

Hebrews 2 then argues with equal power that Jesus was fully human when He lived on the earth. Here Jesus is pictured as:

➤ becoming inferior to the angels

➤ suffering

➤ sharing a common humanity with those He saves

➤ calling us His brothers and sisters

➤ partaking of flesh and blood

➤ experiencing death

➤ being made like us in every way

In a word, the first two chapters of Hebrews are the strongest affirmation in Scripture that Jesus combines the experience of being fully human with the essence of being fully divine.

As we have seen, many first-century Jews had difficulty believing in Jesus because He claimed to be divine. For first-century Greeks, however, the obstacle to faith was often the idea that He was once human. Many Greeks presumed that God would defile Himself by assuming a mortal, human body. As a consequence, some who otherwise believed in Jesus began to teach that He did not have a physical body when He was on earth. The apostle John calls these teachers "false prophets" (1 John 2:22; 4:1-2). From what we can determine, they were forerunners of a group that troubled the church for decades. They contended that Jesus was only a spiritual being, that He never became human. While He resembled a man, He was in fact like those angels in the Bible who occasionally assumed a human appearance.

John therefore began his first letter by pressing the point that he personally witnessed the humanity of Jesus. He was with Jesus repeatedly. Not only that, he touched Jesus with his own hands (1 John 1:1). John knows for a fact that the body of Jesus consisted of flesh, blood, and bone. Consequently, John does not hesitate to denounce anyone who contradicts this truth or who discounts Jesus as the Messiah. He identifies such notions with the antichrist (1 John 2:22; 4:3), a word which denotes a person or power that opposes Jesus.

<< Both God and man

Christ and Satan

In building the case for the humanity of Jesus, the book of Hebrews shows how His physical death was the way in which God overthrew Satan. In the Garden of Eden, God told Eve that one of her descendants would crush Satan's head, receiving a bruise to the heel in return (Genesis 3:15). The Bible says nothing more of this event until Hebrews 2. There we learn that in His death Jesus stripped Satan completely of his power (Hebrews 2:14-15).

But how could Jesus destroy Satan's power by dying? The key seems to be not so much what Jesus did directly to Satan, but what Jesus did for mankind in His death. So long as we fear death, the forces of evil can use that fear to intimidate and manipulate us. But by providing full forgiveness of sins, the death and resurrection of Jesus give us confidence that we possess eternal life. This confidence allows us to cast off the fear of dying, which gives us freedom to withstand any intimidation. The apostle Paul, speaking of the resurrection, words

< Freedom from fear of death gives power

it this way: "Death is swallowed up in victory. Death, where is your victory? Death, where is your sting?" And then he notes, "Thanks be to God who gives us the victory through the Lord Jesus Christ" (1 Corinthians 15:54-57).

Because the fear of death no longer grips us, Satan no longer has us in his power. His authority over us is destroyed. Like a serpent whose head is crushed (remember that Satan appeared in the Garden of Eden under the guise of a ser-

Genesis 3:15 illuminated >>

pent), Satan no longer endangers us. Nevertheless, Satan was able to inflict a death blow on Jesus. But because Jesus returned from the grave three days later, the blow was only temporary. It did no more lasting damage than a bruise to the heel, the kind of bruise one might receive in the process of stomping a serpent's head. At long last Hebrews 2 lets us understand the imagery of the crushed head and the bruised heel in Genesis 3:15.

The Cross: God's Secret Weapon

Ironically, John's Gospel tells us twice that it was Satan who enticed Judas to betray Jesus (John 13:2,27). In one regard, the cross was Satan's idea. Little did he know what God actually intended to achieve through the crucifixion. This may explain why God shrouded His plans and purposes with secrecy during the years of the Old Testament. By telling neither prophets nor angels the specifics of what Christ would do, God also hid His intentions from Satan.

Along these lines Paul speaks of God's hidden wisdom which was unknown to "the rulers of this age," a phrase that Paul and John use for Satan and his cohorts (John 12:31-33; 14:30). Paul goes on to say that if "the rulers of this age" had known God's hidden wisdom, "they would not have crucified the Lord of glory" (1 Corinthians 2:6-8). Had God revealed in advance what the death of Jesus would inflict upon Satan and his forces, they would have known that the cross was their undoing. Far from tempting Judas to betray Jesus, Satan would have worked to prevent the crucifixion.

Christ as High Priest

A vulnerable high priest >>

Even though the Bible describes Satan's blow to Jesus as a bruise on the heel, we must never minimize what Jesus suffered in His death. He went through all the pain and anguish that a tortured body can feel. In doing so, Hebrews says, He qualified Himself to be a perfect High Priest on our behalf (Hebrews 2:17). Under the Law of Moses high priests were chosen to intercede

with God on behalf of the people. Since high priests were subject to the same vulnerabilities as the people they served, they could represent the plight of their people sympathetically (Hebrew 5:1-2).

So it is with Christ. Having Himself suffered in the midst of His own trials, He can relate to us in our times of distress (Hebrew 2:18). The Letters therefore give us an image of Jesus appearing before God the

Father constantly to intercede on our behalf and to plead our case before His throne (Romans 8:34; Hebrews 7:25; 1 John 2:1).

God the Holy Spirit

The Holy Spirit joins Christ in this intercession. Romans 8:26-27 describes the Spirit as searching our hearts, identifying the longings for which we cannot find words, and expressing those feelings to God the Father. This is one of several key passages in the New Testament that ascribe attributes of deity and personality to the Holy Spirit.

When Jesus gave His final instructions to His apostles, He told them to take His message to all mankind, "baptizing them into the name of the Father, and of the Son, and of the Holy Spirit" (Matthew 28:19). He thus seemed to treat the Holy Spirit as distinct from, yet equal with Himself and the Father. We find similar language in Paul's benediction at the end of 2 Corinthians: "May the grace of the Lord Jesus Christ and the love of God and the fellowship of the Holy Spirit be with all of you" (2 Corinthians 13:14).

According to the New Testament, the Holy Spirit is a partner with God in carrying out the eternal purpose, which originated with God the Father. First, the Holy Spirit is the agent through which God guided the prophets, apostles, and others who wrote the Bible. During the last week of His life Jesus promised His apostles that the Holy Spirit would direct them into all truth (John 16:13).

In keeping with what Jesus said, the apostles later maintained that the Holy Spirit had imparted the truth they taught. This would parallel the way in which the Holy Spirit had previously led Old Testament prophets (2 Peter 1:20-21). Paul told the Corinthians that His message was not something he had personally invented or devised. Instead, he merely reported what the Spirit revealed to him (1 Corinthians 2:10-13). Elsewhere Paul claimed that it was the Spirit who disclosed God's eternal purpose to the apostles and early Christian prophets (Ephesians 3:4-5). And Peter, speaking from his own experience, confirmed that fact (1 Peter 1:10-12).

< The Holy Spirit teaches

Second, the Holy Spirit bestowed extraordinary power on the apostles, such as healing people instantly of various crippling diseases (Acts 5:12-16; 19:11-12). According to the book of Hebrews, the Holy Spirit gave them this ability in order to demonstrate that God was indeed behind their message (Hebrews 2:3-4)

< The Holy Spirit validates the message

Third, the Spirit strengthened the church by giving special skills and abilities to individual Christians (1 Corinthians 12:8-10). These gifts permitted newly planted churches to have the resources they needed to survive in a world that was often hostile to them.

< The Holy Spirit gives resources

The Holy Spirit
in partnership ➤

Three-in-one ➤➤
by analogy

Oneness of
purpose and
nature ➤➤

Fourth, the Holy Spirit forms a personal partnership with every Christian, so that the Spirit of God and the spirit of the believer are bound closely together. So close and personal is this bond that Paul calls it the "indwelling of the Spirit" (Romans 8:9-11). It is as though the Holy Spirit has taken up residence within us. On several occasions Paul refers to the Christian's body as a temple that houses the Holy Spirit (1 Corinthians 3:16; 6:19). Through this indwelling the Spirit gives Christians added resources in their pursuit of spiritual growth.

The Relationship of Father, Son, and Spirit

In summary, then, the New Testament affirms that the Father, the Son, and the Holy Spirit are three distinct manifestations of God. This does not mean that there are three Gods. Rather, God's Being reveals itself in three different expressions, each of them bearing the hallmarks of personality. Admittedly, this is a difficult concept to grasp. It is noteworthy moreover that clarifying the precise relationship between the Father, the Son, and the Holy Spirit never preoccupies the New Testament writers. When they address the subject at all, it is only in a passing phrase or two. As a result, Scripture never elaborates on how God can be three, yet One.

This leaves Christians with the challenge of working through that mystery for themselves. Most people who wrestle with this paradox usually propose some analogy to resolve it. They choose an analogy that compares God's nature to some other reality which itself has three distinct manifestations.

One such comparison invites us to look at a piece of fruit, such as an orange. On the outside the orange has a peel. Within the peel are first the fleshy sections of fruit, and then the seeds. The peel is not the entire orange, but it is entirely orange. The same can be said of the flesh and the seeds. They are entirely orange, but they are not the entire orange. Only when we have the peel, the flesh, and the seeds do we have the whole orange.

So it is with God. Jesus is not all the Deity that exists, but He is total Deity. There is nothing about Him (in His present, heavenly state) that is not God. He has the full essence of divinity within Him. In the same way, God the Father and God the Holy Spirit are totally divine. But neither of them, alone, embraces all there is to God's nature. Only when we have all three together do we have Deity in its completeness.

But if these three are recognizably separate, why do we speak of them in the singular? Why do we say there is one God? Because they act as an integrated whole, with one common nature, one will, one unifying purpose. Their beings are so tightly integrated, indeed, that the New Testament sometimes uses the terms "Spirit of God," "Spirit of Christ," and "Holy Spirit" interchangeably.

Yet, while all three are equals in essence, Christ and the Holy Spirit willingly subordinate themselves to the Father's leadership. The New Testament describes the Father as the head of Christ (1 Corinthians 11:3). And both Jesus and the Holy Spirit are pictured as sent by the Father to do their work on earth (John 8:42; 15:26; 16:4). The Holy Spirit further submits Himself to Jesus by serving always to glorify Christ (John 15:26).

We also see this subordination of Jesus in His prayer the night He died. He begged the Father to let Him forgo the crucifixion. But He ended His entreaty by saying, "Not My will, but Yours be done" (Matthew 26:42). We find another picture of His subordination in 1 Corinthians 15:24-28. There Paul tells us that Christ will continue to reign over His kingdom until everything in this world is subject to His rule. At that point He will deliver His kingdom back to the Father, from whom He received it, and subject Himself to the Father's sovereignty.

In conclusion, and at the risk of being far too simplistic, we might say that God the Father represents the ways in which Deity is totally different from us and from the created order. This is sometimes called the "transcendent" aspect of God's nature.

God the Son embodies the self-sacrificing element of God's character. In addition, His life on earth and His function as High Priest demonstrate the commonality that God has with us.

And the Holy Spirit, which Scripture normally portrays as working in the lives of individuals, represents the deep communion between the Divine Spirit and the human spirit. Through this communion God empowers mankind to transcend its past. In the chapters ahead, we will see how God calls us to better lives and how the Spirit works within us to make that better life a reality.

◄◄ Inter-relationships of Father, Son, and Spirit

Chapter Twenty-Four

SIN AND FORGIVENESS IN THE LETTERS

The New Testament teaches that every individual is born with an innate sense of right and wrong (Romans 1:20-32). Paul points out that there are certain human experiences — love, joy, peace, kindness, goodness, trustworthiness, gentleness, and self-discipline — that every society has recognized as proper. No one has ever passed a law against them (Galatians 5:22-23).

God's law highlights imperfections ➤➤

But if we inherently recognize that these things are right, then anything that works against them must be wrong. Thus, even without the benefit of the Bible, mankind recognizes that many types of behavior are wrong and inappropriate. Yet, no one uniformly pursues what is right. As the book of Romans says, "Everyone has sinned, falling short of the glory God intended for us" (Romans 3:23).

Man breaks innate standards ➤

Beyond that, sin becomes habitual. It traps us in its grip. Disclosing his own struggle with sin, Paul notes, "In my mind I agree with God's law and know it is right. But because of the habits that still control my body, I continue to do

Sin is a trap ➤

things that I no longer condone" (Romans 7:14-25).

When God gave His law to Israel, moreover, the awareness of sin intensified. Paul confesses that he never thought of himself as a covetous person until he heard the Ten Commandments say, "Do not covet!" When he started comparing his life to that standard, he discovered that he was coveting on every turn (Romans 7:7-11). God's law is thus like a straightedge. When laid alongside our lives, it reveals how much our moral and ethical conduct is out of line with God's standard. We become more conscious than ever of our problem with sin (Romans 3:20; 5:20).

The Gift of Righteousness

Sin cuts us off from God, for His holiness and purity cannot countenance wrongdoing. Recall the words of Habakkuk, which we visited in the last chapter: "Your eyes are too pure to approve evil, and You cannot look on wickedness with favor" (Habakkuk 1:13). To come before God with sin-infested lives is to feel His condemnation. We wither in His presence. Because of sin, spiritual death has settled on us. Or as Paul describes it, "Sin pays a wage, which is death" (Romans 6:23).

Left to our own resources, we cannot reverse this situation. Sin makes us lawbreakers, and we are powerless to remove our guilt. Through God's mercy, however, guilt can be overcome. God's solution is the person of Jesus Christ. Unlike the rest of mankind, Jesus did live a perfect life, conforming completely to God's law (Hebrews 4:14-16). God therefore chose to do two things with Him.

➤ First, God allowed the death of Jesus to substitute for the penalty of death that everyone incurs for sin. Romans sums this up with a simple but profound phrase, "While we were still sinners, Christ died for us" (Romans 5:8).

➤ Second, God allowed the perfect life of Jesus to be credited to those who follow Him.

Paul borrows language from the field of accounting to describe this process. His imagery brings to mind a great ledger book that contains a personal account for every person. When dealing with those who follow Jesus, God overwrites the misdeeds on their record with the perfect life of Jesus. In effect, the righteous life of Jesus is posted to their account (Romans 4:22-25).

His righteousness becomes their righteousness.

This explains what Jeremiah anticipated when he said the Messiah's people would wear the title "The Lord is our righteousness" (Jeremiah 33:16). Paul alludes to this transfer of righteousness when he tells the Philippians that he longs to be "found in Christ, not having a righteousness of my own, but the righteousness that is ours through faith in Christ, the righteousness that comes from God on the basis of faith" (Philippians 3:8). Romans calls this "the gift of righteousness" (Romans 5:17).

‹‹ Consequences of sin

Justification

To depict the transfer of righteousness from Jesus to us, the New Testament uses the concept of justification. Justification is the process of aligning something with a standard. When a printer justifies a page of type, he forces every line to conform to a set length, a set standard. Similarly, when God justifies us, He makes our lives align with the standard of His law. And He does so by applying the righteousness of Christ to our account.

‹‹ Jesus Christ pays the price

In addition, He does not justify us as repayment for something good we have done. Instead, justification is a gift that flows from His kindness and grace (Romans 3:24; Ephesians 2:4-8). God promises to justify everyone who places faith in Jesus (Romans 3:26). Once justified, we stand before God uncondemned,

‹ A free gift from God

for sin no longer appears on our account. To borrow Paul's words again, "There is no condemnation for those who are in Christ Jesus" (Romans 8:1). Thus, being free from condemnation, those who are in Christ can approach God with confidence (Romans 8:14-16).

Chronicles of faith >>

Life in Christ — A Life of Faith

Since these blessings come to those who are in Christ, what does it mean to be "in Christ"? Basically it means that we yield our entire being to His will. Writing to the Galatians, Paul describes his own life in Jesus by saying, "I have been crucified with Christ, so that in a sense I no longer live. Instead, Christ lives in me" (Galatians 2:20).

Submitting to Christ >

To yield ourselves entirely to Jesus is to put complete trust in Him and His word. The Biblical name for such trust is "faith." Because faith is essential to being in Christ, the Letters always give priority to clarifying the meaning of faith. Hebrews 11, sometimes called "the faith chapter of the Bible," offers the most thorough assessment of faith found anywhere in Scripture.

Faith defined >

The chapter begins by defining faith as the conviction that undergirds whatever we hope for. This conviction, moreover, is based on evidence of what is unseen. As an example of faith in the unseen, the author points to the creation. "By faith we understand that the universe took shape at God's command, so that what we see was not

made from what was visible" (Hebrews 11:1-3).

Next the author chronicles the lives of great men and women in the Old Testament, people whose faith undergirded their achievements: Abel, Abraham, Sarah, Isaac, Jacob, Joseph, and Moses, just to name a few. These individuals all stand as a circle of witnesses, the writer says, testifying to the blessings that come from a consistent life of faith. Encouraged by their example, believers should fix their attention on Jesus, rid themselves of sin, wait patiently for God to fulfill His promises, and prepare themselves to endure any kind of opposition that may come because of their faith (Hebrews 12:1-3).

Abraham's Exemplary Faith

The Letters often explain faith by drawing on the life of Abraham. Three Letters — Romans, James, and Galatians — call attention to pivotal moments in Abraham's life as stellar examples of faith.

In Romans Paul takes us back to the moment when Abraham, old and childless, was told that he would have countless offspring (Romans 4:1-3). Such a thing seemed improbable, if not impossible. Still, Abraham took God at His word (Romans 4:18-22). Genesis tells us, "Abraham believed God, and God counted his belief as righteousness" (Genesis 15:6). This is the essence of faith. To trust God, to believe in Him, even when what

He says exceeds the imagination.

Because Abraham had that kind of faith, God treated him as a righteous man. This is another way of saying that God justified him. In Greek, the original language of Paul's writings, "righteous" and "justify" are two forms of the same word. It is easy to see the connection between the two when we consider that

➤ a righteous person is one who lives according to God's law, and

➤ justification is the process of bringing a life back in line with God's law.

Thus, a person who is justified is treated as righteous.

As for Abraham's righteousness, it was not based on how well he knew God's law, for he lived centuries before the Law of Moses. Nor was he righteous because he performed some religious ceremony, like circumcision. Years would pass before Abraham was circumcised (Romans 4:9-13). No, God treated Abraham as righteous solely because he demonstrated such faith.

This is the same way that God makes us righteous, as Paul plainly states in Romans 4. It is never because of something we are able to do. We can never do enough good deeds to earn the title "righteous." As with Abraham, God treats us as righteous on the basis of our trust in Him, our faith.

The book of James gives us another perspective on Abraham's faith. James makes the point that genuine faith always has a visible impact on behavior. After all, the only way to demonstrate faith is through some type of action (James 2:17-18). Faith that produces no action, James says, is just as dead as a body that has no spirit (James 2:26). He cites Abraham's faith that led him to sacrifice his son Isaac. In that act Abraham's faith came to full completion, James declares. He then adds, "You see from this that a person is justified by what he does and not by faith alone" (James 2:21-24).

◄ Faith impacts behavior

Contrary to first appearances, this statement does not contradict Paul, who said that we are justified by faith. James is simply amplifying Paul's definition of faith, so that we have a fuller picture of what it entails.

James wants to emphasize that mere belief in God is not the same as faith. Even demons believe that God exists, James notes (James 1:19). Not only that, the demons recognize Jesus as the Son of God, for when He encounters them in the Gospels, they hail Him as God's Holy One (Mark 1:24). If mere belief constitutes faith, then, the demons have faith. Yet their continued rebellion against God shows their lack of faith. Faith, unlike mere belief, always has an impact on behavior.

◄ Faith is more than belief

◄◄ God treats faith as righteousness

In Galatians 3 we again encounter Abraham's exemplary

Promises to
Abraham fulfilled ➤

Baptism as death,
burial, and
resurrection ➤➤

Children of
Abraham ➤

Separating from
sin ➤➤

faith. There Paul makes the unequiv-
ocal statement that Jesus is the fulfillment of the promises made to
Abraham (Galatians 3:16). When
God told Abraham, "All nations will
be blessed through you," He was
looking ahead to the day when
Gentiles and Jews alike would be
justified by faith (Galatians 3:7-9).

Later Paul adds that anyone who
belongs to Christ is counted among
the numberless offspring promised
to Abraham. They receive the blessings promised to Abraham's
descendants (Galatians 3:26-29).
They are children of Abraham, not
by physical descent (as with the
Jews), but by spiritual descent, as
people who have the same kind of
faith in God that Abraham did
(Galatians 3:7). As Abraham's children, they benefit equally in the
promise made to him, without
regard to race, gender, or social
status. "There is no longer Jew nor
Gentile, slave nor free man, male
nor female," Paul concludes, "for
you are all one in Christ Jesus"
(Galatians 3:28).

Baptism

In explaining how they came to
be counted among Abraham's
descendants, Paul points to their
baptism. They were "baptized into
Christ," so that they "put on Christ
like a cloak or garment (Galatians
3:26-27). They had clothed themselves with Christ. Their identity
was lost in His. They were one
with Him.

Putting on Christ ➤

Using a different set of meta-
phors, Romans says that baptism
unites the believer symbolically with
Christ's death. Baptism is a symbolic crucifixion of our former life
with its attachment to sin (Romans
6:3-6). That is why Paul says to the
Colossians, "You have died and
your life is cloaked with Christ in
God" (Colossians 3:3)

Additionally, baptism is a fore-
taste of our resurrection. Paul tells
the Romans, "If we have become
united with Jesus in a death like His,
we shall just as surely share in a resurrection like His" (Romans 6:5).
Put simply, being in Christ translates
into eternity with God.

Because baptism denotes a decision to separate ourselves from sin,
Peter compares baptism to the
experience of Noah in the flood.
The flood waters separated Noah's
family from their sinful neighbors
who perished. In a similar way, baptism now saves us, Peter observes
(1 Peter 3:21). Baptism demonstrates our determination to distance ourselves from sin. In
response, God grants us safety from
punishment for sin, just as Noah
was kept safe from God's punishment of his neighbors.

Yet baptism alone is not what
affords such protection. What God
honors in baptism is the faith that
leads to it. To quote from Paul's language to the Galatians, "We are all
sons of God through faith in Christ
Jesus, because all of you who were
baptized into Christ have clothed

yourselves with Christ" (Galatians 3:26-27). To the Colossians he wrote, "Having been buried with Him in baptism, you were also raised up with Him through your faith in the working of God, who raised Him from the dead" (Colossians 2:12).

Peter makes this same point in comparing baptism to Noah's flood. The saving power of baptism is not the physical washing of our bodies, he says, but the appeal we make to God out of a conscience that trusts in the resurrection of Jesus (1 Peter 3:21).

The Resurrection

As you can see, baptism and the resurrection often appear side by side in the Letters. Baptism looks back to the resurrection of Jesus and forward to the resurrection of His followers. Repeatedly the New Testament reminds its readers not to lose sight of their resurrection. Paul tells the Philippians,

> We eagerly await for our Savior, the Lord Jesus Christ, to appear from heaven and to transform the body of our present humble state so that we will have a body that conforms with the glory of His own.   — Philippians 3:20-21

In a similar vein he writes to the Colossians, saying, "When Christ, who is your life, is revealed from heaven, then you will also be revealed with Him in glory" (Colossians 3:4).

It therefore shocked Paul deeply when he learned that some

Christians in Corinth were teaching that there is no resurrection. He responded with an immediate refutation, opening with these words:

> When I preached the gospel to you, I emphasized matters of first importance. First, that Christ died for our sins, just as Scripture had foretold, and was buried. Second, that He was raised on the third day, again in keeping with what Scripture had said.
>   — 1 Corinthians 15:1-3

≪≪ How baptism contributes to salvation

In Paul's estimation, to deny the resurrection is to deny the core of the gospel. The resurrection, he says, declared Jesus to be the Son of God (Romans 1:1-4). If Christ was not raised, then that declaration never occurred and our faith has no value (1 Corinthians 15:16-17). We have put our trust in an imposter. Moreover, it would be foolish to undergo persecution as a Christian. Why accept pain and suffering for believing in Jesus if there is no hope of the resurrection (1 Corinthians 15:19)?

≪ Resurrection, the core of the gospel

In 1 Corinthians 15, the longest chapter on the resurrection in the Bible, we find the fullest description of our own resurrection. Paul pictures it as a moment when our personal spirits become clothed in a new, immortal body, unlike the perishable body that we now inhabit (1 Corinthians 15:41-54). This change will happen instantaneously, in the "twinkling of an eye." This will occur when Jesus returns to earth. At His appearance "those who have fallen asleep" (Paul's phrase for the dead) will immediately be brought back to life (1 Corinthians 15:20-23). With their awakening, the ultimate victory over death will be achieved (1 Corinthians 15:54-57). At the same time, those who are alive when Christ returns will be gathered directly to Him, bypassing death (1 Thessalonians 4:14-17).

Nature of existence after resurrection >>

Paul's second letter to the Corinthians also plays on the theme of the resurrection. He compares our current physical body to a tent which is easily struck down. Or to a clay vessel, easily shattered. By contrast, at the resurrection we will receive a more splendid body, a permanent building, not a flimsy tent. What we long for, Paul says, is to set our tent aside and take up residence in our permanent dwelling, the very purpose for which God prepared us (2 Corinthians 4:6-7; 5:1-5).

The New Testament is never specific about the precise change we will undergo in the resurrection, other than to say that our existence will become more glorious and our nature imperishable. John suggests that we have no way of foreseeing what we will be like after the resurrection. But he assures us that we will have much in common with the resurrected Jesus (1 John 3:2). And this is the hope that has sustained Christians for centuries.

Righteousness   Wages
    Justification   of Sin

Resurrection   Life in Christ

Faith   Forgiveness   Baptism

    Abraham

Chapter Twenty-Five

MORALS AND ETHICS IN THE LETTERS

In the Bible, ethics and morality are drawn from the nature of God's character. He is good, absolutely good, so pure that evil cannot tempt Him (James 1:13). Furthermore, His goodness permits Him to will only what is best for His people. He therefore wills that we become like Him in terms of virtue and integrity.

Many words could describe God's character: just, truthful, loving, compassionate, trustworthy, merciful, to name only a few. But the Bible sums them up in one word — He is "holy." And because He is holy, He is also the ideal of goodness and love. Anything less than perfect goodness and love would compromise His holiness.

Consequently, when God appeals to His people to become like Himself, He enjoins them to be holy. Speaking to Israel through Moses, He decrees, "You must be holy, because I am holy" (Leviticus 11:44). The New Testament extends this injunction to Christians. Peter writes, "Since He who called you is holy, be holy yourselves in all your conduct" (1 Peter 1:15-16).

For God's people personal holiness means separating themselves from whatever is corrupt or immoral in the world around them. Another word for holiness is "sanctification." "God called you to sanctification," Paul tells the Thessalonians, "not to lives of impurity" (1 Thessalonians 4:7).

Elsewhere Paul notes that the Romans were called to be "saints," which literally means "holy people" (Romans 1:7). The New Testament treats every follower of Jesus as a saint, a "holy person." (See Acts 9:13 and Acts 26:10, for example.) In fact, "saints" is the most common name for Christians in the New Testament. Through its preference for this term, the Bible constantly reminds Christians to be holy in all they undertake.

To that end, the Letters use every opportunity to promote lives of integrity and personal morality. The Letters hold up Jesus as an example for Christians to imitate (1 Corinthians 11:1). Because He embodied the essence of Deity in human form, Jesus exemplifies what human

<< God's character

<< Our character to reflect His

personality looks like when stamped with God's holiness.

Battling "the Flesh" and "Darkness"

The Letters recognize, however, that becoming Christlike is a life-long endeavor. Being justified does not mean that sin no longer troubles us. We still struggle against its influence. Paul describes the ongoing struggle with sin as a war between two powerful forces. On one side is God's Spirit, communicating with our own spirit and prompting us to live as godly people. On the other side are the habits and impulses that sin engenders within us. The New Testament gives a collective name to these drives. It calls them "the flesh."

The flesh promotes self-indulgence and self-gratification. It takes bodily appetites to excess. In Galatians, Paul catalogs the types of behavior that the flesh produces. His list includes sexual immorality, impurity, unrestrained pleasure-seeking, idolatry, witchcraft, hatred, fits of rage, selfish ambition, jealousy, envy, strife, drunkenness, and wild parties (Galatians 5:19-21). A mind set on such values is hostile toward God, Paul says, unwilling to submit to God's law. Anyone who lives that way cannot please God or be part of His kingdom (Romans 8:5-11; Galatians 5:21).

The flesh is part of a larger world known in the New Testament as "darkness." This term traces back to

Activities of the flesh ➤

Light vs. darkness ➤

Isaiah, who foretold the Messiah's work by saying, "Those who dwell in darkness will see a great light" (Isaiah 9:2). In the New Testament to live in darkness is to love sin more than God (John 3:19-20). Living in darkness can also refer (as it does in Luke 1:79) to those who have simply never learned of Christ.

The realm of darkness embraces everything that is opposed to God. It is controlled by spiritual forces in the service of Satan (Ephesians 6:12). By contrast, those who are Christians are "children of light" (Ephesians 5:8-11). They have been delivered from the "dominion of darkness and transferred into the kingdom of God's beloved Son" (Colossians 1:13).

Overcoming the World

Peter reminds his readers that they have been "called out of darkness into God's marvelous light" (1 Peter 2:9). That makes it essential for them to restrain the desires of "the flesh," which war against their inner spirit (1 Peter 2:11). John adds that "God is light, and there is no darkness in Him at all." Therefore, it is impossible to walk in darkness and be in partnership with God at the same time (1 John 1:5-6).

For the apostle John, to "walk in darkness" can also be expressed as "loving the world." "The world" is John's name for cravings that pass away when the earth comes to an end (1 John 2:17). These include the drives and appetites of the body, the desire to possess things that catch the fancy of our eye, and arrogant pride (1 John 2:16). When these impulses go unrestrained, they inevitably lead to sin.

Of course, no one can ignore appetites and desires completely. And John is not suggesting that we should. He knows that God placed appetites and cravings in the human body for good. But God never intended for appetites to control us. When finding pleasure becomes more important than living a principled life, when satisfying physical drives and desires takes precedence over being a person of character, we have become people (to use John's words) who "love the world."

The goal for Christians is to *overcome* the world, not *love* it (1 John 5:4). The habits of sin and the enticements of pleasure exert a strong hold on us. When we become Christians, sinful habits and attitudes do not immediately relinquish their grip, as we noted above. We have to overcome them.

Indeed, John says that we are only deceiving ourselves if we claim that we have no sin. What walking in the light requires is a *determined commitment* to overcome the problem of sin. God then honors that determination by forgiving our sins when they do occur. As John puts it, if we walk in God's light, the blood of Jesus continually cleanses us from sin (1 John 1:8).

God grants this cleansing to encourage us. He does not want us to fear that all is lost simply because old habits draw us into things that are wrong. God wants the cause of righteousness to prevail. He wants to see us living sin-free lives (1 John 2:1). And so long as we genuinely work toward that goal, He readily lends His encouragement. He only asks us to be honest about our problem with sin. John writes assuringly, "If we confess our sins, God, being righteous Himself, is faithful to forgive our sins and to cleanse us from all unrighteousness" (1 John 1:9).

God's Indwelling Spirit

To help Christians live sinlessly, God places His Spirit within the believer. (This is the Spirit's "indwelling" that we reviewed in chapter 23.) The Spirit becomes our ally and source of strength in the war with the flesh. At every turn the Spirit urges us to live properly. When we follow those urgings, the New Testament describes us as "walking by the Spirit" or being "led by the Spirit." And if we are led by the Spirit, Paul writes, we will not let the flesh dominate our behavior (Galatians 5:16-18). Galatians describes the qualities of a Spirit-led life as love, joy, peace, patience, kindness, goodness, faithfulness, gentleness, and self-control. Paul labels these "the fruit of the Spirit" (Galatians 5:22-23).

The Spirit does not slavishly control us, however. We can suppress His urgings. Paul depicts this as

◄ A help to live sin-free

◄ Fruit of the Spirit

Freedom of choice ➤

"quenching the Spirit" (1 Thessalonians 5:19). God never does anything to deprive us of our freedom to choose. His Spirit forms a voluntary partnership with us. But we can reject that partnership, even as Christians, and opt for what is evil.

Imitators of God ➤➤

Nor does the Spirit transform our lives overnight. Learning to be like Jesus is a growth process. The New Testament refers to new Christians as "babes in Christ" (1 Corinthians 3:1; Hebrews 5:13). They need to develop and mature spiritually.

Godly family relationships ➤➤

Maturity involves a transformation of our ego and sense of self. Borrowing the imagery of changing garments, Paul tells the Ephesians that they must take off "the old self" and fully clothe themselves with "the new self" (Ephesians 4:22-24). The old self had a darkened understanding of God and was separated from life in Him. For the Ephesians, many from Gentile backgrounds, the old self had included pleasure-seeking that became so addictive that they greedily pursued every kind of impurity (Ephesians 4:17-19).

The new self, by contrast, aspires to have a godly outlook on life. It concerns itself with the pursuit of righteousness, holiness, and truth.

➤ As a consequence, the new self is known for its integrity, resisting the temptation to lie or deceive.

➤ It is trustworthy, forgoing anything that would constitute stealing.

➤ And the new self also learns to manage anger, never allowing bitterness and resentment to get out of control or to stir up evil impulses (Ephesians 4:20-32).

Walking in Love

Paul summarizes the lifestyle he wants for the Ephesians with these words: "Be imitators of God, as children He loves, and walk in love, just as Christ also loved you and gave Himself up for us" (Ephesians 5:1). He then applies the principle of walking in love to specific situations in daily life.

➤ Husbands are to be as loving and self-sacrificing toward their wives as Jesus was toward the church (Ephesians 5:25-29).

➤ Wives are to reciprocate by yielding to the loving leadership of their husbands (Ephesians 5:22-24).

➤ Children are to be obedient and treat their parents with honor (Ephesians 6:1-4).

Walking in love thus requires us to subordinate self-interest to the needs of others. In this, as in so many other areas of Christian service, Jesus is our example. Paul encourages the Philippians to have the same attitude personally that Jesus demonstrated when He gave up His deity, with all of its privilege, to take on human form (Philippians 2:5-8). "Do nothing from selfishness or conceit," Paul tells them. "Instead, treat others as more important than yourself. Watch out for their interests, not just your own" (Philippians 2:3-4).

Peter, too, emphasizes the need to control self-serving impulses, especially in the face of sneers and insults. He addresses his first letter to Christians in Asia Minor, many of them Gentiles who had formerly indulged every pagan vice (1 Peter 4:3). But now they have turned their back on such things.

Having rejected the habits of their former life, Peter invites them to view themselves as visitors to a foreign land (1 Peter 1:1; 2:11). That is, they should treat many of the things they once did as now foreign to their nature. This will not be well received by their peers, Peter admits. He acknowledges that these Christians are being ridiculed and belittled by friends with whom they once socialized (1 Peter 4:4). Yet, this is part of the price to be true to Christ.

Peter then holds up the example of Jesus to illustrate how Christians should react to abuse and ridicule. When Jesus was insulted, He did not retaliate. When He was suffering, He did not respond with threats (1 Peter 2:21-23). And Christians should follow His pattern as their ideal. Peter even applies this principle to relationships in which it would be difficult to sustain a Christlike attitude.

First, he talks about slaves who are owned by a difficult, mean-spirited master. (Over half of the Roman population was in slavery.)

Slaves should treat such masters with respect, Peter says, knowing that God will reward the person who bears up under pain and unjust treatment (1 Peter 2:18-20).

Second, Peter discusses women whose husbands reject Jesus. Such a woman should not use her husband's disbelief as an excuse for being disrespectful toward him. To the contrary, a Christian wife in such circumstances should conduct herself so properly that she wins her husband to Jesus by the power of her example (1 Peter 3:1-4).

Being Born Again

These are, of course, remarkable attitudes for someone to have, especially in the specific situations that Peter cites. Such attitudes are possible, however, because of the change that takes place when a person becomes a Christian. Peter describes this change as being "born again," a term borrowed from Jesus, who used it in a conversation with Nicodemus, a leader of the Jewish Sanhedrin. "To see the kingdom of God," Jesus told him, "you must be born again" (John 3:3-7).

Perhaps Peter overheard their conversation and was struck by the phrase. In any event, it became a part of his vocabulary. In his first letter he writes, "God has caused you to be born again to a living hope by means of the resurrection of Jesus" (1 Peter 1:3). Later he adds, "You have been born again through the influence of God's

◄ Christ transforms us

living and enduring word." Returning to word pictures from Jesus in the parable of the sower, Peter portrays God's "enduring word" as seed that does not perish (1 Peter 1:23-25).

All believers are priests >>

As a figure of speech, being born again highlights the fact that becoming a Christian leads to sweeping change. In one sense an entirely new person emerges. This new person has different goals, different attitudes, and different outlooks on life. Yet, for all of these differences, there is still much to learn. Peter therefore refers to people at this stage of faith as newborn babes. Having been born again through the power of God's word, they need to continue to hunger for that word. By nourishing themselves on God's word, they will grow to maturity in Christ (1 Peter 2:1-3).

Priests must be pure >>

Marks of spiritual maturity >

In his second letter Peter identifies seven traits of spiritually mature people, namely

➤ moral excellence

➤ a deep knowledge of God

➤ self-control

➤ perseverance

➤ a godly outlook

➤ kindness

➤ love

By steadily strengthening these qualities, we ensure that we will always be useful to God and fruitful in His service (1 Peter 1:4-10).

One objective in becoming mature is to proclaim God's excellence to others. Peter tells his readers that in calling them to be His people, God has also made them His new priesthood (1 Peter 2:9-12). Unlike Israel, where only men from one tribe could be priests, every person in Christ is a priest before God, both men and women alike.

And with this priestly calling comes another demand to maintain lives of purity. Priests in Israel could not come before God defiled. Likewise, Peter begs his readers to abstain from sinful desires (1 Peter 2:11). He encourages them to master a Christlike spirit, so that they do not return evil for evil or insult for insult. Instead, as priests, they should use their lives to bless people, even people who mistreat them (1 Peter 3:9).

Prepared to Suffer

Peter has a purpose in raising the subject of mistreatment. He knows that difficult days lie ahead for these Christians. He refers to an approaching "fiery ordeal" that will cause them to share in the sufferings of Christ (1 Peter 4:12-13). This came about a short time later when fierce persecution broke out against Christians all across Asia Minor.

To prepare them for that day, Peter coaches his readers to develop a proper perspective on suffering by doing two things. First, they should keep in mind that Jesus also suffered. Thus, the fact that difficult times come upon them are no sign that they have lost God's approval or blessing. Peter brings up the suffering of Jesus six different times in 1 Peter, saying on one of these occasions, "Since Christ suffered during his humanity, arm yourselves for the same purpose" (1 Peter 4:1).

Second, they are to keep their focus on the reward that awaits them personally when Jesus returns. They will have praise, glory, and honor when Jesus reveals Himself (1 Peter 1:7). In the meantime they should anchor their hope entirely on the reward they will receive at Christ's appearing (1 Peter 1:13). "You were called for this very purpose," Peter assures them, "so that you might inherit a blessing" (1 Peter 3:9).

This passage from Peter follows a pattern that is characteristic of the New Testament Letters. That is, they routinely tie exhortations to live a principled life to reminders of eventual reward. That is why the Letters with the strongest moral tone also tend to include unqualified assurance of Christ's return, the resurrection of His followers, and eternal life.

Christians soon learn, however, that they do not have to wait for Jesus to come in order to experience reward. There is an indescribable peace and joy that comes from a life of principle and integrity. Knowing that we have done what is right, even in times of duress, gives a sense of fulfillment that those who live in darkness can never comprehend.

◄ Peace and joy in holiness

Saints

Integrity

Paul

Self-control

Sanctification

Priests

The Flesh

Peter

Love

Light vs. Darkness

Holy Spirit

Overcoming

Chapter Twenty-Six

THE CHURCH AND WORSHIP IN THE LETTERS

Just as Christians are individually accountable to God, they also have specific obligations toward other Christians. The Bible normally expresses these responsibilities in terms of relationships within the church. From the perspective of the New Testament, being a Christian and being a member of the church are inseparable.

The Church as the Body of Christ

Paul loves to compare the church to a body, with Jesus Himself as its head, so that the church answers to Christ in everything (Ephesians 1:22-23; 5:23-24; Colossians 1:18,24). As a spiritual body the church carries on the task that Jesus began in His physical body. Individual Christians are the joints and ligaments that hold the body together, each one contributing to the growth and well-being of the whole (Ephesians 4:14-16). Or viewed another way, Christians are the arms and legs to accomplish Christ's work in the world about them.

Just as a human body must have a spirit within it to be alive, so also the Holy Spirit must be present for the church, the body of Christ, to thrive. The Spirit begins this work at the very moment a member is added to the body of Christ. "By means of one Spirit we were all baptized into the one body," Paul writes (1 Corinthians 12:13). Thus, when Paul considers the inherent oneness God intended for the church, he calls it "the unity of the Spirit" (Ephesians 4:3).

In both Romans and 1 Corinthians, Paul shows how the Spirit also empowers the church by giving special abilities to individual members. At Corinth some received the power to perform miracles. Others had the gift to teach with exceptional insight or to excel in helping people or to be good administrators. Still another group was able to speak languages they had never studied, an obvious aid to preaching in an international city like Corinth (1 Corinthians 12:8-10).

The Spirit placed such gifts in the church for the common good

Every Christian gifted >>

Every Christian necessary >

(1 Corinthians 12:7), since each gift contributed uniquely to the well-being of the church. Christians have a duty to use their blessings and abilities to benefit one another and the church. As in a physical body, every part plays an essential role if the body is to be healthy and vibrant (Romans 12:3-8; 1 Corinthians 12:14-28).

For that reason, Paul tirelessly warns about rivalries and divisions that would undercut the effectiveness of the church. One purpose for writing the book of 1 Corinthians was to deal with reports that the Christians there had broken into warring camps (1 Corinthians 1:10-12; 11:18-19). Much of their division, it turns out, was over who had received the greatest gift from the Spirit. Paul rebukes such boasting. The Spirit's gifts were given to exalt Jesus and to promote the common good (1 Corinthians 12:7), not to exalt oneself and promote ego-fed competition.

Division in the church is the exact opposite of God's design, as we learn from Ephesians. There Paul offers a majestic sketch of God's eternal purpose and the role of the church within it. God's purpose, framed before the creation of the world, centered on reconciliation and peace. Through the cross God planned to reconcile all people to Himself, bringing them together in one body, the church (Ephesians 2:11-17).

Within this body every individual has unhampered access to God through the Holy Spirit, regardless of ethnic or social background (Ephesians 2:18). The body is also the place where God overcomes alienation and animosity between people. By reconciling warring parties to Himself, God seeks to reconcile them to one another as well. God's goal for the body is to bring an end to racial strife, class conflict, and ethnic tension (Ephesians 2:11-19). This is why the prophets pictured the age of the kingdom as an era of peace.

<< Problems of division

The church, God's body of reconciled people, was thus vital to God's plan from the very beginning. In Ephesians, Paul cannot talk about God's eternal purpose without talking about the church. In fact, Ephesians brings the concept of the church to its highest stage of development in the New Testament.

Turning to a different set of images, Paul portrays the church as the bride of Christ. Jesus, the bridegroom, loves her so much that He was willing to die for her. And the aim of His love is to present the church in "all her glory, without stain or wrinkle or any kind of blemish, so that she is holy and blameless in character" (Ephesians 5:25-27). Beyond that, Paul views God as having set the church, His Son's bride, on cosmic display. Through the church, he says, God is demonstrating to principalities and powers in heavenly places (that is, the angels) the vast wisdom of His eternal purpose (Ephesians 3:10-11).

<< God's purpose – reconciliation

Signs of a Healthy Church

Mutual contributions **>>**

Unity **>**

Since the church plays such a pivotal role in God's scheme of things, it is essential for the church to be healthy. In Ephesians 4 Paul cites several factors that foster spiritual health in the body of Christ. First, *a healthy church is a united church*. The entire life of the church is built around oneness, Paul says. "There is one body and one Spirit, just as God called you to one hope. Likewise, there is one Lord, one faith, one baptism, one God and Father of all, who is over all and through all and in all" (Ephesians 4:2-4). For that reason Paul appeals to the Ephesians to maintain the unity which God had in mind when He reconciled them and gave them His Spirit.

Respect **>**

Second, *a healthy church is one in which there is lasting, mutual respect*. In the interest of unity the Ephesians are to deal with each other in humility, gentleness, patience, and love (Ephesians 4:2). Their duty is to make the church as strong and as loving as possible. They are to show kindness and compassion to one another, being always ready to forgive each other, just as God has forgiven them (Ephesians 4:32).

Spiritual maturity **>**

Third, *a healthy church is one in which each member is seeking personal spiritual maturity*. Paul notes that God put various types of teachers in the church in order to help members mature. The teaching objective of the church is to see that believers grow into spiritual adulthood, attaining the stature that marks maturity in Christ (Ephesians 4:11-15).

And fourth, *a healthy church is one in which each person contributes his or her strengths and abilities to the well-being of the whole*. Christians have an inescapable duty to the church and to one another. Only when they fulfill their individual roles can the body grow and build itself up (Ephesians 4:15-16).

Healthy Teaching

To be healthy the church also needs proper teaching and good leadership. Those are subjects that form the heart of Paul's letters to Timothy and Titus. In writing to both of them, Paul insists that they resist any teacher who works against the interest of spiritual growth and health. This includes teachers who are argumentative, seemingly bent on stirring up controversy and promoting pointless speculation (1 Timothy 1:3-7; 6:3-4; 2 Timothy 2:14-18). Also to be stopped are certain teachers whom Paul calls "rebellious deceivers" who are teaching things that are improper, all for the sake of dishonest gain (Titus 1:10-11). This implies that they had found a way to make money from their teaching and would say anything, just to hold an income.

In contrast, Timothy and Titus are to teach in a way that maximizes health. Paul charges Timothy with proving himself accomplished at handling God's word accurately. Whatever the occasion, he is to be ready to offer correction, rebuke, and encouragement based on Scripture (2 Timothy 2:16). Similarly, Paul instructs Titus to treat God's truth seriously, always maintaining integrity in what he teaches (Titus 2:7).

Paul even spells out for Titus what his teaching should emphasize. The list centers on practical matters, having to do with personal character and conduct (Titus 2:1-10).

➤ Titus should teach older men to maintain balanced, respectable lives of self-control and faith.

➤ He should instruct older women to be reverent, speaking only what is good, avoiding gossip and shunning addiction to alcohol.

➤ Young women should learn how to love their mates and their children and how to be pure and kind.

➤ And all younger adults, men and women alike, should be taught the art of self-control.

Leadership

From these remarks it is obvious that character training was a prime concern for the early church. For that reason church leaders were held to exacting personal standards. They were to embody what the church stood for ethically, since they served as role models for newer Christians (Titus 2:7-8; 1 Peter 5:1-3).

In 1 Timothy and Titus, Paul pays special attention to the appointment of church leaders, particularly elders and deacons. In every city Paul established a council of men called elders to guide the affairs of the Christian community (Acts 14:23; Titus 1:5). Because they had oversight of the church, they were also called bishops, from a Greek word for "overseer" (Titus 1:7). The deacons seem to have been their assistants.

The New Testament says little about the specific duties of elders, but they were apparently charged with the overall well-being of the church. Years after Timothy's work in Ephesus, Paul instructed the elders of that city to be on the alert for dangers to their people, especially from teachers who would lead the church astray. Paul compared their congregation to a flock of sheep and the elders to shepherds (Acts 20:28-30). From this imagery came the practice of referring to elders as pastors (1 Peter 5:1-2).

The New Testament requires that elders be proven family men, with an exemplary home life and a single-minded dedication to their wives. The community is to know them for their integrity, gentleness, respectability, and self-control. Drunkenness disqualifies a man, as does a penchant for greed or quarreling (1 Timothy 3:2-7; Titus 1:6-7).

◄ Duties of elders

◄ Moral standards for elders

◄◄ Character training vital

They must have demonstrated that they hold firmly to the message of Christ. And they must be skilled in using Scripture in a healthy way, especially to encourage others and to refute false teachings (Titus 1:9).

Alongside these elders Paul encouraged Timothy to appoint deacons. Again we lack specific details about how deacons functioned. But the name "deacon" comes from a Greek word meaning "a servant," which suggests that they were special servants of the church.

While the standards for deacons are not so exacting as the ones for elders, deacons should also be exceptional people. They are to be respectable and sincere, holding to Christian truth with a clear conscience. As with elders, deacons should not be known as people who have a problem with alcohol or who show the least dishonesty in business. And again like elders, they are to be respected for their strong, healthy families (1 Timothy 3:8-12).

Worship

Another essential for a healthy church is vibrant worship. Early Christian worship consisted of praying together, singing songs that praised God, hearing Scripture read, listening to explanations of God's word, and sharing the Lord's Supper together.

Our deepest insight into the ideals of Christian worship comes from Paul's first letter to the Corinthians. They had allowed their

worship to degenerate to the point that Paul felt compelled to correct their behavior. They had subverted their worship by turning it into a time to call attention to themselves. Various worshipers were showing off their gifts from the Spirit, trying to prove that they had a better gift than anyone else. Their worship had become self-centered rather than God-centered, self-serving rather than meeting the needs of the body.

To correct this problem, Paul devotes an entire chapter to the subject of worship. He lays out specific guidelines that should govern times when Christians worship together. His guidelines basically reduce to two principles.

➤ First, everything should be orderly and done with appropriate reverence (1 Corinthians 14:40).

➤ And second, worship should include only those things that serve to encourage and build up every person present (1 Corinthians 14:26).

The Lord's Supper

To highlight the purpose of worship, Paul directs their attention to the Lord's Supper with its symbols of unleavened bread and wine. "We are all one body, because we eat one bread," he tells them (1 Corinthians 10:16-17). In other words, by eating this ceremonial meal they are being reminded not only of their covenant relationship

Focusing on self rather than God ➤➤

Standards for deacons ➤

Guidelines for worship ➤➤

with God but their covenant duty to one another (1 Corinthians 11:23-34). How could they celebrate the Supper at one moment in their worship then be so self-centered a moment later?

Carrying his argument a step further, Paul points to the "participation" that surrounds the Lord's Supper. The cup of wine, shared by all, is "a participation in the blood of Christ" (1 Corinthians 10:16). But this is a special kind of participation. Paul's word choice in the original text settles on a term that is translated "fellowship" in other contexts. A very prevalent word in the New Testament, "fellowship" fundamentally means "a commonality." Two parties are in fellowship when they share something in common or when they support a common cause.

Fellowship within the Christian community always implies a close, intimate relationship. In Paul's writings, fellowship is the bond that ties Christians together inseparably (Galatians 2:9; Philippians 1:5). In other settings fellowship is the relationship that binds Christians to God (1 John 1:3, 6).

By describing the Lord's Supper as a "fellowship," Paul calls to mind the "commonality" that unites all who share that meal. The Supper is a symbol of oneness and unity, a reminder that Christians have made common cause with each other. They share a common Lord, a common Savior, and a common hope. They are one body, one blood.

Historically, therefore, Christians have considered the Lord's Supper the most sacred moment of Christian service and worship.

Since they share a common covenant, symbolized by the Supper, Paul presses the Corinthians to spend their time together building one another up emotionally and spiritually, not promoting competition and rivalry. He gives similar counsel to the Romans, when he urges them to work for the well-being of other believers, speaking only those things that serve to build other people up, never to tear them down (Romans 15:1-2).   **◄◄ Fellowship**

The Church as the Family of God

In their worship, as in all other   **◄ A new family** times together, the early Christians thought of themselves as a tightly-knit family. They addressed one another as "brothers" and "sisters" and considered themselves "the children of God" (1 John 3:1). As you might imagine, this outlook grew naturally from the practice of referring to God as their Father.

Because they were family, loving attitudes were absolutely important. The apostle John even goes so far as to deny that anyone can be in the family of God and hate others in that family. He insists that those who fail to love their brothers or sisters in Christ

➤ are still living in darkness (1 John 2:11)

> ➤ are not of God (1 John 3:10)

> ➤ are no different from Cain, who murdered his brother Abel (1 John 3:11-12)

> ➤ do not have eternal life (1 John 3:15)

Motivation for prayer ➤➤

And in one final word on the subject, John adds, "If someone says, 'I love God,' but hates his brother, he is a liar. Anyone who does not love his brother, whom he has seen, cannot love God whom he has not seen" (1 John 4:20).

Selfish prayers ➤➤

John offers the example of Jesus to explain why loving the family of God is so important. John notes, "This is the way we know what love is: Jesus laid down His life for us. And we ought to lay down our lives for our brothers and sisters" (1 John 3:16). Or as he states it later, "We love because He first loved us" (1 John 4:19). John has never forgotten what Jesus told His followers just before His death, "The way everyone will know that you are my disciples is that they will see your love for one another" (John 13:35).

Prayer

Prayer and faith ➤➤

In the family environment that governed the early church, nothing was more common than Christians praying for one another. It is impossible to overstate the priority they gave to prayer. Even a casual reading of the book of Acts makes it clear that Christians gathered regularly, and for long hours, to pray. In this regard they were following the example of Jesus. As the Gospel of Luke shows repeatedly, Jesus often withdrew to a place where He could pray for an extended period of time.

Admonitions to pray appear regularly in the New Testament Letters, nowhere more frequently than in the letter by James. Of particular concern to James are the motivations behind prayer. Unless prayer is properly motivated, he warns, it accomplishes nothing.

For instance, he notes the quarrels that are going on among his readers. "What accounts for this conflict?" he asks. He answers that they have let the pleasure-seeking, self-serving desires, and envy get out of control. "You don't have what you want because you don't ask God for it," James scolds. "Or if you do ask Him, He withholds it, because He knows you plan to use it selfishly" (James 4:1-3). Selfishness invalidates the effectiveness of prayer.

Earlier, toward the first of his letter, James mentions another attitude that undercuts prayer. In this case it is failure to trust God fully. "If you pray, doubting that you will get what you pray for, you will be no more stable than the surf in a driving wind," James warns (James 1:4-6).

To reinforce this point, he returns to the subject of praying in faith as he closes the letter. He cites two specific instances in which his readers need to devote themselves more fully to prayer. First is the case of someone in the church who is ill. Call the elders and let them come and pray for the sick person, James advises. A prayer offered in faith can restore physical health to the one who is ill. Moreover, any sin committed by that person will be forgiven (James 5:14-15).

Second, they need to promote spiritual health in their fellowship by praying for each other. There should be such trust and openness among them that they can confess their sins to one another, then pray personally for the one who has sinned. The obvious purpose of this prayer is to seek forgiveness and greater strength to resist temptation.

James removes any question about the importance of such prayers by reminding them, "The effective prayer of a righteous person can accomplish much." To illustrate, he recalls the story of Elijah in the Old Testament. During his struggle against King Ahab and idolatry, Elijah once prayed for a drought that would cripple the evil king. God responded by withholding rain from the land for over three years. Later Elijah prayed for rain, and it came in torrents.

James comments on the faith of Elijah by saying, "He was a man just like us." In other words, our prayers have the same potential power as the prayers of Elijah, since he was just as human as we are. But as James has stressed from the outset, prayers of such effectiveness are possible only when we pray in faith and pray with proper motives.

Prayer is the conduit for taking any and every concern to God. Paul tells the Philippians to use prayer to combat anxiety. Whatever their worry, they are to express it openly in prayer, seeking God's aid, while also giving Him thanks for the blessings He provides (Philippians 4:6). Alluding to the same practice, Peter says, "Cast all your anxieties on God, because He cares for you" (1 Peter 5:7). ◄ Anxiety

◄◄ Spiritual health

Paul especially encourages prayer as a defense against Satan. In Ephesians he warns that our struggles in life are not merely with other human beings. We also struggle with spiritual forces, wicked by nature and evil in their intent, who support the schemes of Satan (Ephesians 6:10-12). To prevail in this conflict, Christians need to arm themselves with every spiritual resource that God supplies. This includes making prayer a daily priority. "Pray at all times in the Spirit," Paul writes. Nor should we forget others in our prayers. Paul adds, "Persevere, too, in your continuous entreaties to God on behalf of other Christians" (Ephesians 6:18). ◄ Defense against Satan

Sharing Financially

As they prayed for each other, the early Christians were also ready to sacrifice financially to help one another. And they extended their generosity to brothers and sisters far beyond their own community. ◄ Sharing material resources

We see an example of this in 1 and 2 Corinthians, which offer details about a special relief fund for Christians in Jerusalem (1 Corinthians 16:1-4). We do not know the specific financial problems facing the church in Jerusalem, but Christians in Greece had taken it upon themselves to offer assistance. They had gladly collected these funds, even though they knew virtually no one in Jerusalem.

This is in keeping with the generosity that marked Christian communities from their beginning. Only a few weeks after the church started in Jerusalem, members began selling their houses and lands in order to help impoverished believers (Acts 4:34-37). By aiding Christians in Jerusalem, the Greek churches were merely continuing the tradition of sharing with those in need. Paul tells them, "Your abundance at present supplies what they need, so that their abundance can become a supply for your needs, the result being a constant equality" (2 Corinthians 8:14). Paul also assures them that God will reward their generosity, enriching them in every way, physically and spiritually because of their willingness to share (2 Corinthians 9:10-11).

The early Christians, then, had the perspective that their lives were vitally entwined with one another. They depended on one another. And they shared their material resources whenever there was need. They were a family. A body. And to the degree they cared for God's children, they honored the Father whose name they wore.

Body of Christ   Kingdom

Sharing material resources   Worship   Lord's

Fellowship   Supper

Praise

Family of God   Love

Chapter Twenty-Seven
THE BOOK OF REVELATION

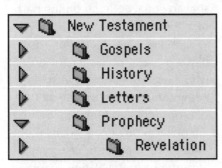

Without a doubt, Revelation is the most unusual book in the Bible. Almost every verse is laced with strange symbols and involved imagery. For 2000 years Christians have struggled to unravel this symbolism, often with very differing results. It is beyond the scope of this introduction to delve into all the ways that people have interpreted Revelation. But we can examine some themes that are obvious to the reader and which most interpreters agree on.

Revelation was written by a man named John, assumed to be the apostle who gave us a Gospel and three letters by that name. Late in his life the government exiled him to the island of Patmos due to his leadership in the church. It was

there that he saw a series of visions that form the heart of Revelation.

In this work John's foremost concern is a major persecution that will soon befall his readers. This is probably the government attack on the church that occurred in Asia Minor toward the end of the first century. Asia Minor was home to devoted cults that worshiped the Roman emperor as a god. Legislation required each citizen to go before an altar dedicated to the emperor, toss a pinch of incense in the fire, and recite the words, "Caesar is Lord."

Normally Christians would not hesitate to call someone lord, if it was only a title of respect. But they knew that the citizens of Asia Minor were using "lord" to mean "divine." To the Christians there was only one Lord in the divine sense, which created a crisis of conscience when they were instructed to participate in this public adoration of the emperor. On the other hand, their refusal to pay homage to the emperor was seen by the government as a sign of disloyalty, or even

◄ Encouragement in face of persecution

Standing firm against evil >>

treason. It was the charge of treason as much as their religion that led to their persecution.

In the first three chapters of Revelation Jesus appears to John and dictates seven letters. He directs them to specific churches in Asia Minor. These letters comprise the second and third chapters of the book. Jesus commends those churches who are remaining faithful to Him, warns those who are slipping into indifference or immorality, and urges a renewed commitment on the part of all. The language found here, while often symbolic, is fairly straightforward and not difficult to understand.

Symbolic numbers >>

Apocalyptic Imagery

All that changes, however, as soon as the fourth chapter opens. For the remainder of Revelation every page is filled with images of beasts, gigantic figures, disasters, and natural calamities that defy description. Playing out in all of these scenes is a showdown between the forces of evil and the forces of good. The constant theme is that evil is making a determined effort to destroy what is holy and righteous. Yet, no matter what it devises, and no matter how long it prevails, evil cannot triumph in the end. God still controls the universe. And at moments of His own choosing, He completely crushes the wicked.

Apocalyptic writing >>

For the Christians to whom John is writing, the important thing is to

stand firm against the intimidating forces of evil. From the very outset of Revelation, John encourages his readers to overcome what the world will throw against them, even if they must stand firm in their faith in the face of death. Some had already died rather than compromise on their commitment to Jesus. And John is using this book to marshal an equal courage on the part of all believers.

In many ways Revelation resembles a modern political cartoon, with exaggerated and oversized beings, images that violate all rules of proportion, and beasts symbolizing political powers or social movements. Numbers also have symbolic importance in Revelation. Events occur in cycles of seven, which represents bringing something to completion. Ten is associated with human powers, while throughout the book twelve and multiples of twelve are connected with spiritual realities.

All of these features are elements of the literary style called "apocalyptic writing," which we first encountered with Ezekiel. John brings that form of narrative and teaching to a new height. His work seems strange to us, just as our modern political cartoons would seem strange to him. He would be no more familiar with the symbolism of an editorial cartoon than we are with the images in Revelation. Yet, in the first century there were many apocalyptic works circulating in Jewish circles. As a result, the people who first read Revelation had far less difficulty with it than we do.

The Seven Seals (Revelation 4–8)

The apocalyptic section of Revelation begins in the fourth chapter, where John is taken into the throne room of heaven and sees God's glory on display. A scroll, secured by seven seals, is in the hand of God, and a call goes out for someone who is worthy to break the seals. The scroll seems to have been the kind that was used in Asia Minor to record a will. Whoever is worthy to break the scrolls is therefore someone in a position to reveal what God's will says about the future.

At this point Jesus appears under the symbol of a lamb who bears the wound of a mortal blow. He is proclaimed worthy to open the scroll, and one by one He breaks the seals. Immediately, with the breaking of each seal, horrifying scenes unfold. War, rebellion, famine, and death sweep over the earth. Meanwhile, Christians are suffering on the earth at the hands of people who oppress them. Indeed, some have already been killed because they held true to their commitment to Jesus. This we learn when Jesus breaks the fifth seal.

With the sixth seal, the heavens themselves start to disintegrate. The sun goes black, the moon turns blood red, the stars start falling, and a vast earthquake shakes mankind. Men see this as a judgment of God coming upon them, and they begin to call for the rocks and mountains to fall on them to hide them from God's presence. God's people, however, are kept safe from this judgment. Before the breaking of the seventh seal, John shows two episodes having to do with those who are in Christ. In the first God sends His angels to put a seal or mark of identification on everyone who belongs to Christ. In the second John sees a scene in heaven where those who have accepted Jesus and have been cleansed by His blood are standing around the throne of God, triumphant over all that happened on the earth.

«« God's throne room

The Seven Trumpets

The purpose of these two stories is apparently to assure John's readers that no matter what punishment God brings on wickedness, His followers are ultimately secure. God knows who they are. He will never lose sight of even a single one, and at the appropriate moment He will bring them before His throne for reward. With that assurance in place, John then returns to the scroll and the seventh seal. When it is broken, silence falls over the entire universe. Then seven trumpets are handed to seven angels, the kinds of trumpets one would hear on an ancient battlefield. The angels sound their trumpets one at a time, and another round of

«« The worthy wounded lamb

« Security in God

calamities come upon the earth and its inhabitants.

With the fifth trumpet even demonic forces are unleashed on humanity to torture mankind further. And in the midst of this an army of unfathomable size moves in to pillage and destroy. Here John makes the arresting comment that

> the rest of mankind who were not killed by these disasters did not repent and give up their worship of demons and idols of gold, silver, brass, stone, and wood, which can neither see nor hear nor walk. Nor did these people repent of their murders, their witchcraft, their immorality, or their thefts.
> — Revelation 9:20-21

Faithful witnesses >

The two great witnesses >>

Recall that John is writing to urge Christians to be faithful witnesses for Jesus in the midst of the persecution that soon would transpire. This hearkens back to God's call in Isaiah for His people to be witnesses to the pagan world. Yet, John wants his friends to know just how hardened the world will be to their message. Even when God's judgment comes upon the earth in the form of unthinkable disasters, like those just described, people who rebel against God will still refuse to repent. The Christians who stay true to their testimony as witnesses should therefore expect a hostile hearing.

To iterate that point, John breaks away from the story of the trumpets for two more episodes of note. The first one centers on an angel, so huge that he stands with one foot on the earth, the other on the sea, and his head in the sun. In his hand is a small scroll or book, which he hands to John and tells him to eat it. John complies, only to find that the scroll tastes sweet in his mouth, but sours his stomach.

The eating of the scroll seems to represent what happens when Christians take God's word to the world. Although the message itself is sweet when spoken, the after effects of persecution and hostility are often quite bitter. Still, God's followers cannot make this an excuse for withholding their testimony as His witnesses. With his stomach still sour, John is told, "Go prophesy again about the various peoples, nations, language groups, and rulers of the earth" (Revelation 10:11).

And then to emphasize the resistance to God's message, John tells a second story of two great witnesses who appear, one with the miracle working power of Moses, the other with the power of Elijah. They speak for God side by side in the streets of the world. But the rulers of the world, far from receiving their message as a word from God, plot to destroy these witnesses. In fact, the two are finally killed and the whole world rejoices, only to be shocked after three and a half days when the two men come back to life. Their reappearance has a jolting impact on some who previously rejected God. Setting their disbelief aside, they now begin to give Him the praise He deserves.

Again John's point seems to be that his readers will encounter resistance in depth when they defend their faith. But they should not blame themselves when men reject their message. People would be just as adamant against the message if it were spoken by Moses and Elijah themselves. Yet, Christians must sustain their testimony, for there are some hearts that can be turned to God, even among those who resist His message most militantly.

The Dragon and the Woman (Revelation 12–14)

With this, the seventh trumpet blows and John sees the kingdom of God emerge victorious over the world, so that no power remains to resist God's will. The dead are judged and God's followers receive their reward. And those who warred against Him are sent away to destruction.

Then suddenly, with the beginning of the twelfth chapter, the series of scenes changes abuptly. Having taken us to the end of time with the blowing of the seventh trumpet, John goes back to a time when the people of God were nourishing a hope that the Messiah would appear. Those who sustained the hope of the Messiah are pictured as a pregnant woman in labor. As the world readies for the appearance of Jesus, Satan positions himself to destroy the child about to be born. Satan appears in this story as a gigantic dragon, so huge that the sweep of his tail knocks a third of the stars from the sky.

But God has prepared a place to protect the woman and her child, so that Satan is unable to destroy them. At the same time a war breaks out in heaven, with the angels of God doing battle against Satan and his angels. In the end Satan and his hosts are overwhelmed and driven out. In rage, Satan turns his fury on the woman. He now changes from a dragon to a serpent, bringing to mind the story of the serpent and the woman in the Garden of Eden. He does everything in his power to destroy the woman, but God continues to protect her. Yet Satan does not give up. He goes off to war against all of her offspring — the ones who now follow Jesus and stand by their testimony as His witnesses.

◄ The woman and her child

Satan's strategy is to enlist the aid of a great beast that he calls up from the sea. This is a seven-headed monster, with ten crowns on his heads, along with names that slander God. This beast is given power to make war against God's people. This beast teams up with another one from the land, who speaks on behalf of the first beast, but with the voice of Satan. He commands everyone on earth to create an image of the first beast, then to bow down and worship it. Those who perform this worship have a mark placed on their forehead. Without that mark, a person can neither buy nor sell goods nor purchase the necessities of life.

◄ Beast with seven heads

◄ Mark of the beast

John's symbolism here surely caused his readers to think of what was happening around them. With the government imposing emperor worship as a condition of good citizenship, the Christians were being compelled to choose between livelihood and loyalty to God. And they could not have missed the irony that those who worshiped the beast received a mark on their head, in contrast to the seal that God had previously put on those who were His people.

But to be certain that they make this association, John changes scenes again to show us Jesus, symbolized by a lamb, standing on Mount Zion (the hill in Jerusalem where the temple stood), surrounded by His followers. On their foreheads is not the mark of the beast, but the name of Christ and the Father. These are the ones, we are told, who have kept themselves pure, who have followed Jesus, and who have stayed loyal to the truth. Overhead, meanwhile, an angel is flying. From high in the sky he calls for the gospel to be preached over the entire earth. And another angel follows, crying a lament. "Fallen, fallen is Babylon the great" (Revelation 14:8).

God's wrath on unbelievers >>

Rome as Babylon (Revelation 14–18)

Babylon = Rome >

At an early date Christians began using the name Babylon as a synonym for Rome. Peter closed his first letter by saying, "She who is in Babylon sends you greetings" (1 Peter 5:13). The angel who proclaims the fall of Babylon is thus foretelling a destruction for Rome. A third angel also sounds a warning. Anyone who worships the beast and his image or receives his mark on the forehead is doomed to feel God's wrath. John's attention then shifts to Jesus, a crown on His head, ordering His angels to go forth like reapers to harvest the earth.

In the midst of this another angel appears who has with him seven bowls, each one bearing a calamity. These calamities represent God's wrath, which is now poured out in stages on an unbelieving world. The disasters that come from these bowls are pictured in language that parallels the plagues that Moses brought on Egypt. Interestingly, when the suffering becomes so intense that men are gnawing their tongues in anguish, John offers the observation, "Still they slandered God because of their pains and their sores, and they did not repent of their evil deeds" (Revelation 16:10-11).

Satan now tries one last stand. Once more in the form of a dragon, he joins forces with the beast from the sea and the second beast who served as his mouthpiece. They bring all the kings of the earth together to battle the forces of God. But when the final bowl, the seventh one, is poured out, Babylon starts to split apart. And then, like Satan who changes forms from scene to scene, Babylon becomes a harlot who invites the nations to get drunk and to practice immorality with her. She herself is also drunk. She has intoxicated herself on the blood of God's people and especially the blood of those she has killed because they stayed true to their testimony for Jesus. And to make sure that we know he is talking of Rome, John identifies the woman as sitting on seven mountains (Rome was known as the city of seven hills) and as the city that reigns over the earth (Revelation 17:9,18).

Having mustered his forces, Satan brings all of them against Jesus, still symbolized as a seemingly powerless lamb. But to no avail. Once more an angel appears to announce the fall of Babylon. And simultaneously a voice from heaven calls for God's people to remove themselves from the vices and sins of that city. As John continues to watch, God unleashes his wrath on Rome. She is consumed with pestilence, mourning, famine, and fire. So thorough is her destruction that the commerce of the entire earth comes to a standstill.

For an entire chapter John pictures how thoroughly Rome will be crushed. And then abruptly he takes his readers to heaven, where a great celebration is underway. Everyone is rejoicing and praising God for finally repaying the city for the persecution she inflicted on His people. And this scene of celebration takes on an even more festive air when the Lamb announces that this is His wedding feast. His bride, the church, has made herself ready for Him through her faithfulness.

Satan's Last Stand (Revelation 19–20)

On earth, all the while, the battle with Satan's forces still continues. Yet Christ steadily prevails. The beast from the sea and the other beast who served as his mouthpiece are thrown alive into a lake of fire and brimstone. Then a powerful angel seizes Satan, once more in the form of a serpent, and binds him with a great chain. He is thrown into an abyss, which is then closed over and sealed. Simultaneously, John sees all those who have been beheaded because they stayed true to their testimony to Jesus, along with those who refused to worship the beast and his image. These come alive and reign with Christ for a thousand years.

◄ Lake of fire

◄◄ Fall of "Babylon"

But at the end of that thousand years, Satan is released. A thousand years in confinement have not tempered his wickedness in the least. He gathers the forces of the world around him once again and makes one more failed attempt to unseat Jesus. Now Satan, too, is thrown into the lake of fire and brimstone. With Satan finally removed, all people, great and small, stand before God for a final judgment. All who have died are there, and each person is judged according to the nature of his or her deeds. Those

◄◄ Rejoicing at God's justice

who do not appear in God's book of life, the book that records the names of those who have gained eternal life, are sentenced to a second and eternal death.

The Heavenly Jerusalem (Revelation 21–22)

Following this scene of judgment, John sees a new heaven and a new earth. Everything is different in this world. There is no longer any death, mourning, or pain. The crowning glory of this new creation is a splendid city that John calls a new Jerusalem. God's glory fills the streets of the city. Everyone is so safe within it that the gates along its walls are never closed. In the middle of the city is a river that contains the water of life, lined on each side by trees that bear the fruit of life. Here the people of God, having proven themselves faithful on the earth, enjoy the peace and tranquility of eternal life and the unending presence of God.

Death and pain gone forever ➤

Total safety ➤

God and man reconciled ➤➤

With this vision of the heavenly Jerusalem still before his eyes, John receives a final admonition from an angel who has been his escort and from Jesus Himself. Jesus tells John that He is coming quickly, rewards in hand, to recompense every person for what that person has done. John adds to the words of Jesus his own statement vowing to the accuracy of what he has written. And then he closes with the words, "Come quickly Lord Jesus."

As we have worked through the ever-changing landscape of Revelation, we have made only a handful of comments about what its language means. But you can doubtlessly see the message that John wanted to convey to his readers. No matter what the cost, they are to stay true to Jesus. They may have to pay with their lives, but what difference does that make, when their eternal life in the new Jerusalem is assured? Time and again in Revelation John speaks of those who overcome. Having written in 1 John about those who overcome the world, he now shows us more fully what that means.

With the conclusion of Revelation, the Bible itself comes to a close. Its conclusion brings us full circle. Genesis opened with God and mankind in a close, personal relationship in a paradise called the Garden of Eden. In the middle of that garden spot was the Tree of Life. At the end of Revelation, God and mankind are again in an intimate relationship, this time in a magnificent city with the Tree of Life in the heart of the city. Death, brought into the human family in Eden, is now banished. Satan has been destroyed, no longer having the power to deceive and mislead. And all that makes for sorrow and grief in the present world is a thing of the past.

Chapter Twenty-Eight
WHERE DO YOU GO FROM HERE?

You now have a basic understanding of the Bible. You are familiar with its major concepts and stories. As you have seen, the Bible is not a dry, dull essay about God and what He wants us to be. Instead, the Bible uses historical episodes and the lives of day-to-day people to teach us vital lessons about ourselves and about our relationship with the Lord.

The stories and language of the Bible contain deep layers of meaning. You can read the Bible for the rest of your life and never exhaust its insights. As you master one level of meaning from its pages, an entirely new level will open to you. Thus, with this introduction to the Bible, you have embarked on what promises to be a lifelong, exciting journey.

In the interest of brevity, the previous chapters have omitted many vital details. There are dozens of valuable stories from the lives of people like Moses, David, Jesus, and Paul that we have not even mentioned. As you begin to read widely in the Bible, you will have the joy of discovering these Biblical moments for yourself.

But where should you begin? Perhaps your first goal should be to learn more about the life and teachings of Jesus, as well as the early history of His followers. You might start by reading through the Gospel of Luke and the book of Acts. They were both written by Luke to a friend named Theophilus to introduce him to Christianity. They can serve the same purpose for you.

In fact, you can think of the Gospel of Luke and the book of Acts as the first and second volumes of a single story. The Gospel of Luke covers the life of Jesus, while Acts traces the work of His apostles after His resurrection. Both books are in the form of narrative, and together they constitute about 40% of the New Testament. They are also among the easiest books of the Bible to comprehend. You will be well along in your grasp of the New Testament, then, once you complete Luke and Acts.

In addition, you will want to begin reading from the Old Testament. It is

<< Begin with Jesus

<< Lifelong learning

already apparent to you that the New Testament builds on the Old Testament. As you read the New Testament, you will find frequent references to events and key figures in the Old Testament. Thus, to understand the New Testament fully, you will need to be familiar with the Old Testament.

Ethical direction >>

Again, you may find it best to begin your Old Testament study by focusing on books that are primarily narratives. Certainly you will want to read Genesis and Exodus, since they lay out so many ideas that are fundamental to the rest of the Bible. As for the other books of Moses, you may want to skip Leviticus and Deuteronomy for the moment. Their heavy compilation of laws is sometimes tedious for first-time readers. But you will probably want to read through Numbers. It traces the history of the Israelites from the time they left Sinai until they were ready to enter Canaan.

Continue your reading of the Old Testament with Joshua, Judges, Ruth, 1 and 2 Samuel, and 1 and 2 Kings. That will give you most of the historical sweep of the Old Testament. Then consider some reading in Psalms and Proverbs. Unlike the narrative books, the individual chapters in Psalms and Proverbs can be read in any sequence. So you can browse through these books, taking in their chapters at random. Many people, indeed, make it a habit to read one of the Psalms and a chapter from Proverbs every day, no matter what portion of the Bible they are currently studying.

When you are ready to deepen your mastery of New Testament teachings, put a priority on the books of Romans, Ephesians, and James. All three of these books are noted for their strong emphasis on how Christians should live. Romans and Ephesians also offer a thorough description of what the early church taught about God, Jesus, and the Holy Spirit.

One final word. In your reading you will come upon statements or ideas that may not make sense to you. That is only natural for anyone. Many passages in the Bible are indeed difficult, a point openly acknowledged by the New Testament itself (2 Peter 3:15-16). People who study the Bible for years still struggle with the meaning of certain verses. But as you continue to round out your knowledge of Scripture, things that once were confusing will become clearer. And with each additional clarification, God's Word will take on deeper and richer meaning for you.

Appendix A
ENGLISH VERSIONS OF THE BIBLE

The Bible is so popular in North America and Great Britain that it is published in a number of different English translations. We often refer to these various translations as "versions," and you will hear the words "translation" and "version" used interchangeably. Christian bookstores typically stock half a dozen English versions of the Bible, sometimes many more.

Behind each version is a specific objective that guided the scholars who did the actual work of translation.

➤ Some versions aim at reproducing the sentence structure and phrasing of the original Hebrew and Greek text as precisely as possible.

➤ For others the goal is to accommodate changes in the English language. Because English (like all languages) evolves over time, Bibles translated decades or even centuries ago have become dated. They are no longer in a style of English familiar to most readers.

➤ Another group of versions seeks to be as readable as possible. They tend to substitute a very informal style, relying on simple sentences, for the more complex sentence structure of the underlying Hebrew and Greek text.

All versions target themselves at a specific reading level. Some translations require high school or college-level reading skills. Others are easily followed by people with only a junior high education.

Early English Translations

The most famous English-language Bible is the King James Version (abbreviated KJV), named for King James I of England. He ordered the publication of this Bible in the early 17th century and authorized it for use in churches across his realm. For that reason it is also known as the Authorized Version (or AV for short).

The King James Version is still more widely read than any other English translation. But its style is increasingly difficult for modern readers to follow. At the time the KJV was translated, the common people spoke Elizabethan English, the English we hear in the plays of Shakespeare. Because English has changed so much over the centuries, the KJV presents the same challenge for modern readers that Shakespeare does. Nevertheless, the phrasing of the KJV is often unexcelled in terms of poetic beauty.

In the late nineteenth century a team of British and American scholars began work to "modernize" the KJV. The result was the English Revised Version (abbreviated ERV) in Great Britain and the American Standard Version (ASV) in the United States. These two translations are almost identical. The primary differences between them have to do with spelling. The ERV respects British spelling conventions, while the ASV follows American usage.

Due to the great popularity of the King James Version, with its Elizabethan English, the translators of the ERV and the ASV felt they needed to retain the Elizabethan style. This decision, unfortunately, limited the period of time in which these two versions would be influential. Even though both were quite popular prior to the Second World War, neither is widely read any more. Their style is too antiquated for most modern readers, and those who like the Elizabethan style have shown a preference to continue using the King James Version.

The Appearance of Newer Versions

The next major step at "modernizing" the KJV came immediately after the Second World War. An international effort to "revise" the King James Version led to what is known as the Revised Standard Version (or RSV). The RSV preserved much of the KJV's sentence structure, but without an Elizabethan style. The Revised Standard has undergone additional updates over the years, the most recent being the New Revised Standard Version (NRSV).

Building on the success of the RSV in the 1950s, the 1960s gave rise to a number of initiatives to produce "modernized" English Bibles. One of these was the New American Standard Bible (the NASB). As its name indicates, it was closely connected to the American Standard Version. The goal of the NASB was to retain the best qualities of the ASV, while generally distancing itself from Elizabethan wordings. (The NASB does retain Elizabethan English for prayers and other statements addressed to God.) Like the ASV before it, the NASB is noted for its effort to duplicate the Hebrew and Greek sentence structure behind any given passage.

Shortly after the NASB appeared, the Catholic Church published another version with a similar name, the New American Bible. Centuries earlier the Catholic Church had underwritten the Douay translation of the Bible. Until the 1960s it was the only English Bible that the Catholic Church authorized its members to study. Catholic authorities have gradually relaxed that stance, first approving the Revised Standard Version for settings in which Catholics and non-Catholics were studying together. With the New American Bible the Catholic community was recognizing the need to overcome the aging style of the Douay translation.

Catholic and Non-Catholic Bibles

When you examine a Catholic Bible, you find that it contains 54 books in the Old Testament instead of 39. These additional 15 books are grouped together right after Malachi. Collectively they are called the Apocrypha, which means "things that are hidden." The books of the Apocrypha were written after 200 BC, primarily in Greek. The Jews accepted them as valuable works, but not of equal authority with the writings of Moses and the Prophets.

In the fifth century AD, when the Catholic Church translated the Bible into Latin, the papacy decided to include the Apocrypha in that translation. Since that time the Catholic Church has sanctioned the Apocrypha as Scripture. In the six-

teenth century, as Protestant churches came into existence, they reexamined the question of which books belong in the Bible. The Protestants uniformly decided to preclude the Apocrypha, accepting only those books of the Old Testament that the Jews recognized. And that judgment has been ratified in every generation since.

The Apocrypha contain no major doctrines not found elsewhere in the Old and New Testaments. They are largely books of history and wisdom literature. Their primary value is the light they shed on developments in Judaism in the centuries between the close of the Old Testament and the beginning of the New Testament.

Other Recent Translations

Apart from Catholic translations, the only other popular English version to include the Apocrypha is the New English Bible (or NEB). It is another product of the 1960s, again part of the effort to modernize the language of the King James Version. Of all the Bibles we have reviewed thus far, the NEB has by far the most advanced reading level. Its vocabulary assumes a well-educated adult reader. In taking that approach, the NEB has sharply limited the number of people who would find its style appealing. As a result, it has established only a rather modest following.

By contrast, the New International Version (or NIV)

targeted itself at the average reader. The NIV is easily understood by anyone who reads a daily newspaper, for its translators took pains to use only simple, uncomplicated sentence structures. To do so they often sacrificed subtle elements that are part of the thought flow in the original Hebrew and Greek documents. But in turn they made the NIV easy to read and comprehend. The NIV has consequently become a perennial best-seller, and several publishers offer it today in a variety of editions.

During the surge of new translations in the 1960s and 1970s, the American Bible Society also underwrote an effort to produce an easy-to-read Bible. The result was Today's English Version (or TEV, for short), first published as the New Testament only under the title *Good News for Modern Man*. Later the Old Testament was added and the entire work renamed *The Good News Bible*. The style of the TEV is so informal that one could almost describe it as "folksy."

Paraphrases

In working to make the Bible easy to understand, some translators have opted to bring Scripture into English in the form of a paraphrase rather than a strict translation. The problem with a paraphrase is that it leaves the reader uncertain as to which words are strictly from the Bible and which ones come from the mind of the translator. Thus, if your goal is careful, in-depth Bible study, a paraphrase is not your first Bible of choice. On the other hand, paraphrases typically have a simple, free-flowing style that makes them quite enjoyable and stimulating for light, casual reading.

By far the most successful paraphrase is *The Living Bible*. It was developed by Kenneth Taylor, whose objective was to produce a Bible that his small children could understand. *The Living Bible* contains both the Old and New Testaments, which makes it somewhat unique among paraphrases, since most of them cover only the New Testament. *The Living Bible* is also printed under other titles. For instance, the New Testament portion has been widely printed in a softback edition called *The Way*.

J. B. Philips, an English churchman, produced another paraphrase of the New Testament that was particularly popular in the 1960s and 1970s and is still widely read today. He later published a translation of four Old Testament prophets before he discontinued his plans to paraphrase the entire Bible. More recently Eugene Peterson has written a widely read paraphrase called *The Message*. He has also begun publishing certain portions of the Old Testament in paraphrase.

Selecting a Bible for Yourself

In addition to the versions and paraphrases we have touched on here, there are dozens of others that enjoy a more limited circulation. As you can see, choosing a Bible for yourself confronts you with a host of options. So how do you make that choice?

You might begin by going to a Christian bookstore, or even a secular book dealer with a sizable inventory of religious titles. Spend some time browsing through the various translations, identifying the ones that you find most engaging. If your purpose is careful and precise Bible study, you will probably want to examine the Revised Standard Version and the New American Standard Bible. The NASB presumes a higher reading level than the RSV. But neither of them relies on a vocabulary significantly more advanced than what you have found in the book you are now reading.

For a compromise between serious Bible study and ease of readability, the New International Version is a good choice. For teenage and elementary age readers it is probably preferable to the NASB or RSV, since it is written for those with junior high vocabulary skills. Although you may want to look at paraphrases, they probably should not be your first choice as your primary study Bible.

And speaking of study, you will also find a number of so-called "study Bibles" on the market. These are not a different translation. Instead, they combine a popular translation (such as the New International Version or the Revised Standard Version) with copious notes and commentary to explain terms and features in the Biblical text. Study Bibles can be quite helpful. But you should always bear in mind that the notes often reflect the particular doctrinal or theological bias of the people who produced them. Feel free to challenge ideas you find in the notes if your own study of the Bible leads you to different conclusions.

HELPFUL RESOURCES FOR PERSONAL BIBLE STUDY

Studying the Bible can be a lifetime vocation. Its depth and richness are truly inexhaustible. Now that you have completed this introductory study of the Bible, you are ready to dig into its pages more deeply. But where do you start? How do you begin?

Fortunately there are hundreds of books whose specific purpose is to examine and explain the Bible. These include introductory guides, dictionaries, encyclopedias, commentaries, Bible atlases, and concordances, just to name some of the major categories. Collectively these are called Bible "study aids." You will want to become familiar with the special assistance that each of these aids can offer.

Many publishers offer "introductions" to the Bible. In fact, these books frequently have the word "introduction" in their title. An introduction provides an extensive background on the authorship, time frame, structure, and major concepts for every book of the Bible. *A Newcomer's Guide to the Bible* is a type of introduction, although it is written at a much more basic level than most others on the market. If you want to learn more about the individual books of the Bible, a good introduction is an excellent place to begin.

Bible dictionaries are also quite valuable. As their name implies, they provide succinct information on the people, places, and events found in the Old and New Testaments. In addition, they contain brief descriptions of theological terms and major doctrines that are common in the Bible. Since Bible dictionaries are generally contained in a single volume, their articles are necessarily short, not giving you as much detail as you might desire.

For a fuller treatment of these same topics, you would turn to a Bible encyclopedia. Most of them are about five or six volumes long, allowing space for articles of considerable breadth and depth. Encyclopedias also address a broader range of subjects than is the case with most Bible dictionaries. Adding to their usefulness, Bible encyclopedias usually include dozens of maps, charts, and illustrations that help explain details in the Bible.

As your interest in the Bible matures, you may also want to look at various commentaries, which offer extensive "comments" on every chapter and verse of the Bible. The purpose of these comments is to give you a deeper sense of the meaning in a given passage.

Given their purpose, commentaries are typically multivolume works. In some cases one author has written the entire commentary. In other cases each book of the Bible has a different commentator. Since they usually encompass several volumes, commentaries can be rather expensive. You do not have to buy all the volumes in a commentary, however, You can buy individual volumes that interest you.

A tool that many people overlook early in their Bible study is a good atlas of the Biblical world. The Bible is filled with names of places and regions you have never heard of. With its dozens of maps and explanatory text, a Bible atlas locates these sites for you and helps you envision the setting in which the Bible's events unfolded. If you have other reference books with good maps in them, you may not need an atlas. But it is particularly helpful, early in your study of the Bible, to avail yourself of an atlas or some other study aid that contains detailed maps for every historical period of the Bible.

Another valuable reference tool is a concordance. These unique books list every word in the Bible in alphabetical order. Following each word a concordance then identifies every instance in the Bible where that word appears. This is especially helpful if you want to study every occurrence of a term or phrase. But be aware that concordances are tied to specific translations of the Bible. A concordance based on the New International Version may not be particularly helpful if your primary study Bible is the New American Standard, or vice versa. When looking for a concordance, therefore, always be sure that it is based on the Bible you most commonly use.

Computer-based Bible Study Aids

On the other hand, if you own a personal computer, you may not need a concordance. For less than a hundred dollars you can buy software that contains as many as a half-dozen versions of the Bible on a single CD. This software permits you to search any translation for every verse that contains a particular word, phrase, or combination of words (something not even the best printed concordances can do). Bible atlases are also available for computers, as well, along with Bible dictionaries and commentaries.

Some software publishers offer translations, atlases, and dictionaries that are linked together, so that they interact seamlessly. For example, as you are reading a passage from the Bible on your computer screen, you come across an unfamiliar place name. You can highlight that name and activate an atlas that will show you its location on a map. Or you might call up an article from a Bible dictionary giving you further information about the site. What a rare privilege to live at a time when so much information about the Bible is readily available to everyone.

Some Cautions

As you look for Bible aids, it is wise to develop discretion in choosing the ones you depend on. This is necessary because religious publications today fall into two broad categories. First are those that show an abiding respect for the credibility, integrity, and authority of the Bible. Books in this category are written from a perspective similar to what you have found in *A Newcomer's Guide to the Bible*.

Other publications, however, hold the Bible in much lower esteem. They see it as a document entirely of human origin that evolved over the centuries as Israel's religious experience gradually unfolded. Included in this number are several well-known introductions to the Bible, Bible dictionaries, Bible encyclopedias, and commentaries. Quite often the editorial bias in books like these serves to undermine the reader's confidence in the Bible rather than affirm it.

While you are still mastering the basics of the Bible, you should turn primarily to reference books that have a high regard for the Bible's integrity and credibility. Certain religious publishing houses specialize in materials written from that perspective. We generally refer to this as an "evangelical view" of the Bible. A minister you trust or the owner of a Christian bookstore can point you to evangelical reference works or the publishers who produce them.

They can also help you determine which commentaries are appropriate for your level of study. Some commentaries are very technical in nature, aimed at readers who are well versed in Greek or Hebrew. Others are written for the average person in the pew, someone with no more knowledge of the Bible than you have after finishing *A Newcomer's Guide to the Bible*. Indeed, you may not need to concern yourself with commentaries at all. Many people study the Bible for years without every reading or buying a commentary. They simply learn for themselves by studying the Bible with the benefit of other aids.

In Closing

You could not have chosen an age when God's word was more accessible, both for reading and for probing study, than today. Take advantage of your privileged position. Become a lifelong student of the Bible. Open it every day, and grow more familiar with its truth and wisdom. Of all the subjects you can study, none will enrich your life more fully than a mastery of God's word.

Resources available from College Press

Bible History Overview: New Testament (Student Book and Teacher's Guide) and *Bible History Overview: Old Testament* (Student Book and Teacher's Guide) by Gary Olsby (1990) go through the entire Bible in summary fashion, with mnemonics and key phrases to help you remember what each book of the Bible contains.

Building Blocks for Bible Study by Peter Verkruyse (1997) is a look at how to set up your own personal Bible study.

The Chronological Life of Christ in 2 volumes by Mark E. Moore (1997) brings the accounts of the four Gospels together in chronological order.

The *College Press NIV Commentary* Series allows a detailed look at the teachings of various Bible books. Contact College Press for information on available titles.

Falling in Love with Jesus: Studies in the Book of Luke and
Falling in Love with Jesus' People: Studies in the Book of Acts by Rubel Shelly (1998) are both helpful study books on the two Bible books written by Paul's companion, Luke.

Genesis: The Beginnings of Faith by Rubel Shelly (1997) looks at various characters in the first book of the Bible and explores how their choices and character are relevant to us today.

New Testament History: Acts by Gareth Reese (1976) is a commentary on this important book of the Bible, with Special Studies on topics of particular interest.

Old Testament History: An Overview of Sacred History and Truth by Wilbur Fields (1998) gives a full treatment of the history covered by the Old Testament, along with a brief view of the time between the Old and New Testaments. Includes many maps, charts, and other illustrations.

College Press *Studies for Small Groups* are available on a number of subjects. Contact College Press for the most up-to-date list.

Studies in the Life of Christ by R.C. Foster (1995) is an older but still relevant study of the life of Christ from all four Gospels. The outline of Christ's life and ministry has been widely used in classes around the world.

Thirteen Lessons in Christian Doctrine and *Twelve More Lessons in Christian Doctrine* by Denver Sizemore (1997) answer some important questions about what Christians believe.

Thirteen Lessons in Christian Doctrine, Youth Edition by Denver Sizemore and John Hunter (1994), not just for children, covers the same material as the adult book but in simpler language.